TO THE FAIRWAY BORN

THE AUTOBIOGRAPHY

SANDY LYLE

WITH ROBERT PHILIP

headline

First published in 2006
by HEADLINE PUBLISHING GROUP

First published in paperback in 2007
by HEADLINE PUBLISHING GROUP

2

Cataloguing in Publication Data is available from the British Library

ISBN 978 0 7553 1472 0

Typeset in Janson Text by Palimpsest Book Production Limited,
Grangemouth, Stirlingshire

Printed and bound in Great Britain by
Clays Ltd, St Ives plc

Headline's policy is to use papers that are natural, renewable and
recyclable products and made from wood grown in sustainable forests.
The logging and manufacturing processes are expected to conform to
the environmental regulations of the country of origin.

HEADLINE PUBLISHING GROUP
A division of Hachette Livre UK Ltd
338 Euston Road
London NW1 3BH

www.headline.co.uk
www.hodderheadline.com

I would like to dedicate this book to my late parents Alex and Agnes Lyle. They were proud of me and never has there been a day in my life I wasn't proud of them. Thank you for your love, support and guidance. Thank you for allowing me to be fairway born.

ACKNOWLEDGEMENTS

At the risk of sounding like an Oscar winner thanking everyone they have ever met 'for making it all possible', I have been fortunate in the abiding support I have received from family, friends, caddies, coaches, business associates and fans during my years of walking the fairways all over the world.

My dear sisters Alison and Anne have spent many an hour awaiting news of my latest tournament results, although sadly for me, to this day Anne can't bring herself to come and see me play because she would be reduced to a jangle of nerves. Actually, I need to apologise to my big sisters for habitually forgetting their birthdays!

My four children – Stuart, James, Lonneke and Quintin – are, needless to say, the greatest prizes I have ever won; far, far more precious than the Open Claret Jug or the Masters Green Jacket could be. Now, more than ever, I have come to realise just how proud of me my mum and dad must have been. It's funny to think that the time comes when the achievements of your children mean as much as, if not more than, your own. Very proud of them I am, indeed.

I am also fortunate in the number of people I can call true friends. From my great pals at Hawkstone Park where it all began so many years ago, to my many friends around the world, thanks for playing such a very important part in my life.

There are a few very special friends I would like to acknowledge individually. Terry and Jo Shingler, I can never thank you both enough for the support you have given me in every way possible – and, please, never stop giving me a good talking-to when I need it!

Cynthia and Joseph Dillane, the ultimate globe-trotters who spend more time in the air than even I do; oh, how I love it when you come to rearrange my garden. Closer to home, all our many friends in Balquhidder and surrounding villages can't do enough for us in keeping a caring eye on Lonneke, Quintin and the dogs when Jolande accompanies me on my travels.

The blessed Carol who has made the impossible possible by organising our home for ten long years. As we say every day, 'What would we do without you?'

I would also like to thank all the caddies with whom I've worked, with one very special thank you to David Musgrove; I will never forget that it was with your invaluable advice and assistance that I won two Majors, old friend.

My gratitude, too, to all the various coaches – especially my current coach, Ken Martin, to whom it falls the task of trying to 'put Sandy together again' before we embark upon the Seniors Tour together in 2008 – plus my past managers, and my present ones: Robert Duck and Rocky Hambric, my future is in your hands, gents.

Robert Philip, thank you for your help in writing this book. As my 'ghost' you had to suffer a lot but I am sure it was all worth it. And at least we had a good excuse to sample the red wine, right? Also, David Wilson, Wendy McCance and Georgina Moore at Headline Publishing Group for their patience with this new author.

Not least I would like to issue a heartfelt thanks to all the spectators, fans and you, the readers of this book. I have drawn great inspiration from your cheers whenever I have hit a great shot or achieved a great victory. It is you who create the atmosphere to inspire and golf would most definitely be lost without you!

Finally, my wife Jolande, for simply putting up with me; if I have something to celebrate, Jolande is there with the corkscrew; if I come home feeling down, Jolande is there to remind me what a lucky, lucky man I am.

CONTENTS

FOREWORD

By Seve Ballesteros

I first met Sandy Lyle when he was my teenage partner in a Pro-Am event some thirty years ago. 'You are very good player,' I tell him at the end of our round. 'Thank you very much,' he tell me, 'I hope to be seeing lot more of you soon . . .'

A few years later, in 1979, he ends my three-year reign as European No.1. 'Now I've seen enough of you,' I feel like saying to him. But, no, he hangs around me winning tournament after tournament and so he becomes one of my best friends.

His record as a golfer is truly brilliant for it takes a very great player to win the Open and the Masters (I should know, ¿sí?) but what always made him stand out on the European Tour was his naturally spontaneous personality and humanity. Sandy is a true champion on and off the golf course.

The spectators recognise this, too. Whenever and wherever he walks up the eighteenth fairway, the cheers for Sandy are filled with real affection.

For decades he was the most difficult golfer to beat because he was a demolishing player with his long irons and putter. His capability of performing birdies was really amazing. Who can ever forget his 7-iron from the bunker on the eighteenth hole at Augusta National to win the Masters in '88 with a fantastic birdie three? One of the greatest shots ever to have won a Major.

During our careers, we held many important duels – sometimes I win, sometimes Sandy win – but we never lost our huge respect and admiration for each other. My victories made him happy and I was extremely happy for him when he won, doubly so when he won something as important as the Tournament Players' Championship. It reminded the Americans that the days when they could look down on European golf was well and truly over.

We have enjoyed many great times, especially as team-mates in the Ryder Cup at Muirfield Village in 1987 when the Americans were beaten for the very first time in the land of the Stars and Stripes and to celebrate I teach Sandy the flamenco Ballesteros-style on the eighteenth green. What a fiesta we have that night! (Away from the public eye, we have had many such parties together . . .)

Sandy's outstanding record – two Majors, twenty-five other titles across the world and winner of the European Order of Merit three times – is basically due to his huge talent as a player but also because he has one of the best virtues when facing challenges: patience. He is not only one of the most patient people I have ever met – with or without a golf club in his hand – but also one of the most generous in spirit.

Sandy is part of golf history as one of the sport's greatest champions and I, his friend, would like to salute him.

CHAPTER ONE

FROM PIG FARM TO ROYAL TROON

Muhammad Ali might never have become the greatest athlete of all time had a neighbourhood bully in Louisville not stolen his bicycle. The 12-year-old Cassius Clay, as he was known then, reported the theft of his ancient but cherished two-wheeler to the nearest cop, Patrolman Joe Martin, who, as fate would have it, ran a boxing gym in his spare time. With Joe Martin's encouragement, the youngster laced on gloves for the first time before setting off to exact revenge on the thief. The rest, as they say, is history.

A far less noble account it may be, but according to Lyle ancestral legend, I might never have picked up a golf club but for the outbreak of foot and mouth disease that struck our family pig farm in Milngavie on the northern outskirts of Glasgow in 1918 – forty years before my birth. The herd was all but wiped out by the epidemic, and my grandfather, Alex, had to find another means of making money to feed his ever-growing brood, which eventually reached a grand total of four sons and five daughters. He had fought in the First World War in a tank division and had never had any opportunity to develop an interest in the game, but he came up with the inspired idea of turning Clober Farm into a golf course.

With the help of his male offspring, Grandfather Alex worked a miracle on the land, transforming the fields and barns, tracks and hedgerows, swills and pig-sties into a twelve-hole golf course which opened for business in 1920, albeit a somewhat rough and ready version of the little jewel that Clober has become a century on. In an era in which Jack Nicklaus can command $2 million and upwards for a single project as a golf architect, using every mechanical and scientific aid, I can't help but relish the romantic image of the Lyles rolling up the sleeves of their farming shirts and setting to with rustic hoes, rakes, spades and hand-mowers, and only a vague notion of what a course should actually look like.

My father, Alex – oh yes, I am just one in a long line of Alexander Lyles – who had never experienced any trouble in nabbing a seat on the school bus because of the less than enticing smell of pigs he carried with him, gave up formal education at the age of 13 in 1933 when one of the greenkeepers at Clober was injured in an accident on the course. Dad was put to work on a tractor cutting the fairways. From these humble beginnings, he later became a golf professional, as did his brothers George and Walter. Uncle Walter partnered Ben Hogan during the first two rounds of the great man's 1953 Open triumph at Carnoustie. Sadly, I never got to know Uncle Walter. He died a few years after I was born, south of the border in England. However, only recently I was watching the Golf Channel in America when on

2

came a grainy black and white clip of the '53 Open and there, two places beneath Hogan on the leaderboard, was the name A.W. Lyle. I must confess, I felt inordinately proud of the old fella.

Clober was hit by several stray German bombs during the Clydebank Blitz of 13 and 14 March 1943, which left over a thousand people dead, 35,000 homeless and accounted for over one third of the buildings in the town. As the anti-aircraft tracer bullets lit up the night sky all over Glasgow, many Luftwaffe crews decided to unload their bombs and turn for home before reaching the shipyards on the River Clyde. Being a practical type, Granddad simply filled in the craters with sand and overnight Clober had sprouted a number of impressive bunkers, which are still ruining many a card today.

The Lyles continued to own Clober until 1987 and I am chuffed to say that the family connection was renewed a decade later when I was invited to become honorary president of the club that had been founded by my grandfather two generations earlier.

My own appearance on the scene is rapidly approaching, so I really should introduce my mother-to-be, Agnes Jameson Fox as was. The Jamesons owned a local bakery. As Clober's popularity gradually grew over the decades, so Mum had come to enjoy, if a long way short of a privileged existence, then what could be considered a reasonably comfortable lifestyle, given the standards of the time. All that was to change dramatically in 1955 when Dad was offered the job of club professional at Hawkstone Park, Shropshire, lying midway between Shrewsbury and Whitchurch.

Fifty years on, Hawkstone is a magnificent golf complex with two championship courses, a par-three layout and luxury hotel, set amid 400 acres of idyllic parkland, woods and hills. When Mum and Dad and my two elder sisters, Alison and Anne, then aged 14 and 13, arrived, there was no doubting the potential of the place, but, in the days before cars and motorways, Hawkstone appeared to have been stuck in the middle of nowhere with little to recommend it to three pairs of suspicious female eyes. But in the mind's eye of my dad, here was a neglected course which only required some tender loving care to transform it into something as visually appealing as it was challenging to golfers of every standard.

Having been accustomed to the support afforded by the close-knit Jameson and Lyle clans gathered around her, my mother found it a particularly depressing time. She was suddenly confined to a small house attached to the pro's shop, a world removed from being even the first word in luxury. Mum swiftly realised the entire house was infested with spiders, and on one of the first few nights in her new home, she caught thirteen mice in the traps she laid on the pantry floor. When she went to have a bath to fumigate herself, she discovered the previous occupant had used the tub as his coal cellar.

And so, on 9 February 1958, into these threadbare surroundings was the latest member of the Shropshire Lyles deposited, Alexander Walter Barr, continuing the family's fascination with first names beginning with the same letter – Dad Alex, Mum Agnes, Alison and Anne. Presumably Mum and Dad had inherited a cherished christening cup engraved with the initial 'A'.

Coincidental to my arrival on the scene, the owners of Hawkstone decided to put it up for sale. A syndicate of twelve, including my father, purchased the golf course, hotel and grounds for what proved to be a bargain price of £60,000. Most of the other members of the group were wealthy businessmen and it was a bold move by Dad to join them. He had to sweet-talk his bank manager into giving him a loan to become a director in the new company.

My first appearance on the golf course was in a pram parked beneath the kitchen window overlooking the eighteenth green, where Mum could keep an eye on me while peeling the potatoes for the evening meal. As I grew into a toddler and, like any inquisitive tot, became fascinated by the tractors, mowers and sheds housing all manner of exciting but potentially dangerous 'toys' spread out before me, child-minding duties passed to our old corgi, Cam. Whenever I gave the first hint of wandering off in search of mischief, Cam would alert the long arm of parental authority with an outbreak of barking of such ferocity that he must have been a rottweiler in a previous existence. Looking back, the faithful Cam was my loyal protector but to a two-year-old bent on adventure, he was nothing but a right, royal pain in the backside.

To the fairway born, blessed with a father who was as canny a teaching professional as ever prowled the practice tee, and reared on tales of an uncle who had played in the Open against Ben Hogan, Peter Thomson, Bobby Locke and Roberto di Vicenzo, it was inevitable that I should find myself drawn to golf at a tender age. I duly made my debut in the first of the many scrapbooks lovingly kept by my mum – posing with an embarrassed grimace and spindly legs in baggy shorts and wellies – under a headline proclaiming 'Sandy, 3½, can hit them all of eighty yards!' I can still remember that day because there had been a storm in the morning and the air was filled with the seductive aroma of wet, newly mown grass, which along with my mother's shortbread, pies, hot-pots and cakes, became one of my favourite smells of childhood.

Armed with a miniature trolley and golf bag containing a cut-down iron, two woods and a putter, I became a familiar sight at Hawkstone, contentedly traipsing around in the company of dog, Dad and big sister, Anne – sixteen years older than me and clearly humiliated by having to play against her wee brother. My mother would occasionally accompany us. During one of these rare outings she gave us an object lesson in what an infuriating sport golf can be. The third hole at Hawkstone is called the Cricket Pitch because during the Second World War British guards used it to try to teach German POWs the mysteries of leather and willow. It's a tricky par-three and, on this occasion, Mum decided it was the ideal place for a hole in one. Dad was suitably outraged and went marching towards the green muttering, 'What a stupid bloody game this is. Plays twice in twenty years and scores a hole in one, when we've got members here playing seven days a week for forty years who've never had a single one.'

I myself took 127 strokes when I completed my first full eighteen holes as an eight-year-old, after which I set myself a series of targets – to break 100 . . . to break 90 . . . to break 80 . . . At the age of 11 (eat your heart out, Tiger Woods), I was again the focus of a newspaper article when I won the August Medal at Hawkstone with a round of 85 net 64. This might have made me one very unpopular little bunny in the clubhouse but, thanks to the way I had been brought up by my dad, in what was basically an adult environment, to respect the etiquette and spirit in which golf should be played, it earned me a number of orange squashes from the grown-ups – not to mention my first silver teaspoon. Over the years, I built up a considerable collection of Hawkstone spoons. They retain a special place in the trophy cabinet at home on the banks of Loch Voil in the Trossachs.

If the Hawkstone members resented being beaten by a primary school kid, they hid it well but I like to think I earned their admiration – aye, and maybe even affection – because I was never a cocky brat. I never bad-mouthed anyone, tried to cheat or threw a tantrum because I knew that if I did, Dad would hear about it, and I would have done anything not to let him down. Quiet and placid as he was, Dad had his little ways. Whenever I went out to play – be it in a friendly foursome or a monthly medal, while I was an amateur or even as a tenderfoot professional – his last words to me would be, 'Don't forget, I'll have my spies watching you . . .' When you think two eyes are watching you from behind every tree and bush, and their owner is ready to report any misdemeanour however minor, you have no option but to behave yourself.

It need hardly be said that I was extremely fortunate in that my dad was not only an accomplished golfer in his own right but possessed a natural gift as a teaching pro. Consequently, I celebrated becoming a teenager by having my handicap lowered to three. Dad coached me from an early age but because he was so busy running the golf side of Hawkstone, he didn't have time to spend hours and hours at my shoulder. He would offer a few words of wisdom now and then, leaving me to put them into practice through application and feel. Dad's guidance proved invaluable over the years. He was a firm believer in the idea that if you had a natural swing, who was he to tinker with what nature had provided? Two decades later I was to regret not remembering this attitude when my game deserted me almost overnight.

Dad was so passionate about golf it was inevitable that I would fall in love with the game. It fascinated me from a young age because it could change so quickly, day by day, week by week. Dad was never one of those overbearing sporting parents, anything but, in fact. If I was on the practice ground on a particularly busy day, he would tell the members just to push me aside. It was on the practice ground that I fashioned all the little skills that stood me in such great stead in the years to come – tricks of the trade I would proudly show off to Dad when the course was a bit quieter and father and son could enjoy an evening round amid the lengthening shadows. Perhaps it was because my dad wasn't forceful or pushy in any way whatsoever that I loved spending so much time with a club in my hands.

The practice range at Hawkstone was of the basic variety – a forty-yard narrow strip that had the benefit of a huge beech tree standing smack in the middle. This is where I learned how to play around a tree, or over a particular clump of branches, or under the hanging leaves – a tremendous exercise and far, far better than simply munching thousands of balls with a 5-iron all day. You learn the subtleties of golf by practising every different kind of shot – downhill lies, uphill lies, fades and draws. Forty odd years further on, sports psychologists now encourage young golfers to have fun on the practice range, clipping 4-irons five feet above the ground and such like, to make those long, lonely sessions more enjoyable, something I instinctively tried to achieve all those years ago.

When I was not playing golf, Hawkstone Park was better than any Disney theme park to a boisterous youngster with boundless energy. Dating back to the Napoleonic era, it was opened by Sir Rowland Hill in 1790 as a country hotel catering to the gentry, complete with the famous ravines, towering cliffs, bridges, archways, caves, grottoes and tunnels. According to local myth, King Arthur is reputed to have addressed his troops in one of the underground chambers before an important battle, while two giants, Tarquin and Tarquinus, lived in the Red Castle, the ruins of which – Giants' Well – are named after them. Their third brother, Sir Caradus, was a renowned fighter and used to make ends meet by kidnapping the Knights of the Round Table and holding them to ransom within what is now Hawkstone. When not practising to become the next Ben Hogan, I would roam my private back garden as Sir Lancelot, in my childish imagination, rescuing maidens in distress. As a hotel and park, Hawkstone fell into disrepair in the early part of the 20th century but, I'm glad to say, it has now been restored to its former glory by the various efforts of successive owners.

I can honestly say I enjoyed a truly blissful childhood, probably because we lived away from any town with all the attendant distractions and peer pressure that might have led me astray. While some of my schoolmates may have hung about street corners for the want of anything better to do, I clambered into our rowing boat and went fishing on the lake in Hawkstone, rode my bike through the woods, took my air rifle and went in search of 'big game' or, in the winter, sledged down the hills.

As an outdoor adventurer, I did not relish being cooped up in a school classroom, especially since I showed no signs of being an Einstein in waiting at Wem Secondary Modern. It was only many years later that I discovered my learning difficulties were due to dyslexia, a problem that I have passed on to all three sons from my two marriages. Fortunately, knowledge of the condition has made such great advances that they have been able to make light of the hindrance. Back in my school days in the early 1970s, we had never heard of dyslexia. Although I have no trouble with hand-eye coordination, putting things down on paper or memorising facts and figures is not easy to this day. Consequently, I spent every day of every school term idly gazing out of the window in the direction of the practice range, where I would have spent an hour or so before breakfast, and where I already knew I would sit my most important examinations.

While I was cheerfully passing my formative years having fun, my parents were working incredibly hard, Mum as housewife, golf club bookkeeper and chief organiser, and Dad as the club pro. Looking back, I cannot remember the five of us ever going on a family summer holiday because the summer months are the busiest on a golf course. At Christmas I always received one special present – Scalextric or Subutteo – but my parents ensured I was not spoiled in terms of golf equipment and I played with old cut-down hickory shafts or Jessie Valentine ladies' clubs until I was 13 when I received my first brand spanking new set of Dunlops. By way of thanks to my parents, I was selected to play for the county senior side in the Staffordshire and Shropshire Alliance. With my shiny new putter I knocked in a twelve-footer on the eighteenth green at Trentham to secure victory for my Hawkstone partner, Les Welch, and myself.

The following year, 1972, I replaced Peter Townsend in the record books when I became the youngest player to be selected to represent England Schoolboys. Since I played my entire professional career under the cross of St Andrew, the irony is that our opponents at Moortown were Scotland. I'm somewhat embarrassed to admit that the scorecard, which I still have in my possession, shows England winning 13½–1½. Among the Scottish reserves for that match was Alloa's Alan Hansen, who could easily have become a highly successful professional golfer but decided to concentrate on a career in football. Winner of three European Cups, eight league championship titles and two FA Cups as captain of Liverpool, plus twenty-six Scotland international caps, Alan obviously made the right choice but gives tantalising glimpses of what might have been on the pro-celebrity circuit, where he is a regular winner.

I was becoming something of a serial winner myself, adding the Hawkstone Club Championship to my growing catalogue of trophies when, aged 15 and with a scratch handicap, I beat defending champion Anthony Smith – who also happened to be the county strokeplay and matchplay champion – in an extraordinary match. My luckless opponent covered the first eighteen holes in one under par only to go in for lunch five down. After the break I completed a 10 and 9 victory, completing the twenty-seven holes played in nine under par. Later that season I also won the Shropshire Boys title at Market Drayton, my level-par 72 being good enough to relegate a tiny but formidable lad from Oswestry into second place – so began a lifelong friendship and rivalry with Ian Woosnam.

If there is one thing worse than a sore loser, it's a bad winner. Again thanks to the manner in which Mum and Dad brought me up, I was never allowed to acquire a big head, and those early victories were probably a good grounding in learning to be a gracious winner. It's so long since I last won a tournament, though – the Volvo Masters in 1992 – I may well turn cartwheels on the eighteenth green should it ever happen again. As a laddie I was never one to punch the air in triumph or roll up to an event proclaiming, 'I'm here. So what's the course record at this joint, then?'

I most certainly did not threaten the course record at Lochgreen where, at the age of 15 years and five months, I tried – and failed – to qualify for the 1973 Open Championship to be played at Royal Troon. My sister Anne drove me north from the Midlands to Ayrshire in her little Mini-van, which was an eight-hour adventure in itself. Anne had been born in Scotland but, needless to say, we became hopelessly lost, whereupon big sis suddenly announced, 'I'm going to follow that lorry – I bet it's going to Troon.'

'Why on earth would you think that?' I asked, which, under our present circumstances, seemed an entirely reasonable question.

'I've just got a feeling, that's why,' replied Anne with her unique brand of female logic.

What can I say? With the aforementioned lorry acting as our navigator, we duly drove into Troon. We were staying with relatives around the corner from Lochgreen, where I shot 74 twice and missed qualifying by a couple of strokes. I was far from despondent, however, for I regarded this qualifier as a 'prelim' for the real examinations ahead. Reduced to the role of spectator, I relished watching the world's greatest players challenging each other at the top of the leaderboard – Tom Weiskopf, the eventual champion, Jack Nicklaus, Johnny Miller, Lee Trevino, Bob Charles. It has often been said that Weiskopf's swing was so sweet you could have poured it over a pancake and, to my eyes, it was a wonder to behold. Thirty-one years later at Troon, I partnered Weiskopf during the opening two rounds of the 2004 Open when the old champ had the misfortune to rack up a quadruple-bogey eight on the very first hole of the championship. As Tom, who is well over six feet tall, grew ever smaller in the greenside bunker as he tried to blast his way out of the sand, I really felt for him and offered him a sympathetic smile on our way to the second tee. I didn't pass any comment for the simple reason I knew there was nothing I could say that would make him feel any better. Being the great champion he is, however, all credit to Tom that he turned up the next day instead of 'developing' a strained back and pulling out of the tournament. Day two dawned and as we stood on the first tee I thought to myself, 'Well, Tom ain't going to do that again . . .' He didn't, but he almost did, topping his drive forty yards into the gorse bushes – and sending a family of bunny rabbits fleeing all over the fairway in panic – on his way to a six.

If Weiskopf had realised what a truly great player he was, he would have won far more Majors than the '73 Troon Open, but he appeared to regard himself as being forever in the shadow of Nicklaus, a fellow graduate of Ohio State University. Runner-up four times in the Masters and second again in the 1976 US Open, it was cruelly said of Weiskopf that he knew more ways to choke than Dracula. I always thought that Dracula bit his victims rather than throttled them but there you go . . . Tom never took himself or the game too seriously. In fact, when he became a course designer at the end of his playing days, his wife, Jeanne, commented, 'It's the first job he's had since we were married.'

Talking to J.C. Snead one time, Weiskopf mused, 'Wouldn't it be great if you could come out here and just pick the tournaments you like to play, never practise, hang out in the bars and have a couple of drinks and simply have fun,' to which came the response, 'Tom, that's what you've done your whole life.'

At the 1979 Open at Royal Lytham, Weiskopf was enduring

a miserable round when, on a whim, he decided to hit his 80 yard approach to the sixteenth with his putter before repairing to the bar of the Clifton Hotel. Tom was enjoying a beer when Nicklaus walked up to ask if what he had heard was true. 'Well, Jack,' replied Tom, trying and failing to keep a straight face, 'I wanted to keep the ball under the wind.' Nicklaus turned those famous ice-blue eyes on his friend, shook his head resignedly, and departed.

My favourite Tom Weiskopf yarn occurred during the 1980 Open at Muirfield where he was watching the BBC's coverage of the event with Jeanne and a group of friends, and friends of friends. Tom was gently teasing the BBC when a woman in the company suddenly stood up and left.

'Do you know who that woman is?' demanded Jeanne.

'Don't tell me – the Queen of England.'

'Close, it's her sister, Princess Margaret.'

When HRH rejoined the company Tom was at pains to be at his most gracious. In conversation the princess mentioned that her late father was a passionate golfer when his 'day job' permitted, and Tom innocently remarked, 'That's nice. What did your father do?'

'He was the King . . .'

I had been enthralled by the Open Championship since 1969 when Dad and I drove to Royal Lytham to witness Tony Jacklin's victory. Jacklin celebrated by throwing his ball into the crowd around the eighteenth. Tiny as I was, aged 11, compared to the rest of the gallery, I almost managed to catch it before being denied this historic memento by the long arm of an adult behind me. Just as Jacklin was the first British winner of the Open since Max Faulkner in 1951, so it would be another sixteen years before another golfer from these shores held the Claret Jug aloft, and that was me. When I made my Ryder Cup debut at the Greenbrier, West Virginia in 1979, I partnered Tony in the opening-day foursomes, and later served under his captaincy in Europe's 1985 and 1987 conquests of the United States.

At Lytham, I took the opportunity of studying not just Jacklin close up and personal, but the way in which all the great players prepared for and approached a Major championship. To anyone born in the fifties, the mere mention of the name Peter Thomson is enough to transport you back to that golden sporting era of Real Madrid, Lew Hoad, Gordon Richards, Roger Bannister, Denis Compton, Floyd Paterson and Stirling Moss. In the seven years from 1952–58, Thomson won the Open four times and finished runner-up on the other three occasions.

Even so, some critics across the Atlantic sought to belittle those triumphs because they were achieved at a time when the Open did not routinely feature on the summer itineraries of Ben Hogan, Sam Snead and the other great Americans of the day. As befitting a man who is a keen student of Nietzsche, Thomson remained philosophical, pointing out with typical Melbournian pragmatism, 'You can only beat those who show up.'

At Royal Birkdale in 1965 they all showed up – Jack Nicklaus, Arnold Palmer, Doug Sanders, Phil Rodgers and Tony Lema, the defending champion. Many believed Thomson, then approaching 36, to be in inexorable decline. At St Andrews the previous summer, had he not finished a distant twenty strokes behind Lema to languish in twenty-fourth place? Instead, it was to be his greatest victory of them all. A master of links golf, Thomson arrived on the seventeenth tee on the final afternoon with a one-shot advantage over Lema and with two 500 yard plus holes between him and a fifth Open Championship. Two flawless fours against Lema's five and six finish and the jug was his to embrace for a remarkable fifth time.

Thomson first came among us in the era of Hogan, but his durability was such that he was still good enough to play all four rounds and occupy twenty-fifth place when aged 50 at the 1979 Open at Royal Lytham. 'That was almost as much fun,' he said at the time, 'as winning the damn thing for the first time twenty-five years ago.' A gifted talent rather than a technician, Thomson paid only lip service to practice. 'Target practice,' he used to say, 'is all well and good and you might get a badge saying you're a real marksman, but that doesn't necessarily mean you will be a good guerrilla fighter. You have to display the ability to compete, to survive and not allow the fear of success to overwhelm you.'

Now a highly respected course designer, Thomson keeps a home in St Andrews, where he won the second of his Opens, and is a 'weel-kent face' in the clubhouse of the Duke's Course, one of his many architectural masterpieces. In his fascinating tome *Golf Heroes*, Peter Alliss wrote of Thomson: 'He is one of golf's supreme champions and life's great companions.'

When I happened upon Thomson practising at Troon, there wasn't a soul watching him but I observed him with an increasing sense of awe, thinking, 'What I'd give to do that,' as he unleashed a succession of beautifully struck woods and irons, as smooth as you like. Thomson did not possess a big swing but even towards the end of his playing career it remained a thing of beauty. I was particularly impressed by the purity of his ball-striking and just standing watching a master at work was a terrific insight into what makes a champion.

At the far end of the range I noticed a huge crowd which,

given the lack of interest in Peter Thomson, suggested the presence of someone really famous. Did I say 'famous'? It was my first sighting of Jack Nicklaus in the flesh with a driver in his hand, launching balls at his caddie, who looked like a pinhead away in the far-off distance. The Golden Bear's drives had a hang-time of about ten seconds after which the caddie would move two yards one way, three yards the other, and I remember saying to myself, 'This is it . . . this is the level you'll have to achieve.'

Seeing Thomson and Nicklaus go about their business made a big impression on me because that is the precise moment I realised that golf, which had always come naturally to me, also involved a heap of hard work if your ambition was to make it to the very top.

Trying to qualify for the Troon Open of '73 and play in the same field as these towering legends may seem an ambition too far at the age of 15, but it was an opportunity to test myself, to see if I could even get close to the standard required, to discover what my weaknesses were, be they of temperament or decision-making. I saw it as preparation for the day when I would qualify for the Open, even if that day was many years hence. I would be ready for it. To a naive teenager accustomed to playing in the Hawkstone Saturday morning medal, just being involved in the Open – seeing the crowds and the marquees, feeling the incredible atmosphere throughout the town of Troon that week – was an invaluable initiation, and to miss out by just a couple of shots suggested I was not all that far away.

CHAPTER TWO

'EXCUSE ME, MR PLAYER . . .'

In the cemetery by the ruins of the breathtakingly beautiful St Andrews Cathedral lies the grave of 'Young' Tom Morris, the first 'great' of world golf. The inscription on his memorial headstone reads 'Deeply regretted by numerous friends and all golfers, he thrice won the Championship belt and held it without envy, his many amiable qualities being no less acknowledged than his golfing achievements.' The son of 'Old' Tom, who was Open champion four times and the oldest winner at 46, 'Young' Tom became the youngest player to win the most treasured prize in golf when he triumphed at the age of 17 years, five months and eight days in 1868, a record that seems certain to survive the sands of time.

'Young' Tom was a Tiger Woods-style phenomenon, winning the Championship Belt outright after his three successive victories in 1868, '69 and '70 (I should add that he was runner-up to his dad in 1867). Prestwick Golf Club, which hosted the event in those days, suddenly found itself without a prize to present and postponed the 1871 tournament while deciding what to do next. After much discussion, it was agreed to invite St Andrews and Musselburgh to join the Open rotation and a Claret Jug was commissioned to replace the Championship Belt, then in the permanent possession of 'Young' Tom. In 1872, it came as no great surprise to anyone when 'Young' Tom equalled his father by winning his fourth Open Championship and adding the Claret Jug to his collection of trophies.

On 11 September 1875, father and son were playing an exhibition match at North Berwick when they received word that 'Young' Tom's wife of one year, Margaret Drennan, had been taken ill during childbirth in St Andrews. Before 'Young' Tom could make it home to be at his wife's side, a telegram arrived announcing the tragic news that she had died of a ruptured uterus. 'Young' Tom never recovered from the shock of losing both wife and unborn son and died of a pulmonary haemorrhage on Christmas morning. He was 24. 'Old' Tom, who lived to the age of 86, was often heard to lament, 'They say Tommy died of a broken heart, but if that was true, I wouldn't be here either.'

When it came to my turn to become champion at Royal St George's in 1985, I was both fortunate and privileged because, as well as receiving the Claret Jug, to mark the 125th anniversary of the very first Open, the Prestwick members generously presented me with a beautiful replica of 'Young' Tom Morris's famous Championship Belt. There are only two such priceless trophies in the world – one in my cabinet at home and the original, which graces the magnificent golf museum directly across the road from the Royal & Ancient clubhouse in St Andrews.

I could not match 'Young' Tom Morris's reported feat of

competing in the Open as a 13-year-old, but less than five months after my sixteenth birthday in 1974, I bunked off school to shoot 79 and 71 in gale-force winds in the qualifying event at St Anne's Old and become the youngest player to compete in the Open at Royal Lytham. Perhaps because I was due to leave Wem Secondary in less than two weeks' time and had already sat all my exams, rather than hauling me before him for being absent without leave, the headmaster Mr Needham sent me a 'good luck' telegram. The head even found something nice to say about me in the local *Shropshire Star* newspaper, describing me as 'modest and likeable'.

I trust I was not being cocky, therefore, when I walked into the clubhouse before the opening practice round and, muttering 'nothing ventured, nothing gained', blithely added my name to that of Gary Player's beside his chosen tee-off time. Although I greatly admired the other two members of golf's Holy Trinity of the day – Arnold Palmer and Jack Nicklaus – I revered the South African as no other. Gary had been a huge influence on me since childhood because, while he may have lacked the natural talent of a Seve Ballesteros, say, he *made* himself a champion through dedication and sheer hard graft – a work-ethic followed by Nick Faldo, another who became the best in the world by sweat rather than inspiration.

Nicklaus may have been the giant of golf but Gary fascinated me because he was the little fella trying to topple Goliath. When Gary Player told the world he did one hundred press-ups on two fingers, I did one hundred press-ups on two fingers. When Gary Player told us he hit bunker shots for three hours, I hit bunker shots for three hours. When Gary Player told us he ate bananas, I ate more bananas than Guy the Gorilla in Regent's Park Zoo.

As Peter Alliss put it so eloquently in *Golf Heroes*: 'I first saw Gary Player in the early 1950s. Just 5ft 7in tall and slight of build, his talent looked very limited. He spent hours hitting balls with the most inelegant swing and although he did have the ability to hit bunker shots reasonably well, his putting stroke was just a jab. I remember watching him, with John Jacobs, practising an impossible chip shot on to a downhill slope, ground like concrete and trying to get the ball to stop within twenty-five feet. We watched spellbound: had the lad lost his reason? He turned to ask for advice and, if memory serves me right, in the nicest possible way we suggested he return to South Africa, enjoy his golf as an amateur and get a steady job that might include a pension . . .'

He chose to ignore that advice, which is why Sandy Lyle (Shropshire Boys champion) bowled up to Gary Player (winner of three Open Championships, three Masters, two US PGA titles and one US Open) to introduce himself.

'Excuse me, Mr Player,' I said, 'I hope you don't mind but I've requested a practice round with you tomorrow.'

'Certainly, son. What age are you?'

'Sixteen.'

'My word, you're a big lad for sixteen. I look forward to our date.'

Gary probably disappeared round the corner of the clubhouse and grimaced at the prospect of playing a full round with a raw amateur but, consummate diplomat that he is, he was a real gentleman throughout our eighteen holes. If I had been of a mischievous bent, I might have shown up on the first tee wearing black from head to toe – Gary's favourite golf ensemble – but wisely chose a yellow sweater and grey trousers, although I accept that many would not regard that particular combination as 'wise'. Imitation may be the sincerest form of flattery but I think Gary would have viewed the appearance of another 'Man in Black' as a gross insult. I was so overawed by being in his company that I spoke only when spoken to, but just watching him like a hawk was another vital lesson in my golf education. When Gary did speak, it was usually to offer me a homily – 'work hard, then work harder. When you've finished work, do some more.'

Naive as I was, I idly fantasised about being drawn with Gary and Jack Nicklaus for the opening two rounds – I was totally unaware that the pairings were seeded – and was somewhat disappointed to find myself teeing off at 1.30 the following afternoon with Ireland's Jimmy Martin and Bobby Walker of Scotland, two fine players but not the glamour companions I had envisaged. Jimmy had played in the 1965 Ryder Cup contest at Royal Birkdale against an American side containing Arnold Palmer, Billy Casper and Tony Lema, so I was more than satisfied to finish the first round within two strokes of him after a highly satisfactory 75 in the wind. Gary Player and John Morgan were the joint leaders on 69 – remarkable scores in the conditions – while I lay equal twenty-seventh and ahead of such luminaries as Americans Lee Trevino, Gene Littler and Gay Brewer, plus former Open champions Bob Charles of New Zealand and Australian Kel Nagle.

After five holes of the second round, I was going along smoothly on level par and cracking jokes with my caddy, my sister Anne's boyfriend George Jones, when I found a fairway bunker on the 486 yard par-five sixth, the ball burying itself in the face of the trap. Instead of playing out sideways and giving myself the chance of salvaging a par, I tried to blast the ball towards the green, took three more shots to escape and eventually staggered off the sixth green with an almost ruinous quadruple-bogey nine. Fortunately, I promptly birdied the 551 yard par-five seventh and rolled in a forty-five-foot birdie putt in front of a huge gallery around the eighteenth green to escape with a 77 and a halfway total of 152, making the cut by a comfortable five strokes; I may have been fifteen shots adrift of Gary Player but, encouragingly, I was only one behind Tony Jacklin.

My mum was among those gathered at the last green, sitting behind two ladies of a certain age armed with a Tupperware picnic and binoculars.

'Who's this?'

'Oh, it's Sandy Lyle, that young amateur everyone's talking about.'

'Oh, my,' she commented as I sauntered on to the putting surface, 'he must have been a ten-pound baby.'

'Ten pounds five ounces to be exact,' interrupted my mother, leaning forward.

Because I was a teenager and the leading amateur, the fact I had survived the first cut with something to spare attracted a lot of media interest, especially when my hero Gary Player generously told the assembled TV, radio and newspaper reporters that 'it was stupendous to take nine then shoot a birdie. There are many players in this field who would have collapsed after taking nine. Young Sandy has the character and guts that make champions.' Less encouraging was my third-round 84, which cost me the silver medal awarded to the leading amateur and, because there were two cuts at the time, an appearance in the fourth round.

'Where did it go wrong?' asked an American voice from the pack of journalists, to whom I was still 'hot news'.

'Everywhere from the first hole,' I replied honestly.

I was still the focus of a lot of attention, however, in demand for newspaper interviews and autographs, which, on top of qualifying and three rounds of my first Major, combined to make it a pretty hard week for a tenderfoot. I was nearly late arriving on the first tee for my second and third rounds because of the swarm of autograph hunters lying in wait. It was a great compliment to be asked – indeed, it still is – but when you are young and innocent you will sign every scrap of paper thrust under your nose because you don't like to say no. At the Masters, they have shaved forty minutes off the time of the practice rounds since banning the signing of autographs on the course.

After the disappointment of my departure from Royal Lytham and the Open Championship, I was home in time to watch Gary Player receiving the old Claret Jug on TV. He beat Peter Oosterhuis by four shots with Jack Nicklaus third.

In many ways, Gary Player was the founder of international golf, being the first foreigner to take on and beat the Americans on their own turf. He was a firm believer that no mountain was too high to conquer if you had the necessary will power. His mother died when he was young and the task of rearing him fell to his beloved older brother, Ian. The two Players were out for a five-mile run one morning when Gary pulled up and sprawled on the ground, gasping that he could run no more. Gary recalls, '"What do you mean, you can't finish?" Ian said, as he hauled me to my feet and cuffed me about the ears. "There's no such thing in this world as can't – you have to eliminate that t."' At the 1978 Masters, Player was well out of contention when he launched a late charge that attracted little interest from the galleries. Turning to his playing partner, Seve

Ballesteros, Player famously told him, 'These people don't think I can win, Seve, but I can.' So saying, Player birdied seven of the last ten holes for a closing round of 64, which won him his third Green Jacket by one stroke from Tom Watson, Hubert Green and Ron Funseth.

A week after Lytham, the happiest day of my first sixteen years dawned – in the afternoon I travelled home on the school bus for the last time, joyfully jammed into the back seat with a bunch of mates and a couple of celebratory bottles of wine, arriving back into the bosom of my family in a slightly sozzled state. Overnight, life had never been better. When not playing competitive golf or practising, I earned a wage by working at Hawkstone as trainee greenkeeper/odd-job man alongside Dad, to whom I was very, very close. It may sound corny but it truly was the perfect father-son relationship. The only time he ever really lost his rag with me occurred when I was about ten years of age and happily searching for worms, splashing about in a foot-deep pond of rainwater that Dad was trying to pump off one of the greens. As he disappeared to begin yet another task elsewhere on the course, his parting words were, 'Don't mess about with either the tractor or the pump.' Somehow or other, I did manage to fiddle with the pipe and, consequently, as fast as the water was pumped off the green it was pumped straight back on again. When Dad came back an hour or so later, he was absolutely fuming. That earned me a thick ear for my troubles. He was not a happy man.

Dad was a lovely, gentle, placid man, who hardly ever swore, which was amazing for a golfer and doubly amazing when he had to teach so many players of differing standards. If a piece of machinery broke down, he might have muttered 'bitch' but never, ever the f word. Even when I not only discovered but literally embraced the distractions of the hotel attached to Hawkstone – there were scores of young girls from all over the country working there to provide a wide variety of entertainment – Dad could put his point across without engaging in a shouting match. Whenever golf was in danger of taking a back seat, Dad would open the front door and gaze across the fairways with the words, 'Oh, weather's nice . . . practice range is pretty quiet . . .' He never imposed a curfew on me – he was way too canny for that – but having allowed me to leave school to pursue a career in golf, in his own quiet way he would remind his son and heir of the serious work to be done if I was going to fulfil Gary Player's prediction that I possessed 'the character and guts that make champions'.

Having opted out of the education system, I had no choice but to begin a full-time apprenticeship that would lead to a career as a professional golfer. I did not leave school with a lengthy list of qualifications, I lacked the skills to become involved in course design and I had no formal training in greenkeeping so, from a young age, I accepted that tournament golf represented my best hope of earning a crust.

With two years to wait until I could turn professional, I combined playing as an amateur with helping Dad at Hawkstone, where, depending upon the season, I could be doing something as gentle as painting the tee-markers on a spring morning, or shovelling snow. As a way of building up your arm and shoulder muscles, nothing beats clearing a golf course of trees after a particularly severe storm. Who needs a gym when you have forty fallen trees to cut up with a chainsaw? We hauled them off, logging them, splitting them – ideal for body-building, perhaps, but it did play havoc with my swing. After three weeks of a lumberjack's life, you tend to become a bit heavy-handed and my divots were like mini-craters when I finally returned to the range.

I hated the winter when the course was closed but even then Dad would find a way to keep me amused. One of our favourite pastimes was to hang up an old carpet on two coat-hangers between the lockers in the changing room and I would fire hundreds of balls into the pile from a mat on the floor. Needless to say, it did not take long to put a few holes in the rug, after which the balls would ricochet around the locker-room like bullets in a Wild West shoot-out.

Dad used the winter months as an opportunity to renew his energies after spending spring, summer and autumn working seven days a week from six in the morning until maybe ten at night. A golf course is a bit like painting the Forth rail bridge – as soon as you think you have completed every task it's time to start at the beginning all over again. With the boiler roaring away, burning an endless supply of logs for heat, and the radio playing, days passed far quicker than you might imagine and the bleak midwinter soon turned to spring again and the new amateur season.

Although I would not qualify for the Open again until 1977 (I carried the bag for my close friend Martin Poxon in both '75 and '76), following my promising performance in the Open at Lytham in '74, I was disappointed not to be selected for the 1975 Walker Cup contest against the Americans at St Andrews later in the summer but, as Dad pointed out, I had only just turned 17 and time was on my side. For the record, a powerful US team, comprising Curtis Strange, Craig Stadler, Jay Haas, Jerry

Pate and George Burns, triumphed 15½–8½ so, with the benefit of 20/20 hindsight, perhaps being overlooked was a blessing in disguise.

Maybe I felt I had something to prove and, partnered by Martin Poxon, who had been named in the team, the month before the Walker Cup we stormed into the semi-finals of the prestigious Sunningdale Foursomes with a series of comfortable victories. Among the other semi-finalists that April were Ryder Cup captain Bernard Hunt and Ken Brown, but our bid for glory was scuppered when the tournament was cancelled with Sunningdale under six inches of snow. England in the spring – wonderful is it not?

I enjoyed rather better luck that same month at Moor Park in the Carris Trophy – the English Boys' Strokeplay Championship – an event I had long dreamed of winning, especially as I finished third and runner-up in my first two appearances. The whole trip was a great adventure because it was one of those rare occasions when Dad had time off from Hawkstone and so we set off together in his ancient Fiat 126, a horrible little box on four wheels – I did not like the look of it, the smell of it or the sound of it. Dad was never into cars. Even in later years when I persuaded him to invest in an up-market model with air-conditioning he looked at me in genuine puzzlement and enquired, 'Can't I just open the window?'

We booked into a small bed and breakfast hotel in Rickmansworth and Dad suggested a night out at the local cinema, which was quite something for him. I remember we went to see 'Towering Inferno' starring Steve McQueen, Paul Newman, Faye Dunaway, Fred Astaire and, long before he became infamous, O.J. Simpson. It was billed as 'The Greatest Disaster Movie Ever

Made', but all I know is that it put me off living in a high-rise for life.

After the snow of Sunningdale, the Carris was played in a mixture of frost, snow and torrential rain with the opening two rounds restricted to twenty-nine holes because of the water flooding Moor Park. Lying four strokes behind Paul Carrigill after the first day's play, I shot 72 and 77 to win by five strokes, and was twelve shots in front of a certain N.A. (Nicholas Alexander) Faldo of Welwyn Garden City.

Although I never actually spotted Dad out on the course, I knew he was there from the plumes of Embassy smoke emanating from behind trees and bushes. I have no idea what Dad was saving the coupons from the packets for but we had boxes full of the things, and if he ever saw a member or guest discarding an empty box of Embassy, I was despatched to trawl through the wastebin in case another priceless coupon was there to be salvaged. Apart from winning the Carris, it was a memorable weekend simply for the amount of time I was able to spend with Dad.

I crossed swords with Nick Faldo again a month later in the English Amateur Strokeplay Championship – the Brabazon Trophy – at Hollinwell, Nottinghamshire. The field included five Walker Cup players plus another future Open champion, Nick Price of Zimbabwe, who was a Family Lyle houseguest on various occasions. After three rounds, I trailed Faldo by a single stroke and Geoff Marks was hovering menacingly at my shoulder. Dad rated Hollinwell as one of the toughest inland courses in the country, so I thought my final round of 72 – which earned me a two-shot victory over Marks – was the finest of my career to date, given the severity of the test and the pressures of trying to become the youngest ever winner of the Brabazon Trophy, a record, so I'm told, that I hold to this day. To my mind, Geoff Marks was one of the two or three best amateurs in the world at the time, as he showed by covering the last four holes in two under par, only to lose ground when the young whippersnapper at his side countered with an eagle and a couple of birdies.

In the *Guardian*, the highly respected golf writer Pat Ward-Thomas kindly said of me: 'Sandy Lyle was born on the golf course and the game has been his life; almost certainly it will remain so. Prophecy of success for one of such tender years can often go amiss, but I fancy not with Lyle. Not for a long time, if ever, will the holder of the Carris Trophy win a national championship a month later . . .'

I returned to Hawkstone clutching the treasured golden trophy, which I paraded around the hotel only to hear later the same evening that, despite finishing top amateur in the Open followed by my victories in the Carris and Brabazon Trophies, I was named as first reserve in the six-man England team for the forthcoming European Championship at Killarney. The selectors opted for the five Walker Cup players – Martin Poxon, Mark James, Peter Hedges, Richard Eyles and John Davies – plus Geoff Marks, and I headed for the range to work off my frustration.

Ah well, at least my efforts were appreciated at Hawkstone where I was invited to partner the legendary footballer Billy Wright – capped 105 times and captain of England at three World Cups – against Martin Poxon and Joe Mercer, who had just enjoyed a successful stint as caretaker manager of England following the departure of Sir Alf Ramsey. The celebrity match was held to mark the opening of the new eighteen-hole Weston course. Wright and Lyle won one up before donning dicky suit and bow tie for a gala ball featuring Rovers' Return regulars

Barbara Mullaney (Rita Fairclough), Bernard Youens (Stan Ogden) and Betty Driver (Betty Turpin).

From 'Coronation Street' to Space City – at 1 p.m. on 3 January 1976, Nick Faldo, Martin Poxon and I boarded British Airways' flight BA661 bound for Texas, having taken up the offer of golf scholarships at the University of Houston, the most successful college in America with twelve National Championships in the past twenty-five years. Among Houston's famous graduates were John Mahaffey, runner-up to Lou Graham in the US Open the previous summer, future Open champion Bill Rogers, plus Ryder Cup players Homero Blancas and Bruce Lietzke, which may be why the university coach, Dave Williams, made our adventure sound like the opportunity of a lifetime. 'You will be asked to put in fifteen hours a week in five subjects and will be required to do well in four of them,' he told us, 'but you will play a great deal of competitive golf in ideal conditions.'

Houston, we have a problem – several, in fact. Whereas I had this naive vision of playing golf on perfectly prepared courses with the sun on my back and a team of coaches on hand to offer expert advice, Houston in January is scarcely any warmer than Hartlepool at the same time of year, and our arrival was a fairly bleak affair. Appearing on campus ten days before the rest of the 28,000 students, we were given a series of preliminary examinations, which, given my dyslexia and modest achievements at school back home, left me scratching my head. Although coach Williams had talked of twenty golf courses in the immediate area, when I left the classroom in search of one, not even a practice range was to be found. Indeed, the nearest course was a forty-minute bus ride away, shattering any illusion I might still have fondly nurtured about Houston being a golfing paradise.

To someone accustomed to looking out of his bedroom window and seeing Hawkstone's eighteenth green, far from being paradise this concrete jungle was a living hell.

When my test results came back marked 'must do better' – I had failed to reach the required standard by 0.2 per cent – it was suggested that I take myself off to a junior college eighty miles down the highway, where I would not even have room-mate Martin Poxon's unfailing good humour to cheer me up. Disillusioned with the American dream, having had my fill of McDonald's and iced tea, and aching for the sight of England's green and pleasant land, I quit after precisely three weeks. If I had stuck it out – and the prospect of being entirely alone in what, for all our similarities, to me remains the most foreign of countries, made that impossible – I would probably have enjoyed a better education but I firmly believe my golf would have suffered, probably irreversibly. Perhaps I had been spoiled in some ways by always having my parents around to sort out any problems but I found the whole experience a very scary business. Nick Faldo was the next to ship out a couple of months later, swiftly followed by Martin, so all in all our American experiment can best be described as an unmitigated failure.

While Nick Faldo went off to pursue a professional career, I concentrated on trying to achieve one of my last unfulfilled ambitions as an amateur by gaining selection for the following year's Walker Cup contest at Shinnecock Hills, New York. My defence of the Brabazon Trophy at Saunton in Devon was going nicely until the tenth hole of the final round. After a fine drive, my approach came to rest on the front slope of the two-tiered green. Putt number one fell four yards short of the hole, number two ran three feet past, number three stopped on the lip, number four was a one-handed 'air' shot, and it wasn't until the fifth of my ugly putts that the ball finally disappeared from sight. (Although I have since four-putted, I am relieved to say that was the one and only time in my career – to date! – I have ever five-putted . . .) The Brabazon was a lesson learned as I ultimately finished four strokes behind the new champion, Peter Hedges.

Having fluffed my lines in the English Amateur Strokeplay event, I was pleased to reach the quarter-final of the English Amateur Matchplay Championship with a hard-fought one-hole victory over Toby Shannon, a measure of revenge for a defeat in the final of the British Boys' Championship at Royal Liverpool two years earlier. According to the headlines in the scrapbook so meticulously stuck together by my mum, I had strolled through the early rounds of that event with 'champion-in-waiting' emblazoned across my floppy, white sunhat: Lyle Is The One To Beat . . . Sandy Lyle Has Dream Day . . . Lyle In Runaway Triumph . . . Lyle Through Despite Illness . . . Sick Sandy Keeps His Head . . . and, finally, Lyle Is Beaten Heavily In Boys' Championship Final.

True, I had been suffering all week from a stomach bug that had swept round the locker-room, but from the moment Toby Shannon pitched in for a birdie at the first until the match embarrassingly ended in a 10 and 9 thrashing on the twenty-seventh green, I was never in contention and it was comforting to settle an old score that had niggled at me ever since. Alas, my championship challenge came to an abrupt end in the semi-finals where I was beaten 3 and 2 by John 'Badger' Davies. The glamorous 'Badger' was an iconic figure to the younger members of the amateur circuit, and when I beat him to win the Berkhamstead

Trophy – the first important event of the 1977 Walker Cup year – I went home with the glittering prize and, as befitting a man of style, John Davies went home in his even more glittering new Jaguar XJS.

I should have all but secured my Walker Cup blazer in the first week of May by winning the Lytham Trophy in front of a posse of selectors but dropped five strokes over the final seven holes to concede victory to Peter Deeble, and the following week I threw away the Midlands Open Amateur Championship – in which I went into the last round at Little Aston with a four-stroke lead – with a ruinous 80. Fortunately, throughout my early years I had the happy knack of bouncing back from such traumas – ten days before my 1985 Open victory I walked off the course during the first round of the Irish Open at Royal Dublin when on my way to a score of 90 plus (much more of which later) – and the weekend after that collapse at Little Aston, at the age of 19 I won my second English Open Amateur Strokeplay title in three years at Hoylake.

Rounds of 71, 74 and 70 gave me a comfortable six-stroke lead over a chasing pack headed by John Davies. Even I could not puncture a cushion of such comfortable proportions, could I? Driving rain and howling winds made the weather on the Wirral that final afternoon anything but spring-like and by the seventh hole John had whittled my advantage down to a mere three shots. The par-five eighth decided the destiny of the title. After two impressive drives into the teeth of the gale, John missed the green to the right whereas my 3-iron found the middle of the target, rolling up to within fifteen feet of the hole. While John had to be content with a par, I nailed the putt for an eagle to move five strokes ahead, a lead I extended to seven shots by the time we shook hands on the eighteenth green.

The flamboyant Davies was rated a 'certainty' for the forthcoming Walker Cup match in Long Island. Unbeaten in singles in his two previous appearances in the competition, he had scored victories over George Burns, Gary Koch and Dick Siderowf and halved his round with Curtis Strange. So, having beaten him in our head-to-head duel in the Brabazon, I was fairly confident the selectors would not overlook me this time around, especially when I qualified for the 1977 Turnberry Open as the leading amateur.

Much is made of golf's current strength in depth but a trawl through the list of 1977's fellow qualifiers suggests that even three decades ago, gaining a place in the Open was a major achievement. They included Nick Faldo, Ken Brown, Bernard Gallacher, Maurice Bembridge, Malcolm Gregson and Des Smyth plus an overseas contingent headed by Bobby Cole of South Africa. I was drawn to play with Greg Norman and American Rik Massengale, who had finished third in the Masters behind Tom Watson three months earlier, and was one very interesting character indeed.

In his youth, Massengale had been a self-confessed 'wild man' at the University of Texas, where he gained notoriety for his club-throwing and heavy drinking at fraternity parties. When he joined the US Tour and became obsessed with life on the professional circuit, his wife sued for divorce but they agreed to attend a Tour Bible Study class during the Kemper Open in one final attempt to resolve their marital problems. As luck would have it, the American evangelist Dr Billy Graham, who was playing in the pre-tournament pro-celebrity event, was the guest speaker and due to the power of his oratory, the Massengales became committed Christians and recently celebrated their thirty-fifth wedding anniversary.

An avid golfer, Billy Graham once revealed, 'Prayer never seems to work for me on the golf course. I think this has something to do with my being a terrible putter.' I had to concur that summer at Turnberry, when not even the Almighty could have prevented me from crashing out at the halfway cut after two miserable rounds of 75 and 80. I was left watching TV spellbound as Tom Watson and Jack Nicklaus engaged in their epic 'Duel in the Sun'.

The two matched each other day by day with a mirror-image score – 68, 70, 65 – until Watson claimed the Claret Jug for the second of what would be five occasions with a 65 over the closing eighteen holes against the Golden Bear's 66. I was not the only spectator of their fireworks. Third-placed Hubert Green was a distant eleven shots behind Watson, followed by Lee Trevino, Ben Crenshaw, George Burns, Arnold Palmer, Raymond Floyd and Johnny Miller. Watching Watson and Nicklaus leave a veritable 'Who's Who' of golf in their slipstream simply reinforced the belief that I was still but a fraction of the player I needed to be if I was to conquer the world.

The crushing disappointment of Turnberry was softened when I received official notification of my selection for the Walker Cup, an honour I celebrated by winning the British Youths' Championship at Moor Park by six shots from my new teammates Paul McKellar and Steve Martin. The British Youths' may sound humble fare compared to the Open but it was another step on the learning curve and a feather in my cap. Previous winners included Brian Barnes, Peter Townsend, Peter Oosterhuis and Nick Faldo.

And so to Shinnecock Hills . . . Up until 1890, tennis, hunting and yachting had been the favoured pastimes of wealthy New Yorkers who fled the heat of Manhattan in the summer months to take up residence in their Long Island mansions. Then millionaire industrialist William Vanderbilt discovered golf on a trip to Biarritz and invited Scottish professional Willie Dunn to build him a similar course, employing 150 local Shinnecock Indians as labourers. Over a hundred years later, Shinnecock has developed into one of the finest championship courses in the United States, with an elegant clubhouse designed by the controversial (on account of his fondness for entertaining young women – single or not) architect Stanford White, who created wondrous Fifth Avenue townhouses for the Vanderbilts and Astors, as well as the Washington Square Arch in New York, which appears in the opening and closing credits of 'Friends', an arch I still see once a week on average given the number of times Joey, Phoebe and Ross still appear on our screens. Whatever his predilections in the bedroom, White was a brilliant architect and many are they who believe the view from the balcony overlooking the first tee at Shinnecock to be one of the most stunning in American golf.

It was there on the first tee that my foursomes partner, Peter McEvoy, and I discovered that our preparations for the biennial contest had been amateur in the extreme as we stood scratching our heads in puzzlement over which ball to use. Peter had been accustomed to playing with the 'small' British ball throughout his long and distinguished career whereas I, believing it to represent the future, had been using the larger-sized American ball since boyhood. Being the new kid on the block, I had no hesitation in agreeing to Peter's preference although I could hardly see the damn thing in the lush fairways of Shinnecock. In the event, the decision had little or no relevance – the final result was United States 16, Great Britain and Ireland 8.

Why Peter McEvoy never turned professional is an abiding mystery – he was the winner of the World Amateur Championship in 1988, conqueror of Jose Maria Olazabal in four matchplay contests and a prominent member of the 1989 Walker Cup team that finally claimed the trophy on American soil after sixty-seven years of heroic failure. Peter almost 'did a Paul Lawrie' in the 1979 Open at Royal Lytham. Lying fourth with seven holes to go, Peter was sneaking up on the blind side when the wheels came off and he eventually finished in a tie for seventeenth place with Lee Trevino, eleven shots behind the new champion, Seve Ballesteros.

Although he still supports Scotland on the football pitch, McEvoy represented England in eighty international singles matches, losing just six. In the Walker Cup he was rather less successful, winning five and halving two of his eighteen matches spanning five contests, although he was invariably placed at the top of the order and consequently came up against Phil Mickelson, Scott Hoch, Jay Sigel and Robert Gamez, among others. Perhaps it was the memory of our embarrassment at Shinnecock, but Peter brought a touch of 'professionalism' to the role of Walker Cup captain when he led our amateurs to successive victories over the Americans in 1999 and 2001 before assuming his latest position as chairman of selectors.

Despite the result, I would always have deeply regretted turning professional without having sampled the unique flavour of the Walker Cup. Unlike so many recent Ryder Cups, the Walker Cup has always been played in the traditional Corinthian spirit.

Once I had done so, and thereby fulfilled all my ambitions in the amateur ranks, I felt I was ready to try to knock Seve Ballesteros off his perch as the European number one – no small ambition for a lad not yet turned 20.

CHAPTER THREE

BIG ASS, BIG TALENT

According to one magazine writer: 'Foxhills is a little bit like heaven. Many people know of it, but only a few of us will ever go there . . .' Set in mature woodland in leafy Surrey, in the summer months Foxhills certainly looks heavenly with its gorgeous collection of beech, birch and pine trees and banks of rhododendron bushes, but come blustery October it can be a hellish place when you are one of 300 hopefuls bidding for a few places on the European Tour via the Tournament Players' Qualifying School. Fortunately, I not only won my 'ticket' but collected my first cheque as a professional – £300 – by winning the event.

I also changed nationality, opting to play under the Scottish saltire in preference to the St George's cross of England, despite having represented the country of my birth at schoolboy, youth and senior level as an amateur. To be brutally honest, this was an entirely pragmatic rather than romantic decision. Although my parents remained passionate Scots despite all their years in Shropshire, the 'selling point' for me was the 'Tartan Tour' north of the border, which comprised fifteen additional tournaments and carried a total of £100,000 in prize money. My mum and dad thought it was a great idea, as did all my aunts and uncles back 'hame', and as both Brian Barnes and Ken Brown had taken a similar route before me, I saw no problem in representing Scotland. The rules have since been changed, so that if you play for England as a schoolboy then an Englishman you must remain. I was the very last golfer to slip across Hadrian's Wall under radar height, although many footballers and rugby players still make the same journey.

Although I detected a few mutterings suggesting 'you come down here, win all our trophies then bugger off', in my defence Dad could not have afforded the cost of sending me up from England to play for Scotland as an amateur on a regular basis, and I have, of course, contentedly lived among my 'ain folk' for many years now on the edge of the Highlands beside Rob Roy's grave. Over the years I have become a Scottish nationalist with a small 'n'; if Scotland had been playing in the World Cup in Germany then there is no doubt who I would have been supporting. But, as we failed to qualify, I was more than happy to root for England unlike many of my compatriots!

Armed with a contract to use Dunlop clubs, bag, balls, shoes and clothing, plus an expenses guarantee from the Hawkstone board of directors, which provided a financial safety net, I joined the stable of Derrick Pillage. He not only managed a squad of European golfers but also looked after the affairs of such leading Americans as Lee Trevino, Billy Casper and Johnny Miller on this side of the Atlantic. Derrick, incidentally, had been taught to play golf by my dad. My first professional engagements took me off to South America as a member of Derrick's 'British Caledonian Golfing Lions', who were sponsored by the B-Cal airline, and a very jolly pride we were. My fellow passengers on that first flight to Buenos Aires for the Argentine Open included Sam Torrance, Brian Barnes, Ewen Murray and Tommy Horton.

Sam Torrance was one of the game's great golfers long before he became 'The Man Who Won The Ryder Cup' at The Belfry in 1985. He was also one of the game's most loved characters long before he captained Europe to another stunning success at The Belfry in 2002. They really should erect a statue of Sam overlooking the eighteenth green, arms raised in triumph, roll-up fag behind one ear, with the first tear trickling down his cheek towards that famous Groucho Marx moustache.

Brian Barnes, another Scot and another larger-than-life character, found celebrity by beating Jack Nicklaus twice in the same day during the 1975 Ryder Cup at Laurel Valley, with the assistance of US non-playing captain Arnold Palmer. The mischievous Palmer, who was forever trying to put one over on Nicklaus, the youthful upstart who had so ruthlessly swiped his crown as the king of golf, approached opposing skipper Bernard Hunt on the final morning of the first of two rounds of singles, to enquire if he might 'have anyone who can give Jack a game?'

The richly talented Brian Barnes, who might have become a serial Major winner but for his tragic battle against alcohol, was nominated as the sacrificial offering, only to reject the role with a stunning 4 and 2 upset. Delighted with the success of his scheme, Palmer sidled up to Hunt during lunch to suggest, 'You know, I think if Brian were drawn against Jack this afternoon, he could beat him again . . .' After much nudge-nudge wink-

wink verbal jousting, Hunt let slip that he was of a mind to name Barnes in the last match, which, by a massive coincidence (not!), was precisely the role Palmer had planned for his buddy.

As Brian delights in recalling at every available opportunity, when they renewed their acquaintance on the first tee, Nicklaus turned his ice-blue eyes, which could burn into an opponent's soul like a laser, on his earlier conqueror and said, 'Well done this morning, Barnsie, but there ain't no way you're going to beat me twice in one day . . .' Brian triumphed again, this time 2 and 1, a result that Palmer could not resist mentioning in his victory speech: 'My thanks to the American team who did an outstanding job – even if Jack did lose two matches today to Brian Barnes. He doesn't mind really . . .' At which point Nicklaus interjected, 'Oh yes I do . . .'

Barnsie – and not a lot of people know this, whereas everyone knows he was the son-in-law of the late Max Faulkner, who won the 1951 Open at Portrush – almost became a movie star through Derrick's friendship with Welsh screen actor Stanley Baker. When not filming blockbusters, including 'The Cruel Sea' and 'The Guns of Navarone', Stanley Baker was a passionate golfer and when actor and golfer met, Baker invited Barnsie to appear in 'Zulu Dawn', the sequel to 'Zulu'. Alas, having taken acting lessons for his Hollywood debut, the big fella was dropped from the cast list when Stanley Baker sadly died before filming began. 'Zulu Dawn' went ahead with Burt Lancaster, Denholm Elliott and Bob Hoskins, while Barnsie went ahead with his golf career.

Ewen Murray – yet another Scot – won the world Under-16 championship and subsequently competed with distinction against the very best of his generation until a double trauma in effect put paid to his playing career. Ewen might have slid off the bottom of the leaderboard and into obscurity had he not been blessed with a second talent, the gift of being able to paint evocative images for the delectation of television audiences on Sky TV.

Ewen turned professional in 1971, a year after claiming that Under-16 world crown, and made his paid debut in a tournament at Prestwick, where he hit his tee-shot off the first approximately 180 miles. How come? I don't know if you are familiar with Prestwick but as Ewen stood on the tee – a young pro ready to take on the world – and unleashed a 2-iron down the fairway, the wind caught the ball. It sailed over the wall towards the railway and straight into a coal truck bound for Newcastle.

Over the next fourteen years, Ewen was invariably up with the leaders. Aged 18, he finished in the top forty at his first Open Championship, at Troon, won by Tom Weiskopf. Thereafter his tournament successes included the Northern Open at Royal Dornoch and the Zambian Open, which should have heralded his big breakthrough but this was when a double trauma hit him in the space of a couple of months – firstly his father, Jimmy Murray, tragically died of cancer, and then Ewen's marriage broke up. It was perhaps as a result of the combination of these two events that Ewen then seemed to lose the desire or what-have-you. I am delighted that Ewen has since found personal happiness and a new and successful career in broadcasting.

Tommy Horton was the leading Briton in the Watson and Nicklaus Open of 1977, and although he finished 'only' ninth, he won a sizeable cheque plus an added bonus – when Tommy returned to his hotel there was a crate of vintage champagne awaiting him, courtesy of the owner, who had a large bet on him to finish as the leading Briton.

Raised within a pitching wedge of the Royal Jersey Golf Club, Horton was largely self-taught. Unable to afford to join the club across the hedge, he built his own four-hole course on a piece of adjoining land, with bamboo poles for flagsticks and Heinz baked beans cans sunk into the grass for holes – complete with candles so he could practise putting long after the sun had gone down. He may have been destined never to win the Open but Tommy Horton remains a member of golf's league of gentlemen.

In our ignorance at the time, we knew nothing of the military junta that ruled Argentina with an iron grip, or of the tens of thousands of students, professional people and outspoken opponents of the regime who had simply 'disappeared', or of the many children from poor families who had been kidnapped and offered for adoption to friends of the generals. In our defence, many people within Argentina did not know anything about the horrors being perpetrated in their own country in the name of 'law and order'. As we were driven to our hotel through the main square, we were totally unaware that six months earlier, in April 1977, a group of women, who became known as Las Madres de Plaza de Mayo, had defied a ban on public gatherings to protest against the abduction of their sons and daughters. Argentina was gearing up to stage the 1978 World Cup finals, so a mighty public relations exercise was in full swing and we were treated like visiting royalty. I never knew steak could taste so good until I sampled an Argentine T-bone straight from the pampas.

Even to our naive eyes, however, the contrast was startling. The streets were packed with ancient jalopies missing the odd windscreen here and there while all the time belching out exhaust fumes, whereas the car park at the Jockey Club – which offered two golf courses, adjoining the racetrack and polo fields – was lined with Rolls-Royces, Bentleys and Jaguars. The ruling classes clearly liked their creature comforts to come from Britain.

The creatures I encountered were less than comfortable, however, and had clearly arrived in Buenos Aires straight from the Amazonian jungle. With the heat and humidity unbearable, on the first night in my hotel room I unadvisedly left my window open in the hope of some relief and awoke next morning to find my left arm covered in about ninety angry, itchy, mosquito bites.

After three satisfactory opening rounds of 72, 72, 72, I was privileged to be partnered by local hero Roberto De Vicenzo, winner of the 1967 Open at Hoylake, on the final afternoon. Although Roberto was no longer the force of old, he remained a very fine player and the loveliest of companions – but then, no one knew better than the amiable Argentinian that golf can be the cruellest of sports, and he had long since learned to smile through adversity. During the last round of the 1968 Masters, American Tommy Aaron cost Roberto his chance of glory when he inadvertently credited him with a par four on the seventeenth hole instead of a birdie three. Having signed his card for a 66 when it should have been 65, Roberto promptly discovered he had lost to Bob Goalby by one shot when, in fact, he should have tied on 277 and qualified for a play-off.

Bobby Jones, the founder of the Masters, spent hours pouring over the rules in the hope of finding a loophole that would grant the immensely popular De Vicenzo a reprieve, but to no avail. 'What a stupid I am,' he admitted in his faltering English, with surprising cheerfulness. 'Tommy feels like I feel – very bad. But I would like to congratulate Bob Goalby – he gave me so much pressure that I lose my brain.' It was a very cruel way to lose a

Major, and the problem of signing a wrong scorecard is one for which the sport is still seeking a fair and equitable solution.

What pearls of wisdom did this great man have for the young rookie at his side? 'I see you have a big ass, just like me,' Roberto commented on our route between green and tee. 'Is good. As I tell my girlfriend, you need a big hammer to hammer in a big nail . . .' Big ass, big talent – despite the advancing years, Roberto finished third while I celebrated my professional debut with a joint-sixth finish behind course-expert Florentina Molina, who won the title for the fifth time in seven years.

Another week, another suitcase, another bedroom hallway – we shortly moved on to Sao Paulo. My image of Brazil had always featured beautiful girls wearing bikinis fashioned from dental floss, frolicking on Copacabana; wondrous footballers – Pelé, Rivelino, Jairzinho – in canary yellow shirts; and the sensuality of the Rio carnival, never forgetting the Caipirinha, sugar alcohol served with slithers of fresh lime and crushed ice – so simple, yet probably the best cocktail in the world. Not being an avid newspaper reader, I knew nothing of the poor black children of the favelas, or shanty towns, lining the depressing crumbling highway leading into Sao Paulo from Guarulhos Airport, a grim twenty-mile ride through the endless concrete high-rise suburbs of the world's third largest city and biggest human rubbish tip. The road into the city has now been cleaned up to an extent and renamed Avenida da Ayrton Senna in honour of the nation's iconic Formula One motor racing world champion, who died in 1994 and lies under a lone ipe tree in the Cimiterio do Morumbi on the genteel southern edge of town. Although I always supported my good friend Nigel Mansell in his various tussles with Senna, as a keen F1 fan I recognise Senna was one of the greatest drivers of all time and no one who enters the cemetery does so without a sense of overwhelming sadness.

I should have enjoyed my second top ten finish in seven days but on the 172 yard par-three ninth of my final round, I pulled my first tee-shot out of bounds, then watched my second attempt land in the heart of the green only to take a crazy bounce into the lake behind the putting surface. My resultant quadruple-bogey seven sent me spinning down the leaderboard to nineteenth place and cost me a fistful of dollars. The Brazilian Open had a rich history of producing quality champions – notably Sam Snead, Arnold Palmer, Billy Casper and Gary Player – a tradition which was continued when Argentine Vicente Fernandez, who is now enjoying similar success on the US Champions' Tour, swept home ahead of Spaniard Manuel Pinero and Lou Graham, the 1975 US Open champion.

Despite my fall from grace in Sao Paulo, someone, somewhere must have been impressed because instead of returning home as intended at the end of my two-week visit to South America, I was invited to compete in the following week's Colombian Open at Barranquilla, where the championship course, far from the city bustle, stands on the shores of the Caribbean. As a curtain-raiser to the main event, I picked up $300 by winning a long-driving competition with a winning effort of 382 yards, which, at sea level, surprised even me. According to the *Guinness Book of Records* of the day, the longest drive ever achieved was a blow of 392 yards set by Tommie Campbell at Dun Laoghaire, County Dublin in 1964.

When battle was properly commenced, Orville Moody, who came through the various local and regional qualifying competitions to win the 1969 US Open unexpectedly, was overtaken on the final afternoon by fellow American John Schroeder. An accomplished player, Schroeder won a single victory on the US Tour – in the 1973 PGA Matchplay Championship – but it was a sad return on his talent. Perhaps he knew that no matter what he achieved in golf, his fame would never match that of his father, Ted, who had won the Wimbledon men's singles tennis title in 1949. Known as 'Lucky' Ted, Schroeder Senior was an amiable, happy-go-lucky character. He only ever extinguished his pipe when called on court, which is why he may always have been happier on the golf course. He won the US Championship in 1942 but, although he boasted an impressive Davis Cup record in tandem with Jack Kramer, winning the trophy in 1947, '48 and '49, he was loath to travel and entered Wimbledon on that sole occasion, surviving four five-set matches and dropping eight sets on his way to the title. That was the most conceded by any champion until Boris Becker in 1985 – hence the appellation 'Lucky'.

I felt lucky, too, when my twelfth place in the Colombian Open took my South American earnings to £3,000. More importantly, the trip had provided me with an invaluable insight into the life of a touring pro. The other members of the 'Golfing Lions' could not have been more welcoming and, with the seemingly endless round of dinners and cocktail parties, I could have burned the candle at both ends then torched the bit in the middle if I had so wished. Steve Martin, known as 'Night Fever' on the tour because, like the John Travolta character in the movie, he seemed to know every disco and nightclub in South America, was commander-in-chief of the merry-making but – sensible lad that I am – I made sure I was in bed every night by 10 p.m. (well, I would say that, wouldn't I?).

With over £3,000 in official earnings – although my 'take-home pay' was considerably less once the Argentine, Brazilian and Colombian tax authorities had taken their cut – I finally returned to England to attend the BBC Sports Personality of the Year awards programme, won by Virginia Wade, the new Wimbledon women's singles champion, and to spend Christmas and New Year back home at Hawkstone, which seemed a world removed from the sights and sounds of Buenos Aires, Sao Paulo and Barranquilla. Christmas lunch at the Lyles was always something to behold because my mum was of the old 'pile it high' school of cooking, which is why I tended to be on the podgy side as a child – that was until I went down with measles at the age of ten and re-emerged from my bedroom two weeks later as a slimmed-down version of my former self.

I still ate more than my fair share, but as a professional athlete now I made sure I burned off the Christmas calories with strenuous cross-country runs through the woods and visits to the gym, where I played five-a-side football. I also spent many happy hours honing my short-game, practising escape shots from bunkers, bushes and trees, and left-handed recoveries, which I hoped would stand me in good stead in the years to come. I even stamped my ball into the ground to reproduce plugged lies.

For relaxation, I went haring around the estate on my scramble bike – that love of speed survives to this day – or racing round the countryside in my 'passion-wagon' Mini-van with my girl-friend of the time, Sian Woolley, daughter of my school English teacher. All too soon, a week after celebrating my 20th birthday, it was time to pack my bags again and leave snowbound Shropshire to begin my rookie season by embarking upon the African Safari Tour with the stated ambition of finishing in the top sixty on the money list, thereby avoiding the pitfalls of returning to the qualifying school the following autumn.

CHAPTER FOUR

BEATING 'QUEENIE' TO BECOME
BOY KING IN NIGERIA

I entered the dark continent through Lagos Airport, where I had first-hand experience of the corruption that was rife in Nigeria under the military rule of the day. We had to tip – no, make that bribe – someone to bring our golf clubs from the plane, produce another tip to have them delivered to the baggage hall, a third tip to have them carried out to the taxi rank, and so on and so on until we were delivered into the keeping of the British ex-pat families with whom we were staying.

Their way of life was tenuous to say the least. Telephones could be cut off for anything up to six months at a time until a suitable financial inducement was offered and accepted, while local vagabonds continually stopped the water supply only to turn up in the driveway a couple of hours later, sitting behind the wheel of a delivery tanker. That kind of racketeering was commonplace, yet the families' hospitality to the visiting golfers bordered on the embarrassing, with every meal including fresh fruit and veg at a time when a humble cauliflower could fetch as much as a fiver on the black market.

As a way of saying thanks for our board and keep, the contingent of British players all packed an array of goodies for our hosts, which is why my suitcase was loaded down with tins of tomato soup, baked beans, HP sauce, bacon, Bovril, teabags, biscuits and – sheer luxury – soft loo roll. I arrived at the Heathrow check-in queue looking as though I should have been in the Sainsbury's check-out line instead.

Lagos (which I discovered means 'lagoon' in one of the many local dialects) is a natural harbour situated on the Atlantic, and one could only imagine how beautiful it must have been hundreds of years ago, before the Portuguese arrived in the 16th century and turned the area into a major centre of the slave trade. An estimated population of just under nine million (some put the figure as high as fifteen million) makes Lagos the eleventh largest city in the world and it was a seething mass of humanity.

The courses, too, were very different, with 'browns' instead of greens, the tiny upturned-saucer putting surfaces being a mixture of sand and oil. These required an entirely different style of golf because if you hit a high approach shot – which you would imagine to be the preferred route to the flag – the ball would break through the soft top layer, hit the baked earth underneath and shoot off God knows where. I had to learn to flight my approaches in low, so the ball would skid and, with luck, pull up ten or twelve feet away. Also, unlike our greens, which tend to play faster in the sun, in the heat of the African afternoon the 'browns' became increasingly stickier and slower as the sand and oil began to cook in the heat. As they were fairly flat, there were very few borrows and they tended to be fairly easy to read because, just like playing in the morning dew at Hawkstone, the ball left a little trail on its way to the hole, so you could follow your opponent's line. A further advantage was that the longer the day went on, the bigger the hole became as the edges gradually wore away. It was common to see the ball spinning round the hole like the little white sphere on a roulette wheel before dropping. When you adjusted to all these differences – and when your putter was hot – you could knock in ten or twelve-foot putts like there was no tomorrow.

Before the Nigerian Open, the visiting professionals split into three groups to compete in thirty-six hole events in Benin City, Port Harcourt and Ibadan. I was fortunate in being drawn to play in the Benin Open because this was staged at the Ikoyi Club, where the Nigerian Open was to be played a few days later. In subsequent years I invariably found myself aboard an ageing turbo-prop plane bound for up-country, which was an experience in itself. Unlike the modern air terminals to which we were all accustomed, even back then, Lagos domestic airport was so primitive the check-in staff were still using ancient scales complete with weights – if you can imagine a larger version of what you would expect to find in a 1950s greengrocer's, you've got it.

Disease was also rife, especially in the outlying areas, and that was where the veterans of the Safari Tour enjoyed a big advantage over us rookies by sticking rigidly to the local beer instead of drinking Coke or orange juice. We thought we were taking the healthier option but, needless to say, the ice in the drinks tended to wreak havoc with our digestive systems. While wise old owls Sam Torrance, Eamonn Darcy and Bernard Gallacher quietly quaffed a few beers with a knowing smile, the younger set beat a steady path to the lavatory, having become the latest victims of the ice-cube tummy bug.

Despite the new surroundings, and twice driving out of bounds during the final round, I shot 70, 69 to win the Benin Open by one stroke from my room-mate, Malcolm Gregson. In the subsequent Nigerian Open I teed off with my confidence soaring, along with the temperature, which was nudging 120 degrees. After pitching in from twenty yards at the first hole, I made an eagle three. Even so, I could hardly have expected to launch my first full year as a pro with a ten under par first round of 61, opening up a four-shot lead over David Vaughan and Brian Evans.

My rich vein of form continued unabated as I compiled a second round 63, to beat the thirty-six hole British tournament record of 126 set by Tom Haliburton at Worthing in 1952. Curiously, the Lagos 'browns' were almost a replica in speed and line of our living-room carpet in Hawkstone, where I had spent the snowy winter months practising my putting while listening to Paul McCartney ('Mull of Kintyre'), Abba ('Take A Chance On Me') and Rod Stewart ('I Don't Want To Talk About It') on my record-player, which, as memory serves, was always called a gramophone in the Lyle household.

Five years earlier in America, Ben Crenshaw had created a little bit of history by winning his first tournament after topping the US Tour School, and perhaps it was the implications of holding a seven-stroke lead at the halfway stage on my European debut that caused me to fritter away six of those shots with a third round 70, leaving me just one in front of Michael King (66, 65, 64). The final eighteen holes were a nerve-racking affair. Having led from day one, I suddenly found myself relegated to second place when I dropped two shots after being bunkered at the ninth and tenth. I clawed my way level at the twelfth, surrendered the initiative once more when I hooked my drive on to the adjoining fairway and ran up a six at the long fifteenth, then drew level when Michael bogeyed the seventeenth after hitting a tree. Having been seven strokes in front after thirty-six holes, I now faced a sudden-death play-off. But although I had surrendered victory in the Brabazon, English Matchplay and Midlands Open as an amateur, I knew I had both the temperament and technique to emerge victorious. Despite those setbacks and my tender years, I firmly believed that my dad had instilled all the ingredients of a champion, all I had to do was put all his lessons into practice.

My rival for the £3,400 winner's cheque was as debonair as Cary Grant, as dashing as Errol Flynn and as roguishly good-looking as William Holden. Michael King is the Great Gatsby of British golf. When he first swept on to the European Tour, Sam Torrance, who subsequently became his closest friend, took one look at the sleek Reliant Scimitar sports coupé, heard one sentence spoken with the English public school accent, and promptly dubbed him 'Queenie'. What none of us knew was that Michael had lost all his money in the stock-market crash of 1974, when everyone was jumping off window-ledges. He had been left stony broke – the car was borrowed from a friend.

When I made my Ryder Cup debut in 1979, Queenie was a member of the team, having finished fifth in the Order of Merit after winning the prestigious Tournament Players' Championship at Moor Park, where he had beaten off the challenge of Seve Ballesteros, Gary Player and US PGA title holder David Graham. Then came another devastating crash. The chronic arthritis in his spine that had begun to trouble him during his days as a

Walker Cup player and high-flying stockbroker forced his premature retirement in 1987. Since then he has passed his time attracting sponsors to the Tour he once graced, offering advice on golf-course design and enjoying life's many pleasures in the members' bar at Sunningdale.

King was an outstanding golfer, who might have been even better had he not been prone to bouts of vertigo whenever he neared the top of the leaderboard. If King was one rung below true greatness on the fairway, he had few equals in the art of relaxation when the day's work was done, an attitude that did not always find favour with those who believe sportsmen should adhere to a monastic existence. Having played in the 1969 Walker Cup as a 19-year-old, he found himself unceremoniously dumped from the side for the '71 contest at St Andrews.

'I was thrown out for bad behaviour apparently,' he later told me, with a disarming lack of embarrassment. 'I was leading the Brabazon Trophy at Moortown and had stayed up late in the clubhouse because I was waiting for my host to take me home. When I got up the next morning, I didn't feel too bright and shot an 81 – I wasn't playing that well, to be honest – whereupon I received a letter from the Walker Cup committee informing me they had chosen Roddie Carr in preference to me because "we weren't very impressed by your training methods at the Brabazon".' They were absolutely spot on probably.

Queenie engaged in a brief flirtation on the US Tour. 'My first event was the Los Angeles Open and as I'd arrived a few days early, I just sort of hung around until all the others showed up from Hawaii, where they'd been playing. As you can imagine, LA is a difficult place to hang around without getting into trouble, so the tournament came as a bit of light relief after all the partying.

I never missed a cut during the few weeks I was in the States, but I didn't really settle in America. I seem to remember there was always a very well-trodden path from the eighteenth green to the practice ground and it was a bit embarrassing to have to ask Jack Nicklaus or whoever "which path goes to the club-house?" Because by the time I'd finished eighteen holes my toot-sies were tired, so when Nicklaus and everyone else turned left to hit a couple of hundred drives, I turned right for a beer.'

That's Queenie for you, still spreading fun wherever he goes, and all credit to him. Michael was still smiling broadly as he shook my hand after I had secured my maiden victory with a birdie three at the second extra hole. Although the Nigerian Open may have been small beer compared to the champagne atmosphere of The Open or the Masters, my excitement and relief when I sank the winning putt knew no bounds, especially as it came in a play-off and against an opponent as redoubtable as Queenie. I had proved to myself – and more importantly to my fellow-pros that I could not only compete but win.

I must have made a hit with the locals because the caddies – all of whom seemed to be called Jesus, Moses, Noah or some such biblical name – carried me back to the clubhouse on their shoulders in triumph (I must have been tipping them too much!). The organisers could not have liked me that much, though, because I had to wait about eight months before my cheque came through the post.

I also made some money – without seriously threatening tour-nament winner Seve Ballesteros – at the Kenyan Open, where Bob Charles and Billy Casper were the two big-name invitees. Both great champions were some way past their best – Casper had won the US Open in 1959 and 1966, and the Masters in

1970, while Bob Charles' Open victory at Lytham had been achieved in 1963 – but it was a thrill rubbing shoulders with such figures in the clubhouse of the Royal Nairobi Golf Club.

Although Casper was victorious in just three Majors, he won fifty-one tournaments on the US Tour, played in seven successful Ryder Cup teams, compiling twenty wins and seven halves from his thirty-seven matches, and is regarded as one of the finest putters the game has ever known. As his fellow US Tour pro Chi Chi Rodriguez said of him, 'Billy was the greatest putter I ever saw. When golf balls left the factory they used to pray they would get putted by Billy Casper . . .'

Quiet, a devout Mormon and eminently likeable, Casper and his wife, Shirley, raised eleven children, six of whom they adopted from the Far East, which says a lot about him as a man. As a golfer, he has always been curiously underrated by the galleries but certainly not by his contemporaries. 'I felt sorry for Billy out there today,' said Gary Player during Casper's 1966 US Open victory at the Olympic Club, San Francisco. 'He couldn't putt a lick – I saw him miss three thirty-footers.'

Bob Charles was another who could charm the ball into the hole from whatever distance or outrageous borrow. The New Zealander, the first left-hander to win the Open, was as meticulous on the greens as he was in the way he dressed on the course. His shoes were always polished to an army shine, his trousers had creases as sharp as a letter-opener and his wardrobe was a palette of complimentary pastel shades.

After Kenya it was on to the Zambian capital of Lusaka, which is one of those seething, steaming cities that are as much a symbol of Africa as the breathtaking scenery and safari parks. Even though around 60 per cent of the two million people living there are unemployed, Lusaka is one of the friendliest places on the African continent. The food stallholders on the streets and the market traders always greet you with a smile, even if you are not interested in sampling their wares.

The highlight of my first trip to Zambia was the annual Golfing Lions v. Staff match at the Presidential Palace. As befitting a member of the Royal & Ancient Golf Club of St Andrews, Dr Kenneth Kaunda had built a nine-hole course in the magnificent grounds, where peacocks, wild boar and all manner of wildlife roamed free. Being the nation's president, Dr Kaunda had laid down a number of local rules – if you hit a peacock you lost the hole – basically designed so that the touring pros were never allowed to win. Dr Kaunda had a particular soft spot for Brian Barnes but although Barnsie was one of the leading players in Europe, he made sure he never beat the President in the big challenge. Lunch was a magnificent affair, offering something for every taste from wild boar roasted on a spit and exotic fish dishes to good old bangers and ketchup.

We were back on the home continent in time for the start of the European Tour. In 2006, the Tour officially began in mid-November 2005 with the HSBC Champions' Tournament in Sheshan, China, but twenty-eight years ago we had to wait until April and the Portuguese Open at Portimao on the Algarve. What an idyllic spot for the kick-off, one would have thought, on a beautiful course designed by Henry Cotton overlooking the Atlantic. I must have been preoccupied – as I have often been throughout my career, it has to be said – enjoying the scenery, for while Howard Clark beat Barnsie and Simon Hobday by one shot to take the £5,000 first prize, A.W. Lyle announced his arrival on the Tour by missing the halfway cut with rounds of 83 and 76. I was in good company, Bernhard Langer and Ian Woosnam accompanying me on the early trip to Faro Airport.

Barnsie reversed that result when he pipped Howard by two strokes to win the Spanish Open in Barcelona the following week when I finished an encouraging joint thirteenth and banked my first European Tour cheque worth £447.46. I appeared to be heading for another cash boost at the Madrid Open when I shot an opening round 69, which left me equal second behind Seve Ballesteros. A miserable eight-over-par second round of 80 put paid to any hopes I entertained of making a major impact on the tournament, however, and I eventually trailed home forty-fifth, a distant nineteen strokes behind Howard Clark, who had soared to the top of the Order of Merit with two wins and a second place from the first three events.

One of the reasons why I have always preferred the European to the United States Tour is the diversity of places we are privileged to visit. After the majesty of Madrid, I luxuriated in the splendour of Costa Smeralda on the north-eastern coast of Sardinia, setting for the Italian Open. Costa Smeralda has been the playground of the glitterati since the Aga Khan arrived aboard his yacht in the early 1960s and, with its crystal clear emerald water, coves, bays, white sandy beaches and astonishing pre-historic rock formations, it is easy to understand why the beautiful people continue to flock to this little-known jewel.

With its cliff-top setting overlooking La Cala di Volpe (the Cove of Vixen), Il Pevero Golf Club is one of the most natural and beautiful courses to be found anywhere in the world. I finished a respectable equal seventeenth to add another few hundred pounds to the Lyle coffers, if a long way behind tournament winner Dale Hayes of South Africa. Hayes showed his consistency by making it two victories in seven days when he won the French Open at La Baule. I, on the other hand, displayed my infuriating inconsistency by missing the cut, following which I engaged in a prolonged 'What Am I Doing Wrong?' (and not for the last time) conversation with my dad at Hawkstone (not for the last time). As ever, my father was nothing less than encouraging, constantly emphasising that my rookie season was merely the first step in a five-year plan, but I was growing increasingly impatient to make my mark.

What to me appeared a dismal season continued with a seventy-sixth place finish in the Martini International at the RAC Club, Epsom, thirty-two shots behind Seve Ballesteros, an encouraging nineteenth in the Colgate PGA at Royal Birkdale, won by Nick Faldo, twenty-fourth in the Jersey Open, where Brian Huggett was the winner, then a lacklustre forty-first in the Greater Manchester Open, where Brian Barnes collected his second title of the season. My performance in Jersey hardly represented the ideal way to prepare for the forthcoming 107th Open Championship at St Andrews, providing, of course, I could negotiate the qualifying competition at Leven, where I had been drawn to compete.

The eleventh oldest golf course in the world, Leven links is tougher than many championship layouts and becomes tougher yet when, halfway through your downswing on the tricky par-four second, your driver snaps in two and the clubhead soars down the fairway while the ball sits untouched on the tee. That cost me a penalty stroke. For the next seventeen holes, I drove the ball into the wind with a 1-iron and downwind with a 4-wood, and duly qualified with four shots to spare. So it was on to the hallowed home of golf.

Entering the secret recesses of the Royal & Ancient clubhouse at St Andrews is like stepping inside a pyramid, and an experience Arnold Palmer once described as 'being admitted to the Hall of the Gods', a hushed shrine where wondrous things are to be found – dark corridors of oil paintings depicting royal and golfing kings . . . glass cabinets crammed with glittering trophies fashioned from kangaroo paws and silver boomerangs . . . a hoard of ancient hickory putters, mashie-niblicks and brassies, all lovingly sculpted by Willie Auchterlonie and his fellow 19th century craftsmen . . . chamber upon chamber of priceless antiquities.

One-time sceptic turned born-again worshipper Sam Snead was of the belief that 'the only place in Britain that's holier is Westminster Abbey'. Jack Nicklaus is one of a select group of former Open champions, including Palmer, Kel Nagle, Gary Player, Roberto De Vicenzo, Tom Watson, Lee Trevino, Tony Jacklin and Peter Thomson, to be welcomed through the hallowed portals as an honorary member of the R & A, and as he puts it, 'Bobby Jones always said your career was not complete unless you won an Open at St Andrews and I'm one proud and lucky fella to have enjoyed two victories at the home of golf.'

That explains why the Golden Bear chose this stretch of the Fife coast to bid farewell to tournament golf, which he did at the 2005 Open. Being a few groups in front of the great man that year, I was privileged to witness his final couple of holes after I'd completed my second round. 'There are two British Opens,' explained Nicklaus, with tangible affection. 'The one played at Muirfield, Lytham, Troon and the rest, and the one played at St Andrews. Ever since I first competed in the Open here in 1964, the people have been real nice to me and that's why I think it appropriate to finish my career at St Andrews.'

Critics will tell you the Old Course lacks the mighty challenge of Muirfield, the manicured glamour of Augusta or the Hollywood beauty of Cypress Point, but surely there can be no more starkly breathtaking or atmospheric spot on the golfing globe.

When Sam Snead first saw St Andrews spread out down below from the window of a light aircraft in 1946, he enquired of his pilot, 'Say fella, there's an abandoned golf course down there. What did they call it back in the old days?' Snead's suspicions proved unfounded, of course, and he won the Open that year by four shots. Bobby Jones was so sceptical that he tore up his card after just six holes and vowed never to come back. That was in 1921, yet return he did to win the Open six years later and the British Amateur title – then considered almost as important as any Major – in 1930.

Like so many who came before or followed after, Jones, later to become one of the sport's most accomplished designers, gradually realised that St Andrews, where they have been playing golf since the 1400s, owed its subtle, deceptively uncluttered layout to the architect's pencil wielded by God. To the uneducated eye, it would appear God was some way short of his imaginative best that first morning he took up golf. The shared first and eighteenth fairway is really not a fairway at all, merely a giant polo field devoid of any geographical quirk save the Swilcan Burn and its tiny stone bridge, which, on a frosty January morning, disappears into a curtain of mist, like the path to Brigadoon.

From the third hole onwards, however, St Andrews becomes a rolling, sometimes cruel, sea of bumps and hillocks, gorse and heather, hollows and swales. Then there are the bunkers, a veritable desert of spiteful sand in the Beardies, Hell Bunker, the Grave. Special? Oh yes. Listen to the late Tony Lema: 'What do I think of St Andrews? It's like going to Scotland to visit your sick grandmother. She's old and she's crotchety and she's eccentric. But look real close and my, isn't she dignified and elegant? I sincerely believe anyone who doesn't fall in love with her is totally lacking in imagination.'

St Andrews sure is cranky; Dad always impressed upon me not to be fooled by first appearances or to jump to conclusions too early because, just as Bobby Jones observed, the more you play the Old Course, the more you come to understand it. For the average club player who travels across the world for the honour of teeing off in front of the clubhouse windows, at times it can be not much fun. I have known of many a golfer who has flown the ball into the heart of one of the massive double greens only to find he has been aiming at the wrong coloured flag and is suddenly faced with a 50-yard putt across various undulations.

I started the 107th Open Championship with a par 72, which put me well up the leaderboard, but I stumbled badly the following day with an error-strewn 78 that left me two shots outside the halfway cut. I was not alone in my misery. Tony Jacklin, Lanny Wadkins and Johnny Miller were also among those who found St Andrews at its most cantankerous on day two and failed to qualify for the final thirty-six holes as the familiar name of Jack Nicklaus loomed large on the leaderboard.

The historic eighteenth green, nestling snugly in the elbow of two narrow public streets and overlooked by an imposing red sandstone students' residence (soon to be turned into luxury apartments I'm told) presents a scene largely unaltered since 1895 when John Henry Taylor clutched the world's most precious claret jug. It was here that Nicklaus secured his first St Andrews Open in 1970 after fellow-American Doug Sanders famously fluffed a thirty-inch 'gimme' when the title was within his grasp. What happened next is one of those yarns that Jack is happy to relate, usually in the clubhouse at Augusta where all the great champions regale us members of the 'younger generation' with tales of their past deeds. According to the Golden Bear, he had been following the drama on a TV set in the R & A caravan and was on the point of leaving the trailer in order to be among the first to offer the victor his congratulations when, on an impulse, he decided to stay and watch. Having meticulously studied his putt from every angle, Sanders was preparing to draw back the club head when he suddenly stopped to pick up a stray blade of grass lying in his line of vision. Even from 200 plus miles away in front of our television at Hawkstone, I could hear my dad's sharp intake of breath. After what seemed an eternity, Sanders was finally sufficiently composed to strike the putt that would have brought him sporting immortality but just as the ball appeared poised to drop into the hole, it slowly trickled away to the right, leaving both men to prepare for the following day's eighteen-hole play-off.

As Nicklaus subsequently came to view events: 'Doug deserved to win because he had played superbly throughout the week – his misfortune was one of the luckiest breaks of my career.' And he took full advantage of it; Nicklaus duly won the resultant play-off 72-73 although the luckless Sanders will forever remain a part of Open folklore.

The Golden Bear's second St Andrews triumph in 1978 – when I missed the cut and again watched the closing stages on television as enthralled as any other viewer – was no less dramatic.

On the sixteenth tee of the final round he trailed unheralded New Zealander Simon Owen by one shot. Owen had begun the last day miserably before sweeping back up the leaderboard with a run of five birdies in seven holes. Then, like so many before him, he wilted in the intimidating presence at his shoulder. By the time Nicklaus made his triumphal march up the eighteenth, the emperor was sitting on a comfortable two-stroke cushion.

'It was one of those magical moments,' recalled the Great One. 'There must have been thirty thousand spectators packed into the grandstands, lining the path along the right-hand side of the fairway, hanging from the windows of the houses, dangling from the rooftops even. I had a lump in my throat and tears in my eyes. After all, St Andrews was my favourite place on earth to play golf. I had never received such a warm and affectionate welcome and don't expect I ever will again.'

While Nicklaus returned to a hero's welcome in America, my miserable run of form continued at the Dutch and Irish Opens, where I again missed the cut. I found a semblance of form at the German Open in Cologne, where three rounds of 68, 71, 66 left me in hot pursuit of eventual champion Seve Ballesteros, until a last round 75 dropped me into a share of sixteenth place. I earned £413.97, which was fifty-two quid more than Tony Jacklin, who, nonetheless, emerged as the week's big winner when he aced the par-three, 182 yard fifteenth during his third round to collect the keys of a Mercedes sports car. At £17,000, that was worth almost three times Seve's first-place cheque. Tony being Tony ordered an eye-catching salmon pink version.

My season's earnings of £5,233.98 were good enough to secure my playing card for the following season with a forty-ninth place finish in the Order of Merit, and I treated myself to a third-hand Porsche 924, the so-called 'poor man's Porsche'. That figure may have been a whacking £50,000 less than European number one Seve Ballesteros, but I had done enough to win the Henry Cotton Trophy as 'Rookie of the Year'. I also qualified for the six-man Golfing Lions team to play a powerful Texan side for the British Caledonian Trans-Atlantic Trophy. That was a double thrill for me because the event was played at Prestwick, one of the most historic courses on the planet and site of the first twelve Open Championships from 1860–72, and it gave me the opportunity to meet the legendary Byron Nelson, the Americans' non-playing captain.

Nelson, who celebrated his 90th birthday in 2002, won the US Open in 1939, the Masters in 1937 and 1942, and the US PGA Championship in 1940 and 1945, the same year he won eighteen tournaments in America including a remarkable eleven in a row during one heady spell of golf. That streak began to take its toll on Nelson's nerves and before leaving for one event he told his wife, Louise, 'I wish I would just blow up and get this over with.' When he returned home that night Mrs N. asked him if his wish had come true and he had, indeed, blown up. 'Yes,' he replied, 'I shot a sixty-six . . .'

Jack Burke, himself a former Masters winner, bemoaned Nelson's form throughout '45, saying, 'The only time Byron left a fairway all year was to pee in the bushes.'

Nelson was not only a great champion, he was also the consummate gentleman. Whenever invited to play an exhibition, he made it his business to find out the course record beforehand. If the record was held by a local club pro, or an amateur, he made sure he never broke it 'because it will mean far, far more to them than it would to me'.

During the return Trans-Atlantic contest the following year, a curious event occurred, one of those cameos that leave you baffled, wondering how they ever came about. While I was in Texas, I was made an honorary member of the Coushatta Indian tribe at a special ceremony at their reservation in Livingston, Polk County, at which I was required to perform a war dance around the totem pole. Now, Gene Kelly I am not and the look on the faces of the then Chief, Robert Fulton Battise ('Kina'), and my fellow 550 tribesmen as I executed what was more Highland Reel than war dance was something to behold.

Having become a Coushatta and achieved my goal of keeping my player's card, as the bells rang out to welcome 1979, my New Year resolution was to qualify for the Ryder Cup at the Greenbrier, West Virginia, by easing my way up the Order of Merit. Little did I dare hope, or even imagine, that over the coming months I would supplant Seve Ballesteros as Europe's number one.

CHAPTER FIVE

'WHEN I WAS TWENTY-ONE, IT WAS A VERY GOOD YEAR . . .'

Sportsmen and women are always quick to admit how lucky they are for being paid to do something they enjoy, and after a highly successful return trip to Africa – unlike the previous season I did not win any titles but finished second, third and seventh in my three events – I felt like a TV holiday-show presenter when the first month of spring 1979 took me to Portugal, Spain and Italy.

Vilamoura on the Portuguese Algarve is where Action Man probably takes his girlfriend on vacation. The activities on offer include tennis, horse-riding, water sports, clay pigeon shooting, sailing and deep-sea diving, and there are six golf courses. When the sun sets, tourists head for the marina, which is packed with the floating gin palaces of the rich and famous, and has every type of bar, restaurant or nightclub. As well as the suntan lotion, I had remembered to pack my good form when leaving Africa, finishing in a tie for seventh place with Tony Jacklin behind tournament winner Brian Barnes.

It was on then to Balmadena near Malaga on the Costa Del Sol, the venue for the Spanish Open. The Arabs gave the village its name, which appears to be derived from Banu Al Madena, meaning 'sons of the mines', a reference to the important mineral deposits that had been found there since Roman times – all right, I admit I read that in the hotel guide to the area. For the second week I was in the top ten, claiming a share of sixth place with victory going to Dale Hayes. Winner of the 15 to 17 age group category at the 1969 Junior World Championships, Hayes was developing into something of a serial winner in Europe. In 1971 he had won the Spanish Open at 18 years and 290 days, becoming the youngest winner on the European Tour, a record that still stands today. By 1973 he was fourth on the European Tour Order of Merit, improving to second in 1974 and first in 1975, before going on to win the World Cup in partnership with Bobby Cole. He surprisingly all but retired from tournament golf in his late twenties but remains involved with the sport as a broadcaster and course-designer.

Madrid has long been one of my favourite European cities. Sipping an ice-cold lager on an early summer evening while people-watching in the Plaza Mayor is the perfect way to while away an hour or two. Now that it is surrounded by trendy street cafés, it is hard to picture this fabulous square as it was when it staged bullfights and public executions during the Spanish Inquisition. I endured a sporting torture of my own by shooting 79, 80 over the Puerta de Hierro course, missing the cut by a distance. Four years later, however, I managed to prove to the good citizens of Madrid that I actually knew my way around a golf course by winning the 1983 tournament. That would have been hard to imagine for those who watched me in '79.

From the architectural splendour of the Spanish capital we

moved to Monticello, a short drive – by car, not golf club – from the banks of Lake Como and the splendid site of the Italian Open. I finished twelfth while the on-form Brain Barnes collected his second title of the season. In Lyon at the French Open, Scots filled four of the top five places – champion Bernard Gallacher, runner-up Willie Milne, David Chillas and Bill Longmuir. You will notice that I was not among them.

I was going through an infuriating spell during which I could not produce two good rounds back-to-back, not even on the hallowed links of St Andrews, where the Colgate PGA Championship attracted a genuinely international entry. Gary Player, Andy North and Raymond Floyd all finished well up the leaderboard behind winner Vicente Fernandez of Argentina, while I managed to miss yet another cut after opening rounds of 78, 72.

I was not without inspiration, though. Frustrated by my inability to hole a putt, between the first and second rounds I took a stroll round the various golf shops in town and bought a Ping putter, which had a nice feel about it, although I persevered with its predecessor for the Martini International at Wentworth, where I was a thirty-six hole casualty yet again. I had started the season with such high hopes of winning a place on the first ever European Ryder Cup team, but on this form, while John Jacobs and his merry men were on their way to the Greenbrier, I would be going back to the qualifying school.

The turning point of my season – actually, one of the most important turning points of my entire career – occurred on Jersey, the island of sun, Bergerac and the legendary Harry Vardon, who was born in 1870 within putting distance of what is now the twelfth fairway at Royal Jersey Golf Club. Vardon rose from humble surroundings to become the undisputed best player in the world, winning six Open Championships (two at Sandwich, where his brother, Tom, served as professional) and, in 1900, becoming the first overseas winner of the US Open.

More importantly perhaps, a century and more after Vardon reigned as the king of swing, there is scarcely a professional in the world today who does not use a subtle variation on the famous interlocking Vardon Grip, which the great man invented and perfected. It was not just in these islands that Vardon was considered golf's original superstar. On his triumphal visit to America he played a series of exhibition matches that drew massive crowds, invariably breaking the course record at every port of call, so much so that when he appeared in New York, the stock exchange bowed to pressure from its employees and closed for the day.

Vardon, it has to be said, might have been remembered as the greatest player in history had his putting been as dynamic as his driving, irons and approach play, but as Gene Sarazen observed: 'He was the most atrocious putter I'd ever seen. He didn't just three-putt, he four-putted.' Then, again, as the British golf writer of the day Bernard Darwin saw it: 'A grand player up to the green and a very bad player once he got there. That said, Vardon gave himself less putting to do than any other man.' Vardon was also one of the game's great characters; when a leader of the Women's Christian Temperance Union tried to persuade him to renounce alcohol as an example to his fellow-golfers – most of whom enjoyed a tipple in those days – a horrified Vardon came back with the rejoinder: 'Madam, I believe that moderation is essential in all things but never in my life have I been beaten by a tee-totaler.' Golf without the nineteenth hole – unthinkable.

Whenever I see the name Bergerac, I cannot help but smile

at the spoof Alan Partridge interview with French racing driver Michel Lambert, which went something like this . . .

'What do you think about, when you're racing your car?'

'Surprisingly, er, I think about the race.'

'Right. Um . . .'

'What do you think about when you're interviewing someone?'

'Well, nothing, umm . . . but, er, do you, when you're driving along, do you ever think, "Oooh, sacre blue! I've forgotten to set the video to record . . ." I don't know, "Top Gear"?'

'What is, er . . . what is "Top Gear"?'

'Oh, er, all right then, erm, you've forgotten to tape "Cyrano de Bergerac" with Gerard Depardieu.'

'I think, er, I think what you're trying to ask me is, "Do I ever get distracted when I'm driving?" No I don't.'

'No, no, no, no, I'm quite specifically asking you, do you forget to tape "Cyrano de Bergerac" with Gerard . . .'

'Depardieu . . .'

'Him, yeah.'

'No, I don't ever forget to tape it because I saw it at the cinema when it came out.'

'Right.'

'Have you ever seen this film?'

'Yes. Yes, I did see it . . .'

'You like it?'

'I'm . . . not . . . so keen on it, I mean, I don't like what they did with the idea, they set it in the 17th century, gave him a long nose, maybe it made it a bit funnier . . . but, but for the British, Bergerac is John Nettles . . .'

What else makes me laugh? No matter how often I watch the old repeats of 'The Morecambe & Wise Show', I never fail to marvel at their sheer genius, and the same goes for 'Fawlty Towers' and 'Mr Bean'. I have also made myself laugh on occasion, such as the time I had to turn down a dinner invitation to No 10 Downing Street where Margaret Thatcher was entertaining George Bush and was famously quoted as saying: 'I was really sorry because I know they are also very busy people.' I knew what I meant, just as I did when I won the Suntory World Matchplay – on my fifth attempt – and told a startled audience, which included our Japanese sponsors, that 'I liked playing in Japan because I enjoyed Chinese food so much . . .' As I say, I knew what I meant even if no one else did!

I digress. Opting to use my newly purchased off-the-shelf putter for the first round of the Jersey Open, I produced my best form of the season, a 66, leaving me joint third, two shots behind Tony Jacklin and Bernard Gallacher. By the halfway stage, Bernie had extended his lead over me and the rest of the chasing pack to four strokes but I was so relaxed before the start of the third round that I supped a pint of Guinness over a light lunch in the La Moye clubhouse before shooting a 66 that brought me within one shot of my Scottish compatriot. My new putter repaid its outlay in spades when I holed from fifteen feet for a birdie on the first, then from twenty-five feet for an eagle three on the second.

With my first victory on the European Tour within tantalising distance, but with a posse of big names around me, the leaderboard at the start of the final round read:

Bernard Gallacher -11
Sandy Lyle   -10
Howard Clark   -8
Willie Milne   -8

Tony Jacklin   -7
Michael King   -7

The day was warm and humid and a thick sea mist shrouded the course. Unexpectedly, Bernie, the most tenacious of competitors, dropped three shots on the first four holes and suddenly I was in the lead with the title to lose. By the time I reached the eighteenth tee, I held a three-shot advantage over Howard Clark and that is the precise moment I went weak at the knees. With my nerves jangling, I managed to steer my drive down the middle of the fairway, at which point my playing partner, Tony Jacklin, had a quiet word in my shell-like. 'Just take your time,' Tony told me as I reached for my 5-iron, 'and make sure you knock it on the green.'

Easier said than done, Tony, when it's your knees that are knocking but I managed to do just that; two putts with my trusty fifteen-quider and I was not only £5,000 richer but had risen to sixth in the Ryder Cup points standings behind Bernard Gallacher, Brian Barnes, Michael King, Baldovino Dassu of Italy and Nick Faldo. Sure, I had won in Nigeria but this victory proved to myself that I could take on and beat the best in Europe. All I had to do now was win another title as quickly as possible, thereby showing I was no one-hit wonder. After finishing equal twenty-fifth in the Belgian Open, equal fourth in the Welsh Classic, equal seventh in the Greater Manchester Open and equal fourth in the English Classic at The Belfry, it was time to turn that consistency into the all-important second Tour win.

At the halfway stage of the Scandinavian Open, played at Vasatorps Golf Club in the southern Swedish coastal town of Helsingborg – just across the Oresund from Hamlet's Castle at

Elsinore (which, like any keen student of Shakespeare, I remember from my school days) – I was one shot behind tournament leader Ken Brown, tied for second with the ominous figures of Seve Ballesteros and Dale Hayes. For nine holes of the third round, I was my consistent self, then I suddenly produced a barrage of birdies on the homeward nine, which I covered in a six-under-par 30, equalling the course record of 65 set by American Mike Krantz earlier in the day.

I knew little about Krantz, who spent most of his career in the chorus-line of the Asian Tour, so although he was only one stroke adrift, I fully expected my main challenge to come from Seve, who was among a pack of players a further two shots back. I was right. The title was won and lost on the long par-five ninth, where Seve, who had trimmed my advantage to just one stroke, produced a sumptuous bump and run to within a yard of the hole for a certain birdie. Having been raised by a Scottish dad, I knew a thing or two about bumps and runs myself, and – just when I needed it – played the same shot to perfection as the ball rolled to a stop six inches from the pin. There was no way back for Seve after I slotted my putt home.

Although my Scandinavian Open victory lifted me into second place in the Ryder Cup points standings behind Barnsie, it was back down to earth with a bump the following week when I reported to Lytham Green Drive to try to claim one of the eighty-six qualifying places for the 108th Open Championship. Just in case I fondly imagined I was above such things as having to qualify for the Open, one of my fellow competitors was the 61-year-old South African Bobby Locke, Open champion in 1949, '50, '52 and '57 and winner of eighty-one tournaments worldwide, including a remarkable fifteen in the United States.

Whereas Tiger Woods is the epitome of an athlete, even at the peak of his powers Locke, who always looked older than his years, was an incongruous sight with his, let us say, chunky physique, luxuriant moustache, white cap, plus-fours and tie, but could he play golf? After winning his first Open, Locke was invited to take part in a series of challenge matches against Sam Snead in South Africa, where he stunned the American – and all America, for that matter – by winning twelve of their sixteen contests.

Encouraged by that success, Locke travelled to the US the following year and won six of the first nine tournaments he entered, inspiring great resentment among his less-than-welcoming hosts. Locke took his revenge in the quietest way possible when, shortly before returning home to Johannesburg, an interviewer asked him if he had found it difficult to adjust to the US Tour. 'Oh yes,' he replied dryly, 'I very nearly lost four of the first five tournaments I played . . .'

In the years before former Open champions were automatically exempt from qualifying until reaching the age of 65, Bobby Locke failed to qualify for the 1979 Open while I managed to claim my place in the field, despite suffering from glandular fever, which necessitated a visit to a local hospital before the first round. Twelve months earlier I would have been highly satisfied to finish the British Major equal eighteenth with Gary Player, Nick Faldo, Ken Brown and Orville Moody, but given my previous form during the summer of 1979, I was deeply disappointed to finish twelve shots behind Seve Ballesteros, who instantly became known as 'the car-park champion' for the circuitous routes he found between tee and green.

Having gained sufficient points to guarantee my Ryder Cup

place, I became the European number one for 1979 by winning the European Open at Turnberry, a victory that brought not only a magnificent trophy but also a massive cheque for £17,500 – second only to the Open Championship prize. With its picture-postcard views across the Firth of Clyde to the mountains on the island of Arran, the volcanic outcrop of Ailsa Craig and Paul McCartney's Mull of Kintyre beyond, it is no surprise that Turnberry is known to golfers around the globe as Scotland's Pebble Beach. In reality, the cliff-top links course in Ayrshire is far more beautiful and a far better test of golf than the Californian version.

During the Second World War, Turnberry was requisitioned by the RAF and three concrete runways were built over the course, from where pilots flew Liberators and Beaufighters in their round-the-clock watch for German U-boats. Having played its part in the defence of Britain, there is an atmosphere about the place like no other. I have always adored Turnberry and three fine rounds of 71, 67, 72 left me nicely placed just one shot behind joint leaders Mark James and Neil Coles with eighteen holes to play.

According to one newspaper report that is when I: 'produced ninety minutes of the most sensational golf ever seen at Turnberry – and that includes the Watson-Nicklaus memorable confrontation of two years ago . . .' well, who am I to argue with this sagacious scribe? '. . . for by 1.45 p.m. on a hot, sunny afternoon, Sandy Lyle stood on the eighth tee at level threes, his astonishing opening burst of six birdies in the first seven holes destroying his nearest challengers and hoisting him above Seve Ballesteros in the Order of Merit table. I, for one, will remember with relish all 21 strokes until the day I die . . .'

For my part, I cannot begin to compare my performance that day but I do know that I achieved the almost unachievable by birdying the fearsome sixth. Of all the Open Championship's great challenges – the Road Hole at St Andrews, Lytham's historic seventeenth, the Postage Stamp at Troon – it is Turnberry's 222 yard par-three sixth, Tappie Toorie as it is affectionately known, that is consistently rated the single most difficult hole in the land. This little jewel in Turnberry's crown soars skywards from tee to green, which is spread out in front of the lighthouse at the highest and windiest point on the links. God once again was the architect but he hadn't placed the flagsticks – that must have been Sir Edmund Hillary. Guarded by four sandy canyons, which the locals laughingly refer to as bunkers, the steep green could serve as a ski-jump in winter. A hook leads to the choppy grey waters of the Firth of Clyde, a slice to a sixty-foot sheer drop of heather, gorse and tangled grass. Adders are said to dwell in these parts, probably alongside some 19th century golfers still trying to fight their way out of this Ayrshire jungle. When you birdie the sixth you just know something special is in the air and I was eventually round in 65 to beat Dale Hayes and Peter Townsend by seven strokes.

I was in a rich vein of form. I'd skipped the Swiss Open the previous week to enter the Scottish PGA Championship, and won in a play-off against Sam Torrance at Glasgow Gailes, and had I taken any of the half-dozen or so birdie opportunities that came my way on the homeward nine at Turnberry – I missed a series of putts of around six to eight feet – I might well have done the unthinkable and scored a sub-sixty round on that great course. Alas for my public image, ITV, who covered the European Tour at the time, did not screen the European Open due to an industrial dispute, so the biggest victory of my career to date was largely overlooked.

Although I was mightily proud to have ended Seve's three-year reign as European number one – after all, here was a great champion who I had only recently known from watching on TV – and I might have been the new king of the hill, his charisma and gung-ho approach to golf meant he was still the undoubted star of the Tour. Whenever I play in a Pro-Am event, I always tell my partners that if they are feeling nervous, how do they think I must have felt as a teenaged amateur when I met Seve for the very first time on the tee at a Pro-Am event at Calcott Manor? I shot a 72 that day against Seve's 74, after which he looked at me through narrowed eyes and said, 'You are very good player.' To which I, with the blithe confidence of youth, replied, 'Thanks very much – I hope to be seeing a lot more of you soon.'

After the Turnberry prize-giving and victory speech – I was delighted to think that I was fast becoming an old hand at this, having just won my third European tournament in four months – I embarked upon a high-speed drive back home to Shropshire where I had two hours' rest before setting off on my travels again at five o'clock in the morning to meet up with my Ryder Cup team-mates at a Heathrow hotel. Despite my hurried arrival, I turned up as requested in official blazer, tie and trousers to be met by the sight of Mark James wearing jeans. Mark has never been one to stand on ceremony but the thought did cross my mind that if we were to travel as a team, we might as well look like a team, but Mark has always been something of a free spirit.

Under John Jacobs' captaincy, we flew first class to the Greenbrier in West Virginia, which was a new experience for me. It was the first time I had ever been given a real knife and fork for an airline meal, more accustomed as I was to plastic cutlery. It was a joy to discover the totally different flying experience that awaits when you turn left instead of right on boarding a plane.

Set in the Allegheny Mountains of White Sulphur springs, the Greenbrier was best known as a health spa, offering detoxifying mud wraps for over two hundred years, until Sam Snead became the resident golf professional whereupon it was transformed into a 'must visit' golf complex much adored by President Dwight D. Eisenhower for one. Many a US president has been a keen golfer but none more so than Ike, who even had a putting green laid down in the gardens of the White House directly outside the window of the Oval Office.

Sam Snead spins the tale of playing with Ike at the Greenbrier on one occasion when the President was enduring a miserable round; the worse he played, the faster he swung and the faster he swung, the worse he played. Eventually, his caddie interjected: 'Slow it down, baldy . . .' Despite the helpfulness of this advice, Ike's play deteriorated even further. 'I told you, baldy, slow it down . . .'

'Listen,' Snead snarled. 'That's the President of the United States of America, you're talking to.'

When Eisenhower finally managed to keep ball on fairway, his faithful caddie was at pains to try and ingratiate himself with the most powerful man in the world. 'Great shot, President Lincoln,' he cooed. No wonder Ike's good friend and golf buddy Bob Hope famously remarked; 'President Eisenhower has given up golf for painting – it takes fewer strokes.'

Although it was not one of America's 'dream teams', their 1979 side had sufficient star names to be an intimidating force, including Lee Trevino, Tom Kite, Hale Irwin, Fuzzy Zoeller, Larry Nelson and Lanny Wadkins. They also had the smug superiority of knowing they had not lost a Ryder Cup contest since 1957 when Dai Rees captained Great Britain and Ireland to a rare victory at the Lindrick Club, Sheffield.

Much has since been made of the so-called 'naughty schoolboys' attitude of Mark James and Ken Brown, who, it has been suggested, did not like the team uniforms, insisted on playing with one another and no one else and attended the various dinners and functions under sufferance. While it is noticeable that Mark and Ken are the only team members not grinning fit to burst in the official team picture, all I know is that after Brian Barnes and Tony Jacklin visited their rooms for a quiet word about the traditions and protocol of the Ryder Cup, they became valued colleagues.

Personally, I thoroughly enjoyed the brouhaha surrounding the opening ceremony, and the round of engagements. It was precisely this kind of experience I had been working towards since Dad first tucked a club into my three-year-old paw. Nothing, however, could have prepared me for the gut-wrenching terror I felt on the first tee when I was introduced to the fray in the afternoon foursomes on the opening day with the Americans already 3–1 ahead from the morning fourballs. Fortunately, I had the battle-hardened Tony Jacklin at my side as we squared up to Dr Gil Morgan (a qualified optometrist who has never had to follow that profession because he earned so much as a golfer) and the living legend of Lee Trevino.

There are probably few such traumatic moments in sport than playing your first match in your first Ryder Cup which is why I remember so little of the experience. But I do remember that with Tony serving as a constant source of encouragement and advice to the rookie at his side, we gained half a point against Morgan and Trevino and followed that up with a resounding 5 and 4 victory over Lee Elder and John Mahaffey on the second day's morning foursomes. By the time of the climactic singles, the Americans were defending a slender 8½–7½ advantage, a lead that was swiftly wiped out when Bernard Gallacher thumped Lanny Wadkins 3 and 2. The scent of an unlikely triumph began to evaporate in the Sulphur Springs air, however, as the US looked bound for victory (and so it turned out) in the next seven matches. Some might have felt the Ryder Cup was over by the time I teed off in the middle of the park – as the luck of the draw would have it – against Trevino, but I was determined to do my bit in the hope we might just pull something out of the fire, even if I was up against one of the most redoubtable match-play competitors the game has ever known.

'Super-Mex' had always been a man to be admired, and he never forgot his humble beginnings. He never knew his father, and neither his mother nor grandfather, who raised him, could read or write, but he emerged from the abject poverty of a shack on the outskirts of Dallas with no electricity, running water or even windows, to become one of the game's great characters. When he won the 1971 Open at Royal Birkdale, he discovered that local tradition called for the new champion to donate a percentage of his winnings to a nearby Roman Catholic orphanage. This Trevino cheerfully agreed to do, providing the orphanage nuns took a glass of champagne with him in the Kingsway Casino. It must have been quite a sight, Trevino sitting there grinning happily, surrounded by the Mother Superior and the cast of 'The Sound of Music'. So impressed was golfer with holy sisters that he auctioned off his Open-winning clubs and doubled his donation to £2,000, more than one third of his first-prize cheque.

Entirely self-taught, Trevino opted out of the Texas education system as a 14-year-old to work on a driving range before enlisting in the US Marines from which he graduated on to the US Tour. Trevino went on to win six Majors – two Opens, two US Opens and two US PGA titles – and was probably responsible for ending Tony Jacklin's days as a contender at the Muirfield Open of 1972. The two men, both playing terrific golf, stood level on the seventeenth tee. The advantage swung firmly towards Jacklin when Trevino found a fairway bunker off the tee, splashed out and was still well short of the green in three in heavy rough. With all Britain willing him on, Jacklin had taken route one and was fifteen feet from the hole in three with the Claret Jug moving ever close to his grasp. Trevino smashed his fourth shot over the putting surface, the ball coming to rest halfway up a steep bank. Super Mex, as he had done so many times previously and would do again, holed his chip for a par. Jacklin sent his birdie attempt three feet past and missed the return. The Open went to Trevino for the second successive year and Tony would never be the same force again.

The galleries, needless to say, loved Trevino because here was a man whose unique swing not only defied every law of nature but who also kept up a steady stream of one-liners even on his backswing. Some of these are just too good not to repeat here and, although I didn't hear Lee deliver all of them during the numerous times we played together, they certainly provide a fair reflection of the man I know, like and admire.

On his upbringing: My family was so poor they couldn't afford

To the Fairway Born

Royal Lytham, 1974. Not quite breaking 'Young' Tom Morris's record – but 16 years old is still pretty young to be in the Open.

We went through a lot of polish in our house.

Brabazon Trophy, 1975. I'm sure I didn't plan on being in that spot – but I must have got out okay. I went on to become the youngest winner of the tournament.

Opposite: Houston, we are about to have a problem. Martin Poxon, me and Nick Faldo head out west on 3 January 1976. But not for long.

EMPICS

MIRRORPIX

POPPERFOTO

Washing up, advertising the course, selling equipment … was there no end to my talents at Hawkstone? Mum and Dad helped a bit, of course.

My first pro gig. South America-bound with the British Caledonian Golfing Lions. *Top row, l-r*: David Ingram, me, Mike Miller, Sam Torrance, John Morgan; *bottom row, l-r*: Ewen Murray, Malcolm Grigson, Dai Rees, Carl Mason, Tommy Horton. Barnsie should be there. I wonder if he's still in the bar …

At Buckingham Palace to receive my MBE. I hope in my life I made Mum and Dad proud of me. They deserved no less.

Dad instilled in me all the ingredients to be a champion. All I had to do was put everything he taught me into practice.

Dad certainly seemed pleased when I won my first US tournament, in 1986. He named his new house after it.

European Open, 1979, Turnberry. Victory by seven strokes. Europe's No. 1. Arm held aloft by organiser Sven Tumba. Pity no one could watch it on TV …

Nailed it. On my way to winning the 1987 TPC at Sawgrass, the 'fifth Major'.

1988 was a very good year. After winning the Phoenix Open I ....

...regained the Greater Greensboro...

... shot a 66 in my opening round with Trevino at Woburn and went on to win the Dunhill British Masters from Faldo by two strokes ...

... met Nick again at Wentworth for the final of the National Ball Skimming Tournament, sorry, the World Matchplay ...

... won, fifth time lucky ...

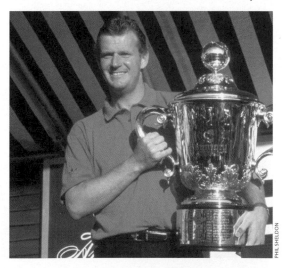

... and I did OK at Augusta that year too.

The Volvo Masters, 1992, Valderrama.
My last tournament victory,
beating Monty in the play-off.

kids. The lady next door had me . . . By the time I was five I was working in the fields. I thought hard work was just how life was. I was 21 years old before I discovered Manual Labor wasn't a Mexican . . .

On his wealth: I'm going to win so much money this year my caddie will make it on to the top twenty money-winners' list . . . I may buy the Alamo and give it back to the Mexicans . . . You can make a lot of money in this game. Just ask my ex-wives . . . You don't know what pressure is until you've played for five bucks with only two in your pocket . . .

On golf-course architects: If I were designing one for myself there would be a dogleg right on every hole. And the first hole wouldn't count – it would be a warm-up hole . . . Spyglass Hill in California? They ought to hang the man who designed it. Ray Charles could have done better . . .

On the Open: This is the one tournament I would play if I had to leave America a month early and swim over . . .

On the occasion his three playing partners all drove into the woods: What's over there – a nudist colony?

I was ready for anything Trevino might throw at me because one of the many aspects of golf that my dad had drummed into me from an early age was to keep my concentration no matter what might be going on around me. To this end, Dad would jangle the coins in his pocket when I was about to tee off, or suddenly rip off his glove with a satisfying velcrose tear if I was standing over a putt. As is his wont, Trevino chipped in a couple of times, beat me 2 and 1 and the United States ran out comfortable 17–11 winners. The 'new' Europe had not been disgraced, however, and as we listened to the Americans' victory speeches at the post-tournament dinner, you could almost hear Seve Ballesteros mutter, 'Just you wait, just you wait . . .' (although with an accent somewhat less Cockney than Eliza Doolittle's).

I met up with Trevino a few weeks later at the end-of-season Lancome Trophy twelve-man invitation event at the St Nom la Breteche club on the outskirts of Paris. I was fortunate to spend some time there in the company of Arnold Palmer, whose best years may have been behind him but who remained a towering figure in the game. It is almost inconceivable that Palmer will turn 80 in 2009 because four decades and more after his final Major victory in the 1964 Masters, he is still one of America's most beloved sporting celebrities. At the height of his powers in the early 1960s, he was positively adored by one and all.

Palmer won seven Majors and remains the main reason why golf has become a multi-million-dollar entertainment industry. Long before the emergence of Seve Ballesteros, it was Palmer, with his dashing good looks, stevedore's physique and riverboat gambler's instinct, who attracted the first huge golf galleries the world over. The peerless *Los Angeles Times* columnist Jim Murray described his hold over Arnie's Army thus: 'Golf was a comparatively sexless enterprise until Palmer came a-wooing. His caveman approach took the audience by storm. He was James Cagney pushing a grapefruit in Mae Clark's face, Gable kicking down the door to Scarlett O'Hara's bedroom . . .'

In any genuine poll to discover the most popular and influential sports personality of the 20th century, I think I would probably vote for Palmer alongside Muhammad Ali and Pelé. Jack Nicklaus might have won more 'Majors' but as Ken Still, the former US Tour veteran, put it, 'He's the sole reason we're playing for all this money today. Arnie single-handedly made it all possible. I'll tell you what I think of the man; if he should walk in the door right now and say, "Shine my shoes," I'd take off my shirt, get down on my hands and knees and shine his shoes. Of course, Arnie would never ask you to do any such thing.'

The public loved him so because they knew every time Palmer reached for a club it was show time! Playing in the Los Angeles Open in 1961, Palmer took a ruinous 13 on one hole when he refused his caddie's advice to lay up short on a par five with victory seemingly certain. 'Take an iron,' pleaded his bag carrier. 'It's my reputation,' replied Arnie, taking a long draw on his cigarette. 'Give me the goddamn wood.' The ball flew into the water guarding the green and from there calamity followed calamity. Asked to explain how he had run up thirteen shots, Palmer grinned and drawled, 'It was easy, I missed a twenty-foot putt for a twelve.'

I managed to finish ahead of Arnie in the Lancome Trophy – well, he was 50 at the time – but could not catch Johnny Miller and had to settle for joint second with Trevino. A question I am often asked is whatever happened to Miller, who for a brief spell in the 1970s threatened to dominate golf. Now approaching 60, Miller shot to fame when he won the 1973 US Open by shooting a stunning 63 in the last round at Oakmont, and added his second Major three years later in the Open Championship at Royal Birkdale. He won twenty-four tournaments on the US Tour, eight in his annus mirabilis of 1974, and with his Robert Redford good looks, a superstar was born.

'I had a stretch back there for a few years when I played some golf that bordered on the twilight zone,' he recalled. 'I can remember getting upset when I was required to putt out.' Then, as suddenly as Miller had burst on the scene, he all but disappeared. From 1977 to 1987, he won but six tournaments before coming out of semi-retirement at the age of 46 in 1994 to record an unlikely victory in the AT & T Championship at Pebble Beach. The following month he missed the cut at the Masters and was gone. He did have a brief crack at the US Seniors Tour in 1997, but walked away after four appearances when his best finish was joint twenty-third. Since then he has concentrated on golf design and television commentary, a field in which he has a reputation for telling it like it is. His condemnatory comments after the infamous 'Battle of Brookline' had the US Ryder Cup team apoplectic with rage.

So whatever happened to Johnny Miller? As Peter Alliss puts it: 'Some sporting gods simply wake up one morning to find that all their magical deeds appear to have been just a glorious dream.' I'm not certain I would classify myself as a 'sporting god', but like Johnny Miller I know only too well what it is like to wake up one morning and find you are a mere golfing mortal.

How did the lyrics of the old Frank Sinatra song go? 'When I was twenty-one, it was a very good year . . .' – 1979 had been a very good year indeed for me. I'd received the Harry Vardon Trophy for winning the Order of Merit, enjoyed three tournament victories in the Jersey, Scandinavian and European Opens, and sampled the flavour of the Ryder Cup. Oh yes, and along with the Christmas greetings that dropped through the letterbox at Hawkstone came an envelope postmarked Augusta, Georgia, containing a tastefully embossed card: *The board of directors formally invite your participation in the 1980 Masters tournament.*

At the bottom a little tear-off section was provided for your acceptance or apology – as if anyone is ever going to say no. As a past winner, I'm glad to say the invitation still arrives at the Lyle household on an annual basis. It goes without saying that I never, ever send my apologies.

CHAPTER SIX

DISQUALIFIED IN KENYA, WORLD CUP WINNER IN COLOMBIA

I began the new decade by recording a first – finding myself disqualified after the final round of the Kenyan Open, with a little help from my playing partner Nick Faldo, in what became known as the 'Sandy Lyle Incident'. We were playing in the heat of mid-afternoon and every time I leaned over a putt, the sun reflected off the top of the putter's blade and dazzled me. Feeling quite proud of myself, I came up with the cunning ploy of peeling off a strip of tape from my hand, which I used to prevent my fingers from cracking, and sticking it over the offending part of my club. I even told Faldo of my wheeze.

'So when did you do that?' he asked.

'On the third hole,' I told him and proceeded on my merry way.

When we came off the eighteenth green, I was approached by George O'Grady, the rules official, who told me, 'I think we've got a bit of a problem, Sandy. What's this about sticking tape on your putter?' Not thinking anything of it, I showed George the fruits of my endeavours – it had never crossed my mind to remove the damn thing – whereupon he informed me I had altered the characteristics of my putter. Now, to my mind, altering the characteristics meant adding a lead weight or bending it over my knee, and I was puzzled that George knew about what seemed a triviality.

In his autobiography, Faldo provided an explanation of sorts to that question when he explained: 'En route to the tenth, past the clubhouse, I bumped into an official and asked, "Sandy has a bit of tape on his putter. Can he do that?"' According to eye-witnesses, however, it would appear that he went out of his way to find an official in order to 'shop me'. I have no idea whether that is the case or not, but I was heartbroken to be disqualified. As anyone who knew my dad will tell you, I had been brought up to respect the first rule of golf that you never, ever cheat. Also, having played in all the Pro-Ams, then four rounds in the African heat and finishing well up in the money, it was annoying that it had all been for nothing.

If I was despondent – and fearful of telephoning my dad to tell him of my disqualification – the feeling among my pals in the clubhouse was one of anger. Brian Barnes, who had consumed a couple of beers by the time news of the furore reached the bar, was all for inviting Faldo to accompany him round the back of the clubhouse to punch his lights out. Now, Barnsie is exactly the type of man you want in your corner, but I managed to persuade the big fella that this was probably not the best course of action. I cannot believe that Faldo was devious enough to bring about my disqualification deliberately. I put it down to the inexperience of youth, but only he knows the motives behind his actions.

You might think I had been foolish or careless but to this day I firmly believe I did not 'alter the characteristics' of the club. In contrast, I was rather pleased with my invention and thought nothing of it until George O'Grady approached me. If I'd thought I was cheating in any way whatsoever then I would never have added the sticking tape in the first place. Certainly, if the roles had been reversed, I would probably have congratulated Nick Faldo on his ingenuity rather than running off behind his back to report the matter. Furthermore, my dad, who would have been the first to tear strips off me if I'd done anything untoward, was as puzzled by both the ruling and Faldo's reaction when I finally plucked up the courage to phone him that night to explain my disqualification.

Again, according to Faldo, who has always been a bit of an enigma to us all on the Tour: 'This was the first time a fellow professional had broken the rules under my nose. In retrospect, what I should have done was query the strip of tape and ask him to check with an official, but it was me who brought it to the attention of the authorities and in doing so I became the snitch. Unfortunately, something of a grudge seems to have grown out of my actions.'

I do not know where Nick Faldo gets that notion because there is most certainly no grudge on my part, although it is fair to say we have never been close friends, even when members of the same England schoolboy team as teenagers. Our personalities are entirely different. Perhaps it was being an only child, but Nick has always been a loner. He was never one to sit down in the clubhouse bar for a beer with the gang at the end of a round whereas, quiet as I may be, there is nothing I like better than the company of my pals at day's end. Nick gives the impression that he believes the world revolves round him and him alone. The only time we socialise together, if you can call it that, is at the annual champions' dinner before the Masters, but I can't recall Nick asking even the most rudimentary question, such as, 'How are the wife and kids?'

Our rivalry in those early years was a terrific boost for British golf and there is no doubt that it spurred us both on. As a champion, Nick Faldo is right up there with the best. It takes a remarkable talent to win six Majors and compile a Ryder Cup record that is second to none, and yet I feel he remains unfulfilled. I do not envy him his success, and when I was called upon to slip the Green Jacket over his shoulders after he succeeded me as Masters champion in 1989, I can honestly say I was pleased for Nick because I knew exactly how he was feeling at that special moment. I suppose we were like two boxers forever challenging for the same title – we grew to respect one another but never to form any notions of friendship. The Kenyan Open and the 'Sandy Lyle Incident' seem like a lifetime ago now. I was certainly puzzled and maybe even a bit hurt that a fellow professional would go behind my back in such a way, but there is not a shred of animosity on my part, although I would not be entirely honest if I did not admit that it made any subsequent victory over Nick Faldo all the sweeter.

In order to prepare for my Masters' debut, I entered the Greater Greensboro Open at Forest Oaks in the Carolinas – a tournament won by Sam Snead a record eight times. This was the traditional warm-up event for Augusta and the greens are specially prepared to resemble the following week's conditions in Georgia. I produced a workmanlike par 72 in the opening round, watched by my mum and dad, who had made the trip from Shropshire in order to witness my first tilt at the Masters. I swept up the leaderboard on the Friday when, despite an unpleasant 7.46 a.m. start time, I eventually rubbed the sleep from my eyes to come home in 32 for a second round 67. That left me joint third, three strokes behind Craig Stadler.

After another solid 72, I was four shots adrift of 'The Walrus' and embarked upon the final round with expectations of a high finish in my first tournament in America. My playing partner was Raymond Floyd, the Sergeant Bilko of golf – a hustler and gambler who learned all the tricks of the trade while his father was serving with the US Army at Fort Bragg, Tennessee. At 13 Floyd was a scratch golfer, so precociously expert that the only way he could lure adult opponents on to the camp's first tee was to play alternate shots right-handed then left-handed. Despite his reputation as 'a shark in short pants', the GIs of Fort Bragg, like Bilko's ever-trusting Dobermann at Fort Baxter, could never see the danger until it was too late. Floyd was not at his best that afternoon, shooting a 73, which bettered my miserable score by three and, after such a promising beginning, I trailed home an abject twelve strokes behind Stadler.

It was a salutary lesson on what it takes to win on the American circuit because while I was playing flawless golf from tee to green, Stadler, gritty fighter that he is, scrambled his way round the course, driving like a high handicapper but chipping and putting like a demon. Although never considered one of the game's greats, Stadler was a vastly underrated golfer and would win the Masters two years later in 1982 when he also topped the US money-winners' list. That gives some idea of his credentials.

He might also have won the Open on two occasions. He walked up the seventy-second fairway in the final pairing, both times ending in disappointment. The Walrus partnered Nick Faldo on the Sunday at Muirfield in 1987 when the pride of Welwyn Garden City made eighteen straight pars. For once, Stadler did not hole a single putt of any consequence and finished third. Then, at Royal Birkdale in 1983, he led at halfway, and was tied for the lead after the third round when partnered with Tom Watson. A ruinous final round allowed Watson to win.

Stadler invariably had a smile on his face, though, even at the Sandwich Open of 1985 when he and Jack Nicklaus both shot 83 in the first round. The Golden Bear then went round in 66 against Stadler's 67 to make the cut by one shot. As Stadler tells it, he returned to his hotel after the first round to find his wife, Sue, shaking her head.

'Hey, the great Jack Nicklaus shot eighty-three as well don't forget,' he was moved to protest. Sue was less than impressed that her hubby was trailing in about 150th place. 'You beat two people.'

Although he gained a reputation for being a firebrand on the course – asked why he was playing with a new putter on one occasion, Stadler replied, 'Because the old one didn't float' – it was his talent to manufacture shots that most impressed me. When I asked him once why he had no more than a single Masters title to show for what should have been a glittering career, Stadler told me, 'For three years I was pretty good but I guess my priorities changed. When I married Sue, we spent our honeymoon at the Bob Hope Classic, but once the boys were born [Kevin and Chris are now in their mid-20s], I valued watching them grow up, even though you never spend as much time with them as you want. Before they became little people, I played maybe thirty events a year, driving them round in a camper packed with buggies and toys and diapers. But after they begin to walk and talk, you're done, it's over. I cut back to about twenty-two events, which was still too many. They're two great kids for the simple reason their mom was an awesome dad. I find it hard to claim any credit for the way they've turned out. I know every dad feels guilty, but being a golfer or an athlete of any sort shouldn't make a difference. At the start, I probably felt being a dad might be kind of bothersome to my career, but the moment these little things start talking, you wonder how in the world you ever got along without them. I wouldn't swap my kids for sixteen Majors.' To an extent, I understand where Stadler is coming from but any professional athlete has to have a selfish streak in him and there have been times when I have been forced to put career before family, although I would like to think that as a dad and golfer, I have managed to retain the right balance most of the time.

And so Georgia would be our next stop. Mum, Dad, my manager, Derrick Pillage, and I crammed ourselves, the luggage and clubs into our big Lincoln Continental hire car to make the journey. Augusta National is not the easiest of courses to locate – perhaps by design – and it took us a long time on that Monday afternoon to find the tree-lined avenue up to the clubhouse. Even now, all these years later, I still struggle – and the addition of a sat nav system in today's modern cars instructing us to make numerous U-turns still can't get me to the front door in one take.

On our eventual arrival for my first Masters, there is no denying I was entering what looked like golfing heaven. My first impression was that it was what I had hoped Houston would have been like four years previously, with its fairways of emerald velvet and creeks of shimmering turquoise. Even the sand – soft, white and so flawless you required sunglasses even to glance at it – looked so enticing that I felt it would be a privilege to land in an Augusta bunker. Then there are the smells – pine, camellia, magnolia, flowering peach, dogwood, azalea. All this is set under a Georgia spring sky, with the whiff of sporting history in the air and a clubhouse straight from the set of 'Gone with the Wind' – no wonder Mum and Dad were totally in awe of the place, which they had previously only ever seen on TV.

Certain things stick in my mind from that first visit. When I went to pick up my playing credentials I was just a number then, one of many competitors never expected to make a mark. There was no 'Hello Sandy, how are you doing? Nice to see you again', as there is now. In those days you were allocated one of the local caddies, who all, rather bizarrely, seemed to go by biblical names – Jonah, Noah, Nebakanezer (only joking on that last one). On going to meet my assigned bag carrier I remember glancing up and seeing a sign that read 'No guns, no knives – anyone carrying will be immediately escorted from the premises'. Hawkstone it most certainly wasn't.

Over the years since that initial entry, I've been lucky to visit Augusta many times for the Masters. And on each occasion, chatting in the clubhouse, reading the history, I've learned more and more about this remarkable tournament. And it's a tale worth recounting. It was the brainchild of Bobby Jones who, despite having played his best golf eight decades ago, is still revered as one of the greatest players in the history of the game. Not only did Jones win four US Open titles – as an amateur competing against the likes of Walter Hagen and Gene Sarazen – but on his three trips to Britain in an era when the journey across the Atlantic took the best part of four weeks by boat, he won the Open in 1926, 1927 and 1930, plus the British Amateur championship. A tantrum and club thrower of Olympic standard, heavy smoker and equally enthusiastic bourbon drinker, Jones described golf as 'a sophisticated game, played with the outward appearance of great dignity. It is, nevertheless, a game of considerable passion, either of the explosive type, or that which burns inwardly and sears the soul.'

Jones may have been a firebrand in his youth, but he always displayed an air of dignity, never more so than in the 1925 US Open at Worcester when he penalised himself during the last round and lost the title to Willie MacFarlane by one shot. 'There is only one way to play the game,' explained Jones. 'You might as well praise a man for not robbing a bank.' At the height of his powers in 1930, Jones achieved what was then considered the 'Grand Slam' by winning the US Open, US Amateur, British Open and British Amateur titles, and then decided to retire at the age of 28 to concentrate on a legal career as a lawyer in his home town of Atlanta and spend more time with his family. 'First come my wife and children,' he said, 'and next my profession – the law. Finally, and never as a life in itself, comes golf.'

It takes a brave man to turn his back on any sport at a time when he was as admired throughout America as Babe Ruth in baseball, Bill Tilden in tennis or Jack Dempsey in the boxing ring, and we can only wonder about how many more Majors Jones might have won had he not quit at such a young age. Remember, Jones was playing at a time when courses were often little more than rough pastures, when bunkers remained unraked and when clubs and balls were primitive by modern standards. He was a renowned putter despite being armed with a rusty, goose-necked implement known as 'Calamity Jane'.

One of his closest golfing buddies was President Dwight D. Eisenhower, who presented Jones with a 40 x 32 inch oil painting of himself in the Oval Office inscribed 'Bob – from his good friend D.D.E 1953'. The painting has pride of place in the Augusta clubhouse. I've looked at it many times. The accompanying letter reads: 'Those who have been fortunate enough to know Bob, realise that his fame as a golfer is transcended by his inestimable qualities as a human being. His gift to his friends is the warmth that comes from unselfishness, superb judgement, nobility of character and unwavering loyalty to principle.'

Friendship meant a lot to Jones – 'Friends are a man's priceless treasures and life rich in friendship is a life full, indeed' – and it was to enjoy an annual get-together with his cronies that he and buddy Clifford Roberts, a Wall Street financier, bought 'Fruitlands', a 365 acre nursery running alongside the Florida-New York rail line during the Depression. The duo employed Dr Alister MacKenzie to turn the land into a golf course. MacKenzie had emigrated to America from Scotland, giving up medicine to become a golf-course architect. His Cypress Point layout had brought him vast acclaim. Jones and Roberts had firm ideas about the type of club they had in mind, one that could be enjoyed by amateur members and leading professionals alike, and one that would be devoted to golf and golf alone, hence the absence of swimming pools, tennis courts or the variety of facilities provided by the average country club.

At first acquaintance, Augusta National is deceptively welcoming with its broad fairways, lack of rough and absence of bunkers – fewer than fifty all told, only ten of which are situated on the fairways (trust me to land in one with my 279th shot of the 1988 Masters!) – but come the week of the Green Jacket when the steeply sloping greens are lightning-quick, Augusta is no place for the faint-hearted. As Bobby Jones put it: 'There isn't a hole out there that can't be birdied if you just think about it, but there isn't one that can't be double-bogeyed if you stop thinking.' Tiger Woods may have reduced Augusta to pitch-and-putt proportions in 1997 when he swept round in 70, 66, 65, 69 but when the pressure mounts over the closing holes of the Masters, it has reduced some of the greatest players to nervous wrecks, most memorably Greg Norman in 1996 when he led Nick Faldo by six shots at the start of the final round only to lose by five strokes after a calamity-strewn 78. Just as Jones intended it to be, Augusta is as fair as any course. At the age of 54, in 1967, Ben Hogan covered the back nine in 30. Gary Player triumphed in 1978 after a preposterous 64 in the last round – and who can ever forget Jack Nicklaus's famous charge in 1986 when he came from a long way back to overhaul the luckless Norman, Tom Kite and Seve Ballesteros with a closing 65?

Unlike the other three Majors, all of which are played on a rota of courses generating differing atmospheres and challenges, little ever changes at Augusta. The grass is green, the hundred-foot pines are green, the paper cups are green, the courtesy cars are green, the tee markers are green. I always find it ironic that neither Ken Green nor Hubert Green ever won the Green Jacket.

Just as the Masters is by invitation only, so membership of Augusta National is granted to a selected few only. It may be the closest thing to heaven in many ways for a golfer, but it is just about as hard to become a member. After Jones had been confined to a wheelchair following two spine operations for chronic arthritis in 1950, Clifford Roberts ruled the club like a sporting dictator, deciding who should be admitted and, more importantly, who should be excluded. If Roberts decided you had overstayed your welcome in the members' lounge, out you went with no notification and certainly no appeal.

According to clubhouse legend, one member rang up Augusta to book a round and to reserve one of the luxury cabins, only for the switchboard operator to put him straight through to Clifford Roberts.

'Is there a problem?'

'Only that you are no longer a member.'

'For what reason, Cliff?'

'Non-payment of your bill.'

'But I haven't received a bill.'

'Exactly, only members receive bills.'

Another member was sitting over a drink with a friend in the clubhouse after a round when he was unwise enough to offer the opinion that 'although Augusta is a great club, as a course I think it's only just above average. In fact, I'd go as far as to say that my home course back up north is a far better test of golf.' Two days later the entire contents of his locker – save for his member's blazer – were duly delivered 'back up north'.

Back in the 1950s, Augusta utilised a system of coloured flags to signify how many guests a member would be allowed on any particular day. A black flag meant one guest would be permitted and a red flag meant three guests. When one member flew in with three chums he was embarrassed to find black cloth fluttering atop the flagpole. Espying Roberts in the distance, he ran up puffing, 'Cliff, I've got a real problem. We've just flown in all the way from New York and I have three friends all ready to tee off.' Roberts studied the hapless hacker as though he was talking in a foreign language.

'I don't understand. Unless you happen to be colour blind, what exactly is your problem?'

Even President Eisenhower found his role as the most powerful man in the world ended at the clubhouse door. Ike was forever driving into a tree at the edge of the seventeenth fairway and pleaded with Roberts on many an occasion to have the offending pine chopped down, or at the very least uprooted and moved to another location. Roberts's reply came in the form of a discreet plaque embedded in the bark: Ike's Tree.

Although television was allowed through the gates of Magnolia Drive, Roberts made the TV people fully aware that they were there on sufferance. Even now, commercial breaks are kept to a minimum, a ruling that Roberts insisted CBS explain to the viewing public on air one year, via an appropriate spokesman. When CBS suggested Ed Sullivan, king of the talk-show circuit, Roberts exploded, 'If I wanted someone from showbusiness, I'd get Randolph Scott!'

When Frank Beard was coming to the end of his tournament career and working for CBS as a part-time commentator, he offered a gentle criticism of Augusta and the Masters in his *Golf Digest* column. Roberts, who did not approve of criticism however gentle, phoned the television station to say, 'I don't want Frank Beard at Augusta and I don't want him at CBS.' Beard was duly out on two counts. Jack Whitaker was another CBS employee to fall foul of Roberts when he referred to a particularly large gallery as 'a mob'. By now, CBS had grown accustomed to Roberts's strident voice booming down the line. 'We do not have *mobs* at the Masters and we will not have Jack Whitaker here, either.'

The most famous on-air sacking was that of Gary McCord, who must have thought he had struck exactly the right note when he described the Augusta greens as being 'so slick they must have been bikini-waxed'. Clifford Roberts was not amused and Gary McCord was heard no more from the Masters.

Not even the players were exempt from Roberts's biting tongue. As the Martin Luther King Civil Rights movement swept across America, so eighteen Congressmen sent a telegram to Augusta National urging the organisers of the Masters to include Lee Elder or Charlie Sifford, the two outstanding black golfers, in the list of invitees. 'Frankly,' wrote Roberts in his withering reply, 'we are a little surprised as well as being flattered that eighteen Congressmen would be able to take time out from trying to solve the nation's problems to help us operate a golf tournament.' As luck would have it, Elder beat Jack Nicklaus and the aforementioned Frank Beard in a play-off for the Monsanto Open twelve months later to become the first black player to compete in the Masters.

Ben Crenshaw, the 1984 Masters champion, recalled his first visit to Augusta as an amateur twelve years earlier, when he marked his debut with a fine round of 73. As he left the scorer's tent bound for the clubhouse bar and a restorative beer, Ben bumped into our Clifford.

'Well, how did you enjoy your first round in the Masters, Ben?'

'Very much, indeed, Mr Roberts.'

'That's good, Ben. And I think you'll enjoy it a whole lot more after you've had a haircut.'

Bobby Jones died at the age of 69 in 1971, six years before Clifford Roberts made his way out to the ninth hole of Augusta National, put a pistol to his head and committed suicide.

The Masters, inaugurated in 1934, is now established as one of the most eagerly awaited and prestigious contests on the sporting calendar. Fortunately for me, I've always sported a neat and tidy haircut, have never likened the greens to bikini wax and have never felt tempted to tell the members that in my humble opinion Clober represents the greater challenge, so I have always been made most welcome. Not that Augusta felt all that welcoming as I prepared to drive off for the first time with palms sweating and throat constricting, hoping the fresh air would arrive soon; apart from the Open, after all, tournaments do not come any bigger than the Masters. I was nervous certainly, but only really on that first tee. Who wouldn't be? The sense of occasion is extraordinary. The relief did come – having sent my ball squarely down the middle of the opening fairway I started to relax. Perhaps surprisingly, I felt very little tension, I was just happy to be there. I hadn't piled pressure on myself to perform – Dad and I had discussed the expectations of success – and so I approached the course with an open mind, ready to enjoy myself. Not that my relaxed style seemed to help much – I took 76 shots on my first competitive eighteen holes around Augusta. I finished Day One of my Masters' experience ten shots behind early leader Seve Ballesteros. I survived the cut with a second round 70, which reinforced my belief that this was a course on which I could thrive once I learned all its little subtleties. Pleasingly, when I studied the halfway leaderboard my thirty-six hole total of 146 was only one behind Jack Nicklaus, Lee Trevino and Raymond Floyd, so although I was now a distant eleven shots behind the flying Seve, I was in the very best of company. Better still, I moved ahead of the Golden Bear with another two-under-par 70 in round three and found myself teeing off with the incomparable Chi Chi Rodriguez on the final afternoon.

Chi Chi is a one-off and no mistake. A child at heart though now in his seventies, he says his proudest achievement is not the $7 million plus he has earned through golf but the Chi Chi Rodriguez Youth Foundation in Clearwater, Florida, a refuge for abused and troubled kiddies. 'If I made it, anybody can do it,' he explains. 'I think I can be a good role model to them because they can look at me and say, "He's a small guy who was born poor but worked hard to get to the top."' Born in Rio Piedras, Puerto Rico, from a young age he worked in the searing heat alongside his dad in the sugar-cane fields. Chi Chi recalls his childhood with poignancy. 'I was never a kid. I was too poor to be a child, so I never had a childhood. The biggest present I ever got was a marble. But we were rich in other ways. My father was my hero. One day he caught one of the neighbourhood boys stealing bananas from a tree in our yard. My father told me to go fetch his machete. I thought something horrible was going to happen. Instead, he climbed the tree, cut down a bunch of bananas and gave them to the boy. That was a great lesson for me.'

Chi Chi began caddying as a six-year-old and taught himself to play using 'clubs' fashioned from guava tree branches and 'balls' made out of tin cans, which he would hammer into as round a shape as possible. 'I could hit that thing a hundred yards but it never was much good for putting. That's OK. I never liked putting anyway. Putting isn't golf. It should be treated the same as a water hazard – hit it on and add two strokes.' Despite his slender physique and lack of height – 'When I first came on the Tour my playing partners would use me as a ball marker' – Chi Chi could smash the ball a country mile and more, a talent for which he had another ready-made quip. 'I once hit a drive five hundred yards – on a par three. I had a three wood coming back . . .' Boy, was he straight off the tee! 'The last time I left the fairway was to answer the telephone, and it was a wrong number.'

Chi Chi's bag came equipped with all manner of stage-props for his one-man show. One of his favourite routines on the first tee, which I have witnessed, much to my amusement, involved asking the gallery if they had seen the newest Puerto Rican credit card. Whereupon he would delve into his clubs and produce a flick-knife. Chi Chi was proud of his heritage but never passed up an opportunity to make fun of his nationality. Partnered by Homero Blancas, another Latino, and Rod Curl, who is a Native American, at one tournament, he offered the immortal observation, 'It looked like a Civil Rights march out there. People thought we were going to steal their hubcaps. After all these years it's still embarrassing for me to play in America. Like the time I asked my caddie for a sand-wedge and he came back with a ham on rye.'

Even in the final round of the Masters Chi Chi kept me entertained with a stream of one-liners, and on my way to a ruinous 78 (I was driving like Jane and putting like Tarzan – oh, yes, I can come up with them, too) I was in need of light relief. 'I used to dream about being a waiter in this place,' said Chi Chi, nodding in the direction of the clubhouse. 'Do you know I shot a sixty-four out here in practice. But Monday and Tuesday at Augusta is like a boxer working on a punchbag – it doesn't hit back. One year I was so nervous about playing the Masters I drank a bottle of rum before I played. I shot the happiest eighty-three of my life . . .' Thanks, Chi Chi, I may have trailed home eighteen shots behind Seve – the first European to lay claim to a Green Jacket – in a tie for forty-eighth place, but that first Masters experience was something I have never forgotten.

My first taste of the US Open two months later, however, is something best forgotten. Baltusrol is named after Dutch emigrant farmer, Baltus Roll (oh yes, I've been doing my homework again, as you can see), who originally owned the land but was killed in 1831 when two thieves, imagining a stash of money was hidden in the house, shot him in front of his wife. It was murder for me, too, with rounds of 76, 73 leaving me on nine over par and well outside the halfway cut. By the time Jack Nicklaus beat Japan's Isao Aoki by two shots, I had long since departed the scene and was preparing for the Welsh Classic at Royal Porthcawl where, armed with a new weapon in the shape of the Dunlop DDH new-age golf ball, I cruised to a five-stroke victory over Martin Foster.

I had picked up three of the DDH balls in America and, because they were still such a rarity, used them sparingly. In fact, the first one I unwrapped I proceeded to use for two and a half rounds whereas I would normally work my way through four or five balls in a single round. The DDH had special dimples that gave you added distance, and superior control in the wind, which is vital at Porthcawl, where you are seldom more than a 5-iron from the breezes of the Bristol Channel. I'd like to think that my swing, concentration, ruthless winning instincts and all-round game played a part in my victory. I'd like to think that, but those balls were awfully good . . .

I then embarked upon a rich streak of form, finishing third in the Scandinavian Open and runner-up behind Spain's Manuel Pinero in the English Classic at The Belfry. That sent me off to Muirfield for the 109th Open Championship with my confidence sky high, and if there is one spot on this golfing earth you would wish to approach with confidence it is the home of the

Honourable Company of Edinburgh Golfers, where only the best need apply. The list of Open winners at Muirfield is a veritable *Who's Who* of the game – Harry Vardon, Walter Hagen, Henry Cotton, Gary Player, Lee Trevino, Jack Nicklaus, Nick Faldo, Ernie Els and, in 1980, Tom Watson. I was well satisfied to finish equal twelfth, and extended my lead at the top of the European Order of Merit with a second place to Seve Ballesteros in the Dutch Open and third spot in the Benson & Hedges at Fulford.

I might have won the Carroll's Irish Open at Portmarnock but for a third round 80 (I was only seven shots behind eventual winner Mark James) and could have made full use of the £11,950 first prize, having announced my engagement to Christine Trew, one of the original band of female professionals known as the Proettes, whom I had met through my manager Derrick Pillage. I celebrated my engagement by abandoning my new fiancée to fly out to Bogota to represent Scotland in the World Cup, an event I treasured if only because you could not fail to be inspired by the names on the trophy – Peter Thomson and Kel Nagle (Australia), Ben Hogan and Sam Snead (US), Jack Nicklaus and Arnold Palmer (US), Gary Player and Harold Henning (South Africa), Seve Ballesteros and Manuel Pinero (Spain).

The previous year, Ken Brown and I had taken the victorious American pairing of Hale Irwin and John Mahaffey right to the wire on the final day in Athens. This time, I arrived in Colombia in the company of Steve Martin, whom I had known from boyhood. Our challenge made the most inauspicious start when Steve, who had been out in South America for three weeks in preparation, unwittingly broke the rules. In all his previous tournaments, players had been allowed to tap down spike marks on the green, a rule not recognised in the World Cup. Steve had made a fantastic opening with birdies on the first three holes and, facing another birdie opportunity on the fourth green, blithely tapped down an offending spike mark with the heel of his putter. 'I don't know if you can do that, my son,' I thought to myself.

The Canadians – Jim Nelford and Dan Haldorsson, who went on to win the event – were obviously of a like mind because out of the corner of my eye I could see them in deep discussion amid much frowning and shaking of heads. When the mighty arm of officialdom came down upon us, we were penalised two shots and poor Steve was suitably shell-shocked. With me serving as a human guide dog – Steve wore Eddie the Eagle style glasses to counter his terrible eyesight – we regrouped to finish three behind the Canadians (I was relieved on Steve's behalf that the margin was more than his two-shot penalty), and I managed to see off the challenge of Bernhard Langer to win the World Cup individual honours. Despite his myopia, Steve might have been a real force on the European Tour, but his father died suddenly and he had to take on the responsibility of running the family engineering business.

I think it is a tremendous pity that the World Cup has since lost much of its original lustre, partly due to the fact the event was extended to include countries with little or no golf traditions. With lesser players shooting in the 90s, rounds became a six or even seven-hour slog. As I had already retained the Harry Vardon Trophy as winner of the European Order of Merit, my victory in the 1980 World Cup individual event proved, to myself and others, that I could compete with the very best on the world stage.

CHAPTER SEVEN

THE AUTUMN CLASSIC

Another once glittering prize that has sadly suffered a marked decline in prestige in recent years is the World Matchplay Championship at Wentworth. Consider these quotes: 'Strokeplay is a better test of golf but matchplay is a better test of character' – Irish amateur Joe Carr. 'Matchplay is more of a joust. It calls for a doughty, resourceful competitor, the sort of fellow who is not ruffled by his opponent's fireworks and is able to set off a few of his own when it counts' – golf writer Herbert Warren Wind. 'A golf course exists primarily for matchplay, which is a sport, as distinguished from strokeplay, which more resembles rifle shooting than a sport in that it lacks the joy of personal contact with an opponent' – 19th century British professional Freddie Tait.

When I reached my first final in 1980 (all told I was a finalist on five occasions but only once a winner) the Matchplay was one of the annual rites of autumn and considered to be just one rung below Major status by the public. Like the Masters, it was strictly by invitation only until the promoters, IMG, brought in a qualification system. Judge its importance in the early days, when it was popularly known as the Piccadilly (in honour of the cigarette company sponsors) by the stature of the champions – Arnold Palmer (1964, 1967), Gary Player (1965, 1966, 1968, 1971, 1973), Bob Charles (1969), Jack Nicklaus (1970).

Although the tournament now offers a winner's cheque worth £1 million, Tiger Woods, Phil Mickelson and the other leading Americans have, in the past, been conspicuous by their absence. This was a great shame in my view because Wentworth in the 'fall' is a delightful setting, when the autumn leaves are transformed into every shade of gold and yellow, rivalling anything you will see in New England. Once the home of the Duke of Wellington's sister, the Wentworth Estate was one of the earliest golf developments to include large houses, all set in an acre of land adjoining the course. It is only a short stroll to the clubhouse, and Ernie Els and Thomas Bjorn are among a number of professionals who live behind the gates of the estate, as are comedians Bruce Forsyth and Russ Abbott, who has been a close friend since the time when I was also a Wentworth resident. You cannot always pick your neighbours, however, and for a spell in 1999 Brucie and Russ had the former Chilean dictator General Pinochet over the garden wall. Nice to see you? I think not.

Sam Snead and Ben Hogan won the World Cup (then known as the Canada Cup) for the US over the famed Burma Road (i.e. Wentworth) in 1956 when a crowd of ten thousand plus made their way to Virginia Water to see the two maestros in action. Wentworth was also the stage for the 1953 Ryder Cup contest, the United States narrowly defeating Great Britain and Ireland 6½–5½, despite final afternoon singles victories for Fred Daly (by a resounding 9 and 7 over Ted Kroll), Eric Brown, Harry Bradshaw and Harry Weetman, a one-hole conqueror of the great Sam Snead.

In fact, it was at Wentworth that the notion of the Ryder Cup was first formed in 1926 after an unofficial contest between two teams of professionals captained by Ted Ray and Walter Hagen, who led a ten-man 'American' team containing two Englishmen (Jim Barnes and Cyril Walker), two Scots (Tommy Armour and George MacLeod) and an Australian (Joe Kirkwood). Can you imagine the furore if Colin Montgomerie or Darren Clarke won the US money list and the Americans tried to claim them as theirs?

Although the result was of massacre proportions – Britain winning 13½–1½ – Samuel Ryder, a millionaire who made his fortune by selling grass and flower seeds in packets, was entranced by the sportsmanship displayed and approached Ray and Hagen in the Wentworth clubhouse with the idea of making it a biennial event. Ryder commissioned Mappin & Webb to design a trophy featuring a likeness of his personal coach and golf mentor Abe Mitchell (who would play in the 1929 Ryder Cup at Moortown, Leeds) on the lid. Hagen was equally enthusiastic and drawled, 'Let's drink to that – but the result will be totally different next time around, that I can promise you.'

I think I would have rather enjoyed a night or two in Hagen's company. I recall a golf magazine article proposing the 'perfect composite golfer', which suggested Tiger Woods' driving, Jack Nicklaus's long irons, Lee Trevino's chipping, Ben Hogan's putting, Seve Ballesteros's vision, Arnold Palmer's charisma and 'the Haig's ability to play when completely smashed'. Given his voracious appetite for life, Hagen did well to survive 76 years on this earth before dying of throat cancer in 1969, a strangely forgotten champion, despite his place in golf's Hall of Fame as winner of eleven Major championships – four Opens, five US PGA titles and two US Opens.

That two of those British victories – 1922 and 1928 – were achieved on the links of his beloved Royal St George's explains why he bestowed the affectionate nickname 'Club Sandwich' upon the remote timber cabin on the shores of Long Lake, Michigan, where he spent his final solitary days. Seldom pictured without a large Scotch on the rocks in one hand and a cigarette in the other – he puffed his way through fifty a day – Hagen's frequently quoted philosophy was 'never worry, never hurry, and be sure to smell the flowers along the way'.

He preferred to smell the flowers in the company of an exclusive circle of like-minded cronies, such as the Prince of Wales, Douglas Fairbanks Senior and Babe Ruth, gaining renown as the first professional golfer to earn a million dollars ('and spend two million') while, in the opinion of his great friend and rival, Gene Sarazan, 'doing more for golf than any player before or since. Haig took the game all over the world and popularised it everywhere he went.'

Hagen, who played with the abandon of Palmer, the quick-witted humour of Trevino and the dress-sense of the late Payne Stewart, gloried in his image as a womanising carouser, and was frequently spotted changing out of his dinner suit and into his plus-fours behind a bush by the first tee. On the rare occasions he allowed his body an early night, he maintained the illusion of dissipation by having Spec Hammond, who filled the various roles of caddie/chauffeur/valet/boozing buddy, roll his neatly pressed tuxedo into a crumpled heap, so that Hagen shuffled into the clubhouse as though straight from a seedy speakeasy. Hagen, whose love of champagne and whisky was matched only by his passion for chorus-girls, was married twice but could seldom resist the temptation to arrange a dinner date with the prettiest woman in the gallery.

As the legend grew, so Hagen turned his attention to the 'stuffed shirts' who ran golf, with the stated intent of improving professional golfers' status as third-class citizens. Eight decades on it is difficult to accept that Hagen, Sarazan, Tommy Armour and their professional colleagues from the 1920s were barred from most clubhouses in Britain at the peak of their fame. On one celebrated occasion, Hagen and Sarazan were invited to lunch at Royal St George's by the Prince of Wales. As the trio were browsing through the wine list, they were approached by an elderly member, seeking to remind the heir to the throne of the club rules. 'If you don't stop this nonsense,' replied the Prince in a regal bellow that could be heard on the ninth green, 'I'll take the Royal out of St George's.'

Hagen was involved in a moment of golfing history at Sandwich in 1922 when he became the first American-born winner of the Open, after surviving the strenuous challenge of George Duncan, who had needed a four at the eighteenth to force a play-off. The Briton's second shot landed in the same little depression at the side of the green from where a certain Sandy Lyle would fluff his chip in 1985. Duncan's approach shot had been an equally miserable mishit, the title went to Hagen and this accursed spot on the Kent landscape became 'Duncan's Hollow'. Hagen, meanwhile, was so underwhelmed by the size of the winner's cheque, he took one look at the sum involved and handed his prize to caddie Hammond.

Unlike many of today's great champions, Hagen never bothered to take himself or his sport too seriously. In the 1919 US Open at the Brae Burn Country Club in Massachusetts, Hagen made up five strokes on third-round leader Mike Brady and had an eight-foot putt on the seventy-second green to force a play-off. Ever the showman, Hagen insisted Brady be summoned from the shower to witness the event, and Brady duly arrived in time to see his beaming tormentor rattle the putt into the middle of the hole. To hammer home his psychological advantage, on the night prior to his eighteen-hole shoot-out with Brady, Hagen threw a 'victory party', which continued well into the following morning. When Hammond offered the quiet observation that it might be time to halt proceedings as Brady had now been in bed for 'six hours or more', Hagen replied, 'He may be in bed, but knowing he has me to face later today, he sure as hell ain't asleep.'

Hagen, inevitably, won his second US Open title by one shot after a classic piece of gamesmanship on the seventeenth, when he sliced his tee-shot into the rough and a spectator stepped on his ball, treading it deep into the mud. An official ruled the ball must be played where it lay, but Hagen insisted it was not his ball and only when it had been lifted and cleaned – thereby ensuring an easy approach to the green – did he voice recognition.

When the throat cancer that was to kill him was diagnosed in 1965, Hagen's larynx was removed and he lost his voice. He did not, however, lose his spirit. Accompanied by his only son, Walter Junior, Hagen had insisted on stopping off in ten bars on his way to hospital for the operation.

'He was loaded by the time we finally got Dad inside,' recalled the younger Hagen, 'and I'll be damned if he didn't make a pass at the nurse.'

That, then, was Walter Hagen and, true to his word, the Americans duly thrashed the British 9½–2½ when the two countries met in earnest in 1927, spawning a contest that has become a global phenomenon in sporting terms.

The Burma Road, incidentally – and I know this from my time living on the estate and boning up on its history to impress house visitors (I'm not sure my ploy worked, by the way, but we did serve a fine malt by way of compensation for having to listen to my carefully rehearsed spiel) – had been known as the West Course until 1945 when a squad of German prisoners of war were brought in to clear the vegetation that had turned the closing six holes into a jungle. The reluctant greenkeepers did a remarkable job because Wentworth is a stunning venue by any standards. Seve Ballesteros holds it in the highest esteem. 'The Burma Road is one of the few courses with the capacity to continually extract the best from the best. I rate Wentworth at the very top of my list of favourite places, alongside Augusta.'

Since Palmer won the inaugural World Matchplay in 1964, in an era when the players were given sumptuous suites at the Ritz and were whisked to and from Wentworth in Rolls-Royces, eighteen of the twenty-two players to have won the title possessed a total of sixty-seven Major titles. Two of the matches that have become part of Matchplay folklore give a flavour of the event.

In the 1965 semi-final, Gary Player played Tony Lema. Lema had won the 1964 Open Championship at St Andrews with a five-stroke triumph over Nicklaus, and was on his way to becoming a golfing great when he died in a plane crash in 1966. In that 1965 semi-final, he ripped round Wentworth. With seventeen holes to play, he stood seven up when Player suddenly went into overdrive. The South African birdied the next four holes but, even so, remained five down with nine to play. Whittling away at the American's lead, Player levelled the match on the thirty-sixth with a majestic 4-wood to the final green, won the match at the first extra hole and went on to claim the first of his five World Matchplay titles. Seve Ballesteros has also triumphed on five occasions, one behind the Wentworth Wizard, Ernie Els.

In 1983, Seve played Palmer in the first round. To celebrate the twentieth World Matchplay, the first-round matches were reduced to eighteen holes because of the number of former champions invited to compete. The new master did not disappoint. One down with two to play, Ballesteros kept the match alive by winning the seventeenth. Then, after a wild drive on the eighteenth, he conjured up a 'miracle' shot through the trees, the ball landing just short of the green. With Palmer pin-high after three, it was advantage America until Seve chipped in for an eagle three. He defeated the old champion amid nerve-tingling excitement at the third extra hole.

Bidding to become the first Britain to win the title – Neil Coles had been our only previous finalist when he lost to Palmer in the inaugural competition – I swept through the early rounds in 1980, only to find Greg Norman at his most redoubtable in the final. Two up after ten holes in the morning, I found myself two down at lunch after the Australian unleashed an unanswerable birdie blitz. He retained the lead until the thirty-third when he three-putted before I managed to square the match on the thirty-fifth green. In the rough from the tee on the final hole, I took three to reach the edge of the green whereas Norman was just two feet from the pin. When my birdie attempt from twenty-five feet shaved the hole, all that was left for me was to concede defeat.

I reached the final again in 1982 but only after the mother of all first-round battles with Nick Faldo, who holed an eagle putt from thirty feet on the last hole of the morning, while I contrived to miss from four feet. That left me six down, facing an ignominious defeat. Curiously, I had played well except on the greens, and over a leisurely lunch – I saw no point in heading for the practice green when I could be heading home before afternoon tea was being served in the clubhouse, so thought I might as well have one final meal on the sponsors – decided to change putters. The bookies, who are very seldom wrong, were offering 12-1 against my winning but my change of putters paid off immediately when I sank an eight-footer on the nineteenth to prevent going seven down. By that stage, my sole ambition was not to go down by a humiliating 10 and 9, or suchlike.

The gallery by then was noticeably thinner than it had been on the very first tee for this long-awaited all-British clash, but they began filtering back when I proceeded to win six of the first twelve holes, and we proceeded to the thirty-first all-square. When I won two of the next three holes, those who had rashly invested any money on me at the halfway stage must have been congratulating themselves on their astuteness. On the sixteenth, even I had begun to believe in miracles when Faldo found a horrible lie in a greenside bunker, while I was perfectly placed on the green about twelve feet from the hole. The drama was not yet over, though. With the cart lined up beyond the ropes in readiness to drive us back to the clubhouse, Faldo's escape from the bunker came out at what seemed 100mph, hit the pin at a height of about four feet and dropped straight into the hole.

Given his lie in the bunker and the position of the pin, to land the ball within twelve feet would have been outrageous good luck. To hole out represented a fluke of monumental proportions. Seriously unnerved, I missed my twelve-footer for a half but immediately birdied the thirty-fifth for a 2 and 1 victory. To beat any player from six down is deeply gratifying but when that player is Nick Faldo, it is doubly satisfying, especially so when he could not bring himself to meet my eyes as I proffered my hand and said, with an admirably straight face, 'Thanks very much, Nick.'

When I finally made it back to the clubhouse for a celebratory beer after the round of press and TV interviews, Faldo was long gone from the scene but not before, so I was told, he had kicked his holdall the length and breadth of the locker-room. I know it is bad of me, but I do like to think that is true.

Wentworth's British jinx continued unabated, alas, when I lost to Seve at the thirty-seventh in the final, and finished runner-up for a third time in 1986, losing 2 and 1 to Greg Norman. By that time I was living on the Wentworth Estate, alongside Nick Faldo and South African Mark McNulty, so was able to drown my sorrows in my own home while partaking of a splendid dinner cooked by Judy Simpson, who ran a wine bar and restaurant in Chiswick and had been hired by IMG for the week.

Twelve months later, I was back in the final, this time against my boyhood chum Ian Woosnam, guaranteeing a British World Matchplay champion for the first time in twenty-three years of noble defeats. My route to the final was not without its little dramas along the way. In my first-round encounter with David Ishii, who was the second leading money winner in Japan that year, I was four down after eighteen holes and facing an ignominiously early exit until a hearty lunch sent me back out on the course with renewed determination. With six holes to play I had managed to draw level when, after finding a fairway bunker on the thirteenth, a sudden deluge forced play to be suspended for the day and I had to mark my ball.

Although weather forecaster Michael Fish famously told the nation that, despite predictions, there was no hurricane on its way, on the night of 15/16 October 1987 the wind reached 108mph, making the storm the worst to hit England since 1703. Eighteen people were killed and overnight Sevenoaks in Kent was reduced to Oneoak, as fifteen million trees were destroyed, including a huge birch in the garden of what caddie Dave Musgrove jokingly referred to as 'Lyle Towers'. Chaos reigned at Wentworth the next morning. Seve Ballesteros had to walk to the course because his courtesy car could not make it through the mayhem.

To the sound of chainsaws clearing away the debris, play resumed in the afternoon and I finally defeated Ishii at the thirty-ninth before going straight out to beat new Masters champion Larry Mize. In the semi-final, I was again staring at a heavy defeat when I trailed Mark McNulty by three holes with four to play before staging another unlikely recovery – 'You'll have to start calling me "the Ice Man",' I told caddie Dave – to reach my second successive final and fourth in eight years. My friendship with Woosie dated back to 1973 when I had beaten him into second place to win the Shropshire Boys title at Market Drayton, but on this occasion there was rather more at stake.

Although he has been known to clamber up on the snooker table in his Jersey palace for putting practice, Ian Woosnam was never one for golfing gimmickry. He won the US Masters and became world number one by virtue of a preposterously simple philosophy – whack it, go find it, whack it again, go find it again. Blessed with an energetic but elegant swing that an envious Seve Ballesteros described as 'the sweetest in Europe', Woosie combined Popeye's power with Fred Astaire's poise.

As we all know, Woosie had no right to be the best. He was raised on an austere dairy farm on the English-Welsh border, a world removed from the pampered lawns of Augusta, where he was to achieve sporting immortality. He never grew beyond 5ft 4½ in and, like his father before him, the boxing ring represented his preferred sporting arena during his formative years. At seven he was winning free holidays by walloping taller and older opponents at Butlin's and the family photograph album shows a tiny, scowling tyke in white singlet and shorts, resplendent in gloves the size of water melons – Just William with his dukes up.

The other boys might have been bigger, but none of them were accustomed to starting each day in the milking shed at five o'clock in the morning. 'It was a tough life on the farm but it was also a lot of fun,' says Woosie of his childhood. 'I look at what kids have now compared to what I had. We used to go looking for birds' nests, fishing, swimming in the river, all that sort of thing. You never see kids do that any more. But we had to work hard when it came to harvesting or driving the tractor or carrying bales of hay or milking the cows, from first thing in the morning 'til half past ten, eleven o'clock at night – weekends and holidays, too. Cows never know when it's Christmas.'

By the age of 14, Woosnam was a schoolboy footballer and golfer of county standard. The local industries of mining and farming held little appeal for him. 'If I'd never swung a golf club, I'd probably have been a joiner or something like that. My brain wasn't too good at school but I was pretty good with my hands.' Then fate decreed that he should be picked to represent Shropshire Schools at football and golf on the same Saturday. 'I was a good little footballer – Gordon Strachan with attitude – but in my heart I wanted to be a millionaire and I wanted to win major championships. So I chose golf.'

After turning professional in 1978, Woosnam's early years were a rumbustious romp through Europe in a rusty old Mini-van – used for eating, sleeping and 'courting' – in the joyous company of fellow rookies D.J. Russell, Martin Poxon and Joe Higgins. Sustenance, i.e. beer and baked beans, came out of tins, funded by his first season's total prize money of £284. Now Woosie flies to tournaments in private planes – from caravanette to executive turbo-prop with a few thousand swishes of that honeyed swing. In 1987, he earned more money than any other golfer while becoming world number one, even though he said that the only way he might achieve the same recognition as 'The Great White Shark', Greg Norman, 'would be to peroxide my hair and call myself the Great White Tadpole'.

Although we had been good pals in our youth when we would regularly get together for a round at our respective home courses – Hawkstone and Oswestry were only about twenty miles apart which I guess made us neighbours in golfing terms – from when we turned professional, we saw less of each other. Mostly this was due to the fact that Woosie wasn't an instant hit on the European Tour and was consequently haring about the continent in his ageing Mini-van whereas I could afford to fly courtesy of my early tournament wins. But if I walk into a clubhouse anywhere in the world and spot Woosie holding court, then that's the table for which I will make a bee-line.

He may be almost a foot smaller than Nick Faldo in height, but in his heyday Woosie was a giant in world golf and I am proud to have been part of what many regard as one of the finest – and certainly the friendliest – of Wentworth's Matchplay finals. I finished the morning round birdie, birdie, eagle and repaired for lunch with a one-hole advantage, a lead I quickly doubled as the shadows lengthened. Then Woosie knocked in two long birdie putts on the twenty-sixth and twenty-eighth to draw level with eight holes to play. It was thrilling stuff and when I miscued my approach to the thirty-third green for a bogey five, it was the first shot either of us had dropped to par during the afternoon session.

We were back to all-square at the next where I sank a birdie putt, halved the thirty-fifth with matching birdie fours, and came to the last tee to the resounding cheers of the gallery. Down the thirty-sixth fairway we went, two friends locked in combat. Woosie found the centre of the green with a beautifully controlled 3-wood, whereas I sent my 2-iron shot plummeting into a bunker on the right. I splashed out to eighteen feet, missed the putt and the title went to Wales when Woosie rolled in his five-footer for a one-hole triumph in Wentworth's 'Battle of Britain'. A year later, and less than six months after my 1988 Masters victory, in my fifth World Matchplay final appearance, I finally saw my name engraved on the trophy when I won another 'Battle of Britain' with victory over Nick Faldo.

I began Matchplay week that year by playing a practice round with Seve, who has always been one of my favourite pre-tournament partners because, like me, his motto is 'play as you practice and practice as you play', which means he hits one ball and gets on with it, rather than holding an inquest after each shot. We attracted a large following and after we had walked off the ninth green, Seve turned to me and said, 'How about a cup of tea and a roll and sausage?' A cuppa and a banger – the breakfast of champions. Thoroughly enjoying the fun of it all, our 'gallery' also swarmed round the food stall and, although I do not know who paid, I do know it was neither Seve nor me. After our round, Seve and his then fiancée, Carmen, returned to Lyle Towers for tea and scones.

Having played Woosie in my last World Matchplay outing, I was drawn against another good friend, Zimbabwean Nick Price, in the second round, having been given a bye as one of the seeded players. Nick and I had first met thirteen years previously when playing in the Brabazon Trophy, during which he stayed with us at Hawkstone. Not that we saw much of him – at least not for the first few days of his stay anyway. He basically hid himself away in his room and we just assumed he was feeling homesick. The wide open plains of Shropshire presumably didn't match up to what he was used to in Zimbabwe. On one occasion he did venture downstairs and headed straight out to the range. World Junior Champion he may have been, but you wouldn't have known it from watching him that day – he had a very fast swing that was getting quicker and quicker by the second. Divots began flying in every direction and he must have hit nine straight shanks in a row, all destined for the famous beech tree on the course. Nick was not a happy boy and stomped back into the house, up the stairs and we never saw him again for the rest of the day.

Dad decided this couldn't go on and stepped in, after he'd finished up work for the day, to give Nick a few pointers. Something in what Dad said obviously stuck and Nick went on to achieve tremendous success. All those years later I confess I was beginning to curse Dad's kindness when I found myself five down after twenty-one holes but, as Nick tired and I grew stronger, I proceeded to win eight of the next eleven holes to complete a 3 and 2 triumph.

Next up was Seve in the semi-finals. As a four-time World Matchplay champion, Seve was the original Wentworth course specialist and the one man most of the other pros preferred to avoid. I was delighted when he beat Mark McCumber in the second round, however, because I had a nagging suspicion this was my year and wanted to pit myself against the very best. Round in 64 in the morning, I was fully aware that if I left the door even slightly ajar, Seve would burst through it like a charging rhino, so I was tremendously chuffed to walk off the twelfth green as the 7 and 6 conqueror of one of the greatest matchplay competitors in history.

Eager to resume against Faldo, who had beaten Woosie in the other semi, where I had left off against Seve, I was frustrated when the final was postponed for twenty-four hours until the Monday due to torrential rain, which had saturated Wentworth. On a beautiful autumnal morning, with the course shrouded in an atmospheric mist, I am glad to say we produced golf worthy of the setting. After halving the fourteenth with birdies, I moved one ahead when Faldo scored a rare bogey on the sixteenth, and I doubled that advantage with an eagle at the next. On the eighteenth, I sent my drive miles left and the ball would have sailed out of bounds had it not crashed into some bramble bushes. Short of the putting surface in three with Faldo on the green with his second shot, I promptly chipped in from over forty yards for an unexpected half and retired for lunch with my two-hole lead intact.

Perhaps I should not have had that half pint of Guinness, for I proceeded to bogey a couple of holes early in the afternoon and thereafter the match swung one way and then the other. One down with five to play, I holed a long putt on the fourteenth for a birdie two, and nudged one in front again on the fifteenth when Faldo three-putted. The seventeenth at Wentworth is a 571 yard par-five monster. I unleashed the perfect drive right down the middle of the fairway, while Faldo pushed his tee-shot to the right from where he could not match my birdie four and the World Matchplay title was mine at last, courtesy of a 2 and 1 victory over my oldest rival. It had been a long time coming and I would have deeply regretted reaching the end of my career without joining players of the calibre of Palmer, Player and Nicklaus as a Wentworth champion. It is a fervent wish of mine that the World Matchplay is restored to its former glory.

CHAPTER EIGHT

ASTRONAUTS, PRESIDENTS, PRINCES AND THE 'DREAM TEAM'

Having finished joint forty-eighth on my Masters debut twelve months previously, I moved up twenty places on the leaderboard in 1981 and despite trailing champion Tom Watson by twelve shots, I was greatly encouraged to finish as leading European with rounds of 73, 70, 76, 73. Increasingly, I felt Augusta was a course I could do business with, and I flew back across the Atlantic in good heart. That sense of well-being intensified when I won the French Open at St Germain Golf Club on the outskirts of Paris.

Playing consistently good golf, I completed the four rounds in fourteen under par, beating Bernhard Langer by four. Seve Ballesteros and Howard Clark were another two strokes away in a tie for third place. Then it was a swift return to Wentworth for the Martini International. I began and ended that tournament with 69s – the best scores of the week – but sandwiched in between were ugly rounds of 78 and 76. Two solid par rounds of 72 would have given me the title by five shots, instead of which I was joint sixth, five behind Greg Norman.

I won my second title in a month, however, in the inaugural Lawrence Batley International at Bingley St Ives, Bradford, where I partnered the founder in the Pro-Am. Lawrence, who passed away peacefully in his sleep at the age of 91 in 2002, was a fine golfer even in his seventies, and a great friend to sport and the arts. A millionaire through his cash-and-carry business (it was he who coined the phrase 'cash and carry' so I'm told), as well as sponsoring the golf tournament that carried his name, he extended his generosity to his home town of Huddersfield, where stands the Lawrence Batley Theatre and, at one end of Huddersfield Town FC's Galpharm Stadium, the Lawrence Batley Stand.

Lawrence was only one of many accomplished golfers with whom I have been paired in Pro-Am events over the years, not all of whom, it is fair to say, have played to their full potential when asked to perform in front of the paying public. Then again, how funny would I be if required to stand in front of an audience at the London Palladium and have them rolling in the aisles, like my pal Russ Abbott, say? Like Russ, Max Boyce is an avid golfer, although you might not have known that during our outing together before the 1981 Bob Hope Classic at Moor Park. Poor Max was held up in traffic on his way to the course and was subsequently late on the first tee. Having started badly, his afternoon deteriorated swiftly.

On the second tee, Max – defying all laws of physics, let alone golf – somehow contrived to send the ball at 180 degrees backwards through his legs. It struck an unsuspecting woman spectator on the chest, and ricocheted five yards behind the tee. With the crowd trying desperately to control their sniggers, Max then tried to smash a 3-iron down the fairway, only to top the ball and send it hurtling into the tee-marker from where it careered another thirty yards in the wrong direction, back towards the first green. He had now played two, converted a par-four into a par-five, and thereafter he became a serious threat to the safety of others. By the time we walked off, poor Max had almost decapitated two spectators, knee-capped three others and was ready to be taken away by the men in white coats.

I tend not to offer advice on such occasions unless expressly asked to do so because it is always tricky to decide exactly how much information to give, not to mention the person's ability to act upon it. You have to remember that whatever the level of celebrity – and it can be Michael Douglas and Catherine Zeta Jones arriving at the first tee – these people are highly successful and often fiercely competitive in their own sphere, but they are likely to be overcome with nerves when asked to tee off with a professional in front of the eyes of a gallery. Some pros dread the Pro-Ams, which can make it a very long four or five hours out on the course, but I have always enjoyed the experience and try my best to make sure my partners derive similar enjoyment from our round.

At the Bing Crosby tournament in Pebble Beach one spring, I was fortunate to be paired with astronaut Alan Shepherd. He had smuggled a 5-iron and ball aboard Apollo 14 and became the only man since the dawn of time to play golf on the moon, 'hitting it miles and miles and miles . . .' Alan told me an amusing tale of the night he and fellow astronaut Edgar Mitchell were woken by a strange clanging noise in the lunar module.

'Did you hear that?' Alan whispered.

'Yeah, what do you think it was?' Mitchell replied in a similarly hushed tone.

'I don't know. Neither do I know why we're whispering when the nearest life form – I hope – is a quarter of a million miles away on Earth.'

Another amateur partner watched me reach a par-five green with a driver and 1-iron before casually asking, 'Are you a pro?'

'Yes. As a matter of fact, I'm the British Open champion.'

'I thought I recognised the accent.'

Talking of accents, on another occasion at the Bing Crosby I partnered Sean Connery – or perhaps more accurately he partnered me as when he was initially invited to attend he said he would only do so if he played with yours truly. Needless to say I was very flattered. Mind you, I almost walked straight past when we met up for the tournament. Not exactly the ideal start. But it wasn't my fault. He'd just finished filming 'The Hunt for Red October' and was sporting that 'Russian' beard. He didn't look anything like James Bond. It wasn't until he called out 'Shandy' that I recognised him.

Sean is a great competitor, very determined, and a fabulous companion, even when things don't go too well on the course. That time at Pebble Beach we were playing in a four with Andy Bear and Clint Eastwood (good name-dropping, eh?). Clint went out like a dream but I'm afraid that sure couldn't be said for my partner. He was fine tee to green on the first but that's where it fell apart, holing eventually with his fifth putt. He never recovered all day from that, but his good chat and humour remained constant.

Sean, as you may remember, featured in (another?) one of golf's most famous 'matches' when he defeated Goldfinger, caddied by

Oddjob, at Stoke Poges Golf Club near Pinewood Studios, where the film was shot. Stoke Poges now has a James Bond theme bar in the clubhouse, if you care to sample 007's favourite dry Martini.

The three BBC 'Celebrity Golf' events I've played in have afforded me many other opportunities to partner stars of TV, film and sport. Those events were played over a couple of days and there would never be a round without some scary, funny or serious incident – be it Peter Cook entertaining the crowds with his outrageous dress code, John Virgo trying to kill every spectator in sight (and indeed us) with a swing that could send the ball frontwards, backwards or sideways at any given moment, or the ever-lovable Jimmy Tarbuck cracking everyone up with a joke.

I found that what all these celebrities had in common was a great determination to succeed – be it in their own chosen field or on the golf course. This is a trait they share with the greatest winner of them all – Sam Snead – who collected over 140 titles across the globe, including 81 in the US, during a scarcely credible career. Before the Millennium Open at St Andrews in 2000, I partnered the original Slammin' Sam in a televised foursomes against Tony Jacklin and Roberto de Vicenzo on a glorious July afternoon at Royal Hoylake. Sam was 88 at the time, only two years before his death, with wobbly legs, failing hearing and fading eyesight but with the same undimmed desire to win every time he teed up.

On the first hole, I left Sam, who by then had adopted a curious sidewinder putting style as though brushing leaves, with a ten-footer for a half. As I studied the line over Sam's shoulder, I could not fail to notice that everything was shaking – the left hand was shaking, the right hand was shaking, the head was shaking, the broom-handle putter was shaking, at which point he looks at me and, in that famous Virginian drawl, enquired: 'Where's the hole . . .?' I crouched down behind him and lined up his putter head: 'Left a bit . . . left a bit more . . . no, a tad to the right . . . stop . . . FIRE!' The ball flew six inches into the air and was travelling like an express train when it slam-dunked into the hole with a resounding *smack!*

On to the second hole, I chipped to sixteen feet, leaving Sam another awkward putt for a half and the same routine . . .

'Where's the hole . . .?'

'Three inches to the right.'

'What? I can't hear you.'

'THREE INCHES TO THE RIGHT!'

'Okay?'

'FIRE!' Straight in the hole.

And thus did we make our way round the course, Shakin' Sam and Shoutin' Sandy finally reaching the eighteenth – by which time I was exhausted and in genuine danger of losing my voice – all square. Risking everything, I unleashed a monster drive seventy yards short of the green – a good 180 yards past Tony's ball – but even that close, Sam could not see the flag.

'Front left, seventy yards,' says I.

'Fine,' replies Sam, firing the ball fifteen yards through the back of the green from where, with four different borrows to negotiate, I knew I would be doing well to leave the ball within six feet of the pin. Clearly, Sam's putting heroics had rubbed off on me and the ball disappeared into the hole, as though by divine intervention, for a birdie three and the unlikeliest of one-hole victories.

Through my friendship with Russ Abbott, forged when we

were neighbours in Wentworth for a spell, I have served as his unpaid coach on occasion, a favour he has since returned by advising my daughter, Lonneke, about her stage ambitions. Although he plays off a very respectable thirteen, we have spent many frustrating but highly amusing hours trying to turn him into a single handicap player. Russ has the perfect physique for a golfer and also possesses natural timing and co-ordination. But I am afraid to say golf comes as third rather than second nature to him so he has stretched my coaching talents to the limit. Russ can find ways to hit bum shots I never knew existed but, as you can imagine, we do have a laugh on our way round, especially when he suffers the golfing equivalent of road rage.

Another occasional partner is HRH The Duke of York whom I first met on a Concorde flight to New York en route to a tournament in Chicago. I was idly studying the breakfast menu and looking around to see which celebrities might be aboard when I received a sharp jab in the shoulder from the row behind. I peered through the small gap between the seats and thought, 'I know that face. It's him, isn't it . . .?'

'What are you doing here?' I blurted out mindlessly as though there could be more than one answer to the question. Not 'Good morning, Your Highness' or even 'Nice to meet you, Sir.'

'The same as you – going to New York. More to the point – I need a golf lesson.'

And so I passed the rest of the flight showing HRH the correct grip using a Concorde knife for a club. When we subsequently shared a table at a charity dinner for the annual finals of the Sandy Lyle Children with leukemia event at Wentworth, the Prince turned to me and said: 'Do you fancy playing golf tomorrow at my course?'

'On a Sunday? Every tee-off time will be booked,' I replied, blithely forgetting that as an HRH, Andrew's name would carry a bit of clout. I lost the first two holes to a net eagle and a net birdie but managed to drag him down to my level after that and we had an honourable draw. One thing I learned is that there is a little nine-hole course in the 'back garden' of Windsor Castle where Andrew and Edward have been known to bang away in challenge matches against the Royal staff.

Prince Andrew is a bandit playing off his handicap of seven whereas former US President Gerald Ford is a serious public nuisance in any Pro-Celebrity event. Bob Hope would weave an entire stand-up routine around poor Gerry's reputation as the least expert golfer in the world . . .

He'd give up golf if he didn't have so many nice sweaters . . . the last time I played a round with Gerald Ford he hit one birdie, an eagle, a jack-rabbit, an elk and three pensioners . . . there are 42 golf courses in Palm Springs and President Gerald Ford waits until he hits his first drive before announcing which one he's playing that day . . . when Russian premier Andrei Gromyko gets down to disarmament talks, the first item on his agenda will be taking away Mr Ford's clubs . . . he's the most dangerous driver since Ben Hur . . . it's not hard to find the President on the course – you just follow the walking wounded . . . and on the first tee, Gerry Ford, the man who has made golf a contact sport and with whom the word 'Fore!' is synonymous . . .

I was staying with friends in Palm Springs during one American jaunt and over dinner husband asked wife what kind of day it had been in the local hospital where she worked as an administrator.

'It was quite interesting, really. We had four golfers, all of whom had been struck by golf balls hit by . . .'

'Let me guess,' I intercepted. 'Two by Gerald Ford.'

'Yes . . .'

'And two by Kojak – Telly Savalas.'

'Right again.'

Golf has become so tremendously popular with the glitterati – Bob Dylan, Alice Cooper, Samuel L. Jackson and Tom Cruise spring immediately to mind, plus a host of British actors and athletes – that the BBC might consider reintroducing the 'Celebrity Golf' programme. It attracted terrific audience figures. If they do, they can consider this a serious job application on my part.

Throughout 1981, I continually finished near the top of the leaderboard without adding to my two early season victories. Fourteen top ten finishes from my seventeen appearances in Europe meant I came third in the Order of Merit, behind Bernhard Langer and Nick Faldo, and secured my berth in the Ryder Cup team. Unfortunately, one of my lowliest placings was in the Open Championship at Royal St George's, where I tied for fourteenth and was never in serious contention.

The title went to Bill Rogers, who also won the Sea Pines Heritage, the Texas Open and the World Series of Golf that year. After that, he disappeared almost as quickly as he had arrived on the scene. Although he won another event on the US PGA Tour in 1983, he was the original shooting star who burned out and quit the tour five years later at the age of 37 to become a club pro in San Antonio, Texas.

In 1981, however, he was a valued member of the greatest Ryder Cup side ever assembled, a twelve-man 'Dream Team' that represented golf's equivalent of Pelé's 1970 Brazilians who won the World Cup in Mexico. When the Europeans lined up for the opening ceremony at Walton Heath, Surrey, our jaws dropped lower and lower as non-playing captain Dave Marr (and Muffin the Mule could have led this team to glory) read out their names with due reverence – Jack Nicklaus, Tom Watson, Lee Trevino, Raymond Floyd, Johnny Miller, Tom Kite, Hale Irwin, Jerry Pate, Ben Crenshaw, Bill Rogers, Larry Nelson and Bruce Lietzke. Bruce was the only one of the twelve destined never to win a Major but he had won the Bob Hope Classic, the San Diego Open and the Byron Nelson Classic in the preceding months and was anything but a lightweight invited along simply to make up the numbers. Between them, the eleven other Americans would win forty-two Majors throughout their careers (against the ten claimed by Nick Faldo, Bernhard Langer and myself), whereas Europe's sole Major winner at the time, Seve Ballesteros (the 1979 Open and 1980 Masters champion), was left out of our side by captain John Jacobs, owing to a festering dispute over appearance money. Talk about shooting yourself in the foot!

Although the final result was an 18½–9½ drubbing, curiously we began well . . . the golf that is. Sartorially, not so good. We'd all been given tailor-made trousers as part of our team outfit. Ideal you'd think, and I took full advantage of it by requesting a bit more room around the thigh to help me with my swing. I don't know what happened – centimetres mixed up for inches? – but when I pulled them on that first morning they were way too tight. We only had one pair of trousers per day and so I realised I'd just have to carry on, however uncomfortable I felt – carry on, that is, until I approached the first tee. In limbering up before we started our match, I was stretching by pulling my knees up to my chest when suddenly – rip! I'd split my trousers right across the backside with the world's greatest golfers around me, not to mention a gallery of thousands. I had no choice but to slip behind a hut, strip off, stash the ruined trews and re-emerge in my waterproofs, ready to do battle.

I was paired with Mark James (suitably attired in regulation clothing) in the opening round of foursomes on the first morning against Rogers and Lietzke, whom we defeated 2 and 1. We followed that up with an unexpectedly trouble-free 3 and 2 victory over Crenshaw and Pate in the afternoon fourballs, at the end of which Europe led 4½–3½. The contest was turned on its head on day two, however, when the Americans won seven of the eight points on offer. The winning run for 'Jesse' and me came to an end in the foursomes when we were beaten by one hole by the formidable partnership of Nelson and Kite.

Larry Nelson was just about the last player you wanted to be drawn against in matchplay. He had collected five points out of five at the Greenbrier two years previously and he left Walton Heath with his 100 per cent record in the Ryder Cup intact. Having fought and been decorated in the Vietnam War, Nelson, winner of two US PGA titles and the US Open, relished the dogfight atmosphere of matchplay golf and, although he eventually surrendered his perfect Ryder Cup record in his only other appearance, at Muirfield Village in 1987 – when he took just half a point from his four matches – he remains one of the most successful competitors in the contest's long and rich history.

With the Ryder Cup inexorably heading into American hands yet again, Jesse and I had to contend with Rogers and Floyd in the afternoon fourballs, whereupon Mark decided that if we could not beat them at golf, we could certainly threaten them in psychological warfare. Whenever Floyd drove into the rough, there would be Jesse standing at his shoulder offering sympathetic tut-tut-tuts before ambling off, whistling a tuneless melody. No one can adopt a hangdog expression quite like Jesse and he trooped round the course, shoulders hunched, head down, looking as downtrodden as humanly possible, and muttering, 'Am I looking miserable enough?' If he was hoping Floyd and Rogers would drop their guard and take pity on us, however, he was grievously mistaken and we were on the wrong end of a 3 and 2 thrashing. Our one-point advantage turned into a five-point deficit.

The final day singles brought no respite in our fortunes. Drawn against Kite, I was six under par after ten holes yet found myself all-square. For the sixteen holes played, we combined to score seventeen birdies and three eagles and I have never played better in being roundly cuffed 3 and 2, such was the brilliance of Kite's golf. Although you are always disappointed when you lose a match in the Ryder Cup, I knew I had performed to the best of my abilities but had come across an opponent in truly inspired form, so I certainly did not feel any sense of disgrace.

I completed the European season by finishing joint second with Isao Aoki of Japan behind Australian David Graham in the Lancome Trophy at St Nom la Breteche. Then I returned to Shropshire for a very important date – my marriage to Christine on 24 October. Following the reception in the hotel at Hawkstone, it was off to Hawaii on honeymoon, where, being the old romantic that I am, I had entered the Kapalua Open. Being a professional golfer herself – good enough to finish sixth in the 1977 Women's British Open – Chris was more than understanding about this mixing-business-with-pleasure arrangement.

That same year, I entered into another union, which lasted rather longer than my first marriage. After trailing home joint forty-sixth in the Carroll's Irish Open at Portmarnock – an embarrassing eighteen shots behind tournament winner Sam Torrance and my worst result since the Martini International at Wentworth back in 1978 – I decided on a change of caddie before the Benson & Hedges International at Fulford. On the practice green, my eye fell upon Dave Musgrove, who had recently split with Seve Ballesteros after a successful four-year partnership during which Seve had won the Open and the Masters. As likeable as he is, and I regard him as a good friend, in the caddie shed Seve is not renowned as the easiest man to work with, and before and after his association with Dave, the popular joke was that he worked his way through more caddies than Joan Collins did husbands.

One yarn, which is probably apocryphal, centred around an incident at the Spanish Open one year when Seve turned to his then favourite, Martin Gray, and asked for a piece of fruit.

'Too bitter,' complained Seve, tasting the proffered orange.

'Too brown,' he bemoaned rejecting a banana.

'Too soft,' he grimaced, handing back an apple.

'Listen Seve,' Gray finally snapped. 'I'm a caddie, not a friggin' greengrocer.' Divorce came swiftly . . .

Caddies are a breed of their own, descendants all of the legendary old-timers of folklore, such as 'Fiery' John Carey, Old Da', 'Pawky' Corstorphine, Lang Willie, Tweedly Sweenum and 'Daft' Willie Gunn, a notorious but harmless eccentric who accepted tips in the form of clothes. His peculiar idiosyncrasy was to wear them all at the same time, which is why he bestrode Carnoustie in four tail coats, five pairs of trousers and a leaning tower of tartan bunnets and top hats. Lang Willie, by contrast, cared nothing for such sartorial elegance as he teetered around the Old Course at St Andrews. His taste ran only to whisky. Caddie to a classics lecturer at St Andrews University, Willie was rightfully disdainful of the professor's prowess with a 5-iron. 'Ach, Latin an' Greek's wan thing, but ye need brains to be a golfer,' he would mutter darkly over a pint of frothing ale in a local hostelry.

According to legend, it was the most famous golf celebrity of all, Mary Queen of Scots, who instituted caddying by employing a band of favoured French students – known as *les cadets* – to tote her clubs over the length and breadth of France almost five centuries ago. *Les cadets* becoming 'caddies' when translated into auld Scots. If you would like to learn more about the curious characters of a bygone age, may I recommend *A Wee Nip At The 19th Hole*, a history of the St Andrews caddie brilliantly written by Rick Mackenzie, the current caddie manager at the Old Course. A publishing sensation both here and in the US, where it out-sold Oprah Winfrey's autobiography (to her credit, America's first lady of chat invited Rick on to her show), this is a priceless little masterpiece, crammed with hilarious anecdotes. One of my favourite stories, which underlines the importance of paying the caddie a decent tip, tells of an incident at the end of a round when the golfer gave his caddie three pennies. The caddie laid them in his palm, saying to the player, 'Sir, are ye aware I can tell yer fortune from these three coins?' The caddie went on to volunteer that the first one told him, 'Yer no' a Scotsman,' to which the golfer nodded assent. 'An' the second that yer no' married,' continued the caddie, to which the golfer nodded as well, asking about the third. 'Weel, the third wan tells me that your father wisnae married either!'

Dave Musgrove's admittance into the masonic brotherhood of caddies came through his local course, Hollinwell in Nottinghamshire, where he caddied from the age of 12 – 'because you earned a lot more carrying golf bags than delivering milk or newspapers'. Dave was still caddying part-time while working as a draughtsman in the aerospace engine division of Rolls-Royce when he was offered voluntary redundancy in 1972. A single handicap golfer, Dave had always harboured a yearning to sample life as a caddie on the European Tour and quickly became a popular figure in the pros' locker-room. Due to work with Vicente Fernandez at the 1976 French Open, Dave found himself without a bag when the Argentine pulled out of the event, whereupon he offered his services to Manuel Ballesteros, who replied, 'You might want to wait for my young brother who's playing better than I am.'

I had always admired Dave's professionalism, honesty and pithy humour, so when he and Seve came to the end of the road, I had no hesitation in offering him a full-time job. Like all players, I had employed numerous caddies over the years and, at the time, I had a casual arrangement with Jimmy Dickinson, but he was never available for the Open, say, because Jack Nicklaus had first call on him when playing in Europe.

Although Dave is wont to dismiss his role as 'show up, keep up and shut up', he has always been far more than a 'bag carrier'. On the course, his advice and judgement are invariably spot on – never more so than during the final, climactic holes of my 1988 Masters victory – while off the course, he has become one of my closest and most trusted confidants.

I'm thankful that the regard in which I hold Dave appears to be mutual, judging by a rare interview he granted the *Sunday Times* after I had won the Open at Sandwich in 1985. He is quoted as saying, 'Sandy is the best bloke in the world to caddie for. I'll tell you what my life is like with Sandy – my wages must be the best on the Tour, must be, and when I stay at his house in Wentworth he brings me tea in bed in the morning. That can't be bad, can it? Who's got the best job in the world? Sandy Lyle, of course. And the second best? Dave Musgrove.'

Dave went off to America at the beginning of the 1990s to work with Tom Watson and Lee Janzen – who became his fourth Major winner when he collected the US Open in 1998 – but we have since partnered together at various events, always providing Dave does not have to travel far from his Kirby-in-Ashfield, Nottinghamshire, home where his beloved Hilary has always, and no doubt still does, spoilt him rotten (deservingly so).

Following Dave's departure as my full-time caddie, I've gone on to work with a number of others, many of whom were by my side for only a short while, or even on a one-off basis, but all played an important part in my career. Roger Morgan, my current partner in crime, was also there to support me back in 1992 when we clinched victory in the Volvo Masters. Terry Holt, who for a long time worked with Brian Barnes, was a great character and would never hold back his opinions, which was exactly what I needed in times of despair when the game was kicking me in the teeth.

And then there was Max Cunningham – the New Zealander who almost saw victory in the Open at St Andrews with Michael Campbell and who was meant to be at Bob May's side at the 2000 US PGA when he took on Tiger Woods in a classic duel, but who missed the event because of high blood pressure. Our time together didn't produce quite that level of success but there was never a dull moment and both Julie, his wife, and Max are still, to this day, great family friends and often feature as the subjects of our dinner conversations.

Julie actually assisted us in the selection of our first dog, Gyp, from the Edinburgh Rescue and Gyp became our regular rabbit-shooting companion. On one of Max's visits to Dolphinton, our home in the Scottish borders at the time, he decided to take Gyp out for a stroll – but was suitably equipped to shoot a bunny if the opportunity arose. A rabbit was duly spotted and Max took aim and fired, and not quite sure if he'd got it first time round, fired again. Sadly Gyp by then had thought it was her turn to get in on the act and she caught the second shot in the leg. I am happy to report that poor Gyp survived the trauma and it did not put her off our adventure – to the point that she later decided to jump from a second storey window to follow me on another rabbit hunt. For a dog that cost £35 she seems to have come with more than the basket the rescue home provided – nine lives seems to have been part of the package as well. And now that I come to think about it, who did settle that vet's bill for repairing her leg?

Of course I can never forget the best caddie of all – I really have to say that or I would be in big big trouble – Jolande, my dear wife. She has now featured in my life for almost twenty years and I'll come on to how we met later in the book. So for now, let's concentrate on her caddying. The truth is we had a very successful spell together on the fairways of Europe. In 1991 she caddied for me as I recorded a number of Top Ten finishes on the Tour and was by my side when I won the Italian Open in 1992. It wasn't all sunshine and roses, mind you. At the PGA at Wentworth in 1992 I was about to take my second shot to the eleventh green and asked – not unreasonably – for the yardage. Jolande gave me the number but something seemed wrong. I'm a good judge of distance – as a golfer you have to be – and her information didn't feel right.

'Are you sure?' I asked.

'Yes.'

'Sure sure? We can't afford to get this wrong.'

'Sure sure,' she replied, a little exasperated, I felt.

'Okay, you're one hundred per cent happy that is the correct yardage? It's just that looking at the pin it doesn't seem . . .'

'I've told you. Either take my word or you can carry your own bloody bag.'

Perhaps the light was playing tricks on me, I thought, as I selected my club and prepared to play. Just as ball and club connected I heard an all-too audible gasp from behind. As my ball soared through the back of the green it seems 'Little Miss Sure Sure' had been looking at the wrong marker!

Poor Jolande was distraught. And I wasn't too happy myself, although I've never really been one to let such things get me down. But I was going to enjoy myself and make her sweat a bit. The twelfth brought comments along the lines of 'Perhaps you should think about getting a professional caddy'. The thirteenth brought 'Do you still love me?' and by the eighteenth I had to relent. 'I don't know what you are worried about, normal caddies make plenty of mistakes in one round, you've made one mistake in plenty of rounds.' Friends again.

Having your wife as a caddie can potentially get you into trouble, mind you. If things weren't going well for me on the course, and I'd either lost a ball or saw it disappear into water, Jolande would sometimes hand me a new one with the words 'I love you' written on it in an attempt to make me smile. I am not sure if that constitutes interfering with your equipment but I certainly had to put a stop to that little lark when I shanked a long iron into a group of spectators and the personalised ball landed at the feet of a rather large lady who suddenly broke into a beaming smile!

Jolande was also caddying for me when I uttered one of my classic lines. It was at the 1992 LA Open and a certain 16-year-old named Tiger Woods was playing and had just missed the cut. I was in the press tent after finishing my round when one of the journalists asked 'Sandy, what do you think of Tiger Woods?' Odd question I thought, saying as how we're here at the Riviera Country Club, but all right, I'm always happy to answer. 'Sorry,' I said, 'don't think I've played that course.' Jolande, who was outside wandering around looking for me, swears that when she heard the howls of laughter emanating from the tent she knew exactly where I must be.

I loved having Jolande on the bag and even though she might not be a pro caddy, she at least is always one hundred and fifty per cent committed to a fun time out on the course. Maybe soon she'll be back by my side again, on fairways around the world.

CHAPTER NINE

MUSSIE AND THE BLUEBELL GIRLS

With a new wife and caddie to support – plus a new marital home in Hawkstone Park to upkeep, about a 1-iron distance from the first tee – I embarked upon one of those curious phases of my career during which, pleasingly, I could not stop making money week in week out but, frustratingly, found tournament victories somewhat more elusive. Although I retained my Lawrence Batley International title at Bingley St Ives – and it is always satisfying to win a trophy in successive years – that was my only success throughout 1982.

I enjoyed a total of fourteen top ten places out of twenty-one appearances in Europe, finishing runner-up in the Order of Merit to Greg Norman, meaning I had regained my place as the top European. Had it not been for the occasional poor round, I might have won several other events but my inconsistency was infuriatingly consistent. At the French Open in Paris I followed up a fine second round of 64 with a bogey-strewn 79, losing the tournament to Seve Ballesteros by four shots. In the Martini International at Lindrick, Yorkshire, I put together a miserable last round of 80 whereas an eminently achievable 70 would have put me in a play-off against Bernard Gallacher. In the PGA Championship at Hillside, Southport (just to prove I was adaptable), I opened with an 81 when a level-par 72 would have left me in another play-off, this time against Tony Jacklin.

While reclaiming my place as European number one as a relatively fresh-faced 24-year-old was gratifying, to win just a single tournament in a year when I missed only one cut and was invariably in the hunt on the final day, left me with a sense of what might have been. I should also point out that had I matched Tom Watson's final round of 70 in the Open Championship at Royal Troon – instead of which I ended up in a tie for eighth place after a lacklustre 74 – I would have walked off with the Claret Jug.

My disappointment must have been nothing compared to that of American Bobby Clampett, though. From a young age, Bobby Clampett – known as 'Tiger' by friends and family – had been labouring under the yoke of being dubbed the 'new Jack Nicklaus' by the American media. For forty-one holes at Troon he certainly gave every appearance of being golf's latest superstar, opening up a seemingly unassailable seven-stroke gap at the top of the leaderboard.

With his blond curly hair, fire-engine red sweater, natty plus-fours and Argyle socks, Clampett approached the game as flamboyantly as he dressed and, in his third round, had attracted a massive gallery as he stood on the sixth tee – at 577 yards (recently extended to 601 yards) the longest hole in British championship golf. When Clampett's drive found a fairway pot bunker down the left-hand side, instead of splashing out, he tried to be too ambitious, smashed the ball against the lip of the trap and succeeded only in sending the ball scurrying into another bunker a few steps forward. By the time the luckless Clampett staggered off the green after a triple-bogey eight, his lead had been slashed to four shots and his confidence wrecked.

By day's end, the scoreboard read:

1. Bobby Clampett   66 67 78 – 211
2. Nick Price   69 69 74 – 212
3. Sandy Lyle   74 66 73 – 213
   Des Smyth   70 69 74
5. Tom Watson   69 71 74 – 214

Although he featured in the final pairing with Nick Price for the final round, Clampett was never in serious contention and a closing 77 left him joint tenth. The Open title appeared as though it was heading off to Zimbabwe in the company of my boyhood pal Nick Price, who led by three with six holes to play, only for Watson to emerge from the pack to pip him by one. At the age of 22, Clampett's career was effectively over, although he won the Southern Open a few months after his collapse at Troon, wearing, incidentally, the same wardrobe he had sported in Scotland to disprove any theory of a jinx. After that, 'the new Nicklaus' quietly drifted out of the game, becoming a television analyst.

Whenever you finish eighth in any Major, or are thereabouts on the final afternoon, it has to be regarded as a great achievement, but nevertheless I felt that 1982 was an 'almost but not quite' season. I was desperate to start '83 by throwing down the gauntlet, especially as it was Ryder Cup year and I did not want to have to depend on being Tony Jacklin's 'captain's pick' for my place in the team. I came out of the blocks with a first round 70 at the Madrid Open, which left me one shot behind Spanish duo Juan Anglada and Antonio Garrido, and American Tom Sieckman. As the weather deteriorated, I entered the final round in second place, two shots in arrears of Gordon J. Brand.

When play was suspended – in all, the final 'afternoon' lasted the best part of eight hours – Dave Musgrove, as only he could, disappeared to enjoy a four-course lunch, including roast lamb and mint sauce, reappearing with a huge self-satisfied grin on his face. Replete or not, Dave was always sound in the advice he gave. Gordon, however, wasn't so lucky. His caddie at the time was a retired teacher, popularly known as 'Snitch' because of his curious nasal tones – sadly, long since dead because he would have enjoyed this anecdote as much as anyone. On the par-three seventeenth, 193 yards into a stiff wind, and with me holding a slender one-shot lead, Gordon was uncertain about the right club to select and wisely asked Snitch his opinion.

'Take what you like, Gordon,' came the reply, 'they're all in there.'

Mussie bent double with his hand covering his mouth to stifle his laughter while I studiously surveyed the surrounding countryside. After scratching his head in puzzlement, Gordon eventually settled for a 4-iron, the ball flew the green for a bogey and I won the tournament by two strokes. I have to admit that win was partly thanks to Snitch's less than helpful reply to a perfectly reasonable question. Perhaps he was feeling miffed that he didn't follow Mussie for a grand nosh-up when he had the opportunity.

I then entered a spell of good form, following up my victory in Madrid by claiming third place in the Italian Open, fourth in the Martini International, joint second in the Car Care Plan International, equal ninth in the PGA Championship and fourth in the British Masters, all but guaranteeing me my spot on the Ryder Cup team. That was just as well because at the very worst time, a week before the 112th Open Championship at Royal Birkdale, I suddenly began playing like a weekend hacker. By way of preparation for the Open, I trailed home joint sixty-fifth in the State Express Classic, a dispiriting nineteen shots adrift of tournament winner Hugh Baiocchi of South Africa, and set off for Southport with much to ponder, not least the fact that Christine was due to give birth to our first child at any time, which tends to put even a Major into perspective.

Open week began in a most unusual fashion when, on my way to the clubhouse from the practice ground, I was approached by a comely young damsel in a raincoat, seeking my autograph. When I readily agreed, she whipped open said coat to reveal a pair of small knickers and a large chest while proffering a felt-tip pen. It was a put-up job, needless to say. My 'admirer' was a well-known *Sun* Page 3 'face'. Quite how Christine felt when she opened the newspaper the following morning while lying in the labour ward is open to conjecture. Out of sorts with my golf and understandably fretting about the forthcoming birth, any faint hopes I had of making an impression at Birkdale evaporated after a first round 73 left me a distant nine shots behind the early leader, Craig Stadler. I duly failed to survive the cut and missed Tom Watson being presented with the Claret Jug but, after a high-speed car journey, was back in Shropshire in time to witness the birth of Stuart who, like father like son, threatened to break the hospital scales at a shade over ten pounds.

Perhaps it was the responsibilities of fatherhood, but I never regained the form I had shown at the start of the season. I missed the cut in the Dutch Open and failed to make any impression at the Irish Open (thirty-fifth) or the European Open (fifty-seventh). When I did display signs of regaining my touch – I was runner-up to Nick Faldo (whom I had led by elelven shots at one stage – ouch!) in a play-off at the European Masters in Switzerland – it promptly disappeared again the following week when I was joint fifty-second in the Tournament Players' Championship at St Mellion. Consequently, I did not travel to Florida for the Ryder Cup at the PGA National in Palm Beach Gardens with my confidence as high as I would have wished. With 107 bunkers plus water hazards on sixteen holes, when you are ailing as I was, the PGA National is not the type of course you would choose for a rest cure.

Tony Jacklin was an inspirational captain even before we left these shores, insisting that we cross the Atlantic aboard Concorde and that we were dressed in the very best cashmere. He left nothing to chance, ordering hand-made absorbent shirts to counter the effects of humidity in Florida, where the temperature would be in the mid 90s, and involving all the leading players in 'team talks' in the months leading up to our departure. A £300,000 sponsorship deal, which was a huge amount of money at the time, allowed our personal caddies to accompany us, which had not happened before in a Ryder Cup 'away' match, and so for the first time in the history of the contest, we squared up to the Americans feeling their equals rather than second-class citizens.

The US team may not have been quite as formidable as two years earlier but the four survivors from 1981 – Tom Watson, Raymond Floyd, Ben Crenshaw and Tom Kite – had been joined by a powerful array of youthful talent, including Curtis Strange, Lanny Wadkins, Craig Stadler and Fuzzy Zoeller. Jack Nicklaus, who lived less than twenty minutes away from the PGA National, was pulling the strings as non-playing captain, so we knew we would need to produce something out of the ordinary to push them to the limit. We did just that, even if Europe received precious little help from an out-of-sorts Sandy Lyle.

In the opening foursomes on the first morning, I partnered Bernard Gallacher against the number-one American pairing of Tom Watson and Ben Crenshaw. Watson was at the very peak of his powers, having just won his second successive Open Championship (his fifth in all), while six months later, Crenshaw would win the Masters at Augusta. Even at our best, Bernie and I would have faced an almighty challenge. Sadly for European hopes, we were both well short of our best, losing 5 and 4. Quite why we failed to gel is impossible to say. Some Ryder Cup partnerships, like marriages, appear made in heaven – Seve Ballesteros and Jose-Maria Olazabal spring to mind – whereas others may be the result of luck or good judgement on the captain's part. Who would have thought that Ian Woosnam and Nick Faldo – fire and ice – for example would become such a devastating unit at Muirfield Village in 1987?

I had known Bernie for years and although at that time we were not yet bosom buddies, we enjoyed an easy relationship and have always been comfortable in one another's company, but we never holed a consequential putt of any distance. We each abjectly failed to produce the type of shots that would inspire the other to new heights. Even so, Europe emerged from that first morning on level terms at two points apiece, and I felt confident I would be selected again for the afternoon fourballs, which are better suited to my game because I am always likely to shoot a few birdies no matter how I am playing.

As it turned out, neither Bernie nor I featured again until the final day's singles, but at least we had sampled the atmosphere at the PGA National, unlike the unlucky Gordon J. Brand who sat out the entire first two days before being sent into the firing line against Bob Gilder. Obviously, I think Tony was wrong to leave me out for three sessions, but that said, we entered the climactic singles with the overall score reading 8–8, so it is impossible to criticise his judgement.

That final afternoon was one of crushing disappointment after we had started so promisingly. In the opening singles, Seve appeared destined to lose to Zoeller when, all-square at the last, he hooked his drive into heavy rough then hacked out a few feet straight into a fairway bunker. Still 240 yards from the green, the bold conquistador let rip with a 3-wood from the sand. The ball flew the water hazard and came to rest pin-high on the fringe of the putting surface from where he was able to salvage a par-five, and a half point. In terms of difficulty, it was ten times harder than I have just described, inspiring Jack Nicklaus to call it 'the greatest single shot in Ryder Cup history'. I am not about to argue with the Golden Bear.

Although the ring-rusty Gallacher, Brand and Lyle were all beaten (in my case 3 and 1 by a brilliant Crenshaw), the Ryder Cup was tied at 13–13 with two matches remaining when Lanny Wadkins, trailing Jose-Maria Canizares by one hole, produced a little miracle on the eighteenth. His sumptuous chip over a bunker landed as gently as a snowflake and stopped less than a foot from the hole. Such was the importance of Wadkins' magic, Nicklaus felt moved to trot across the fairway, kneel down and kiss the divot where the ball had lain. Another precious half point gone and when Watson completed his 2 and 1 defeat of wee Bernie, the Americans had won the trophy by the heartbreaking margin of 14½–13½.

Heartbroken we may have been but we were also tremendously proud and, anyway, it was difficult to remain stony-faced when Seve burst into our locker-room, eyes blazing with passion, to proclaim, 'Why you sit there like that? We have won a great victory – and next time we fuck them good . . .' Nicklaus offered the same sentiment but used different words when he breathed a sigh of relief and told the assembled newsmen, 'The Ryder Cup will never again be a foregone conclusion. What we now have is a real match once more.'

In many ways, of course, Jack Nicklaus was the man who saved the Ryder Cup. When Samuel Ryder founded the contest in 1927, he did so in the hope it would 'influence a cordial, friendly and peaceful feeling throughout the whole civilised world' and no one came to epitomise that spirit more than Jack. In a now famous incident during the 1969 Ryder Cup at Royal Birkdale, Nicklaus sank a treacherous putt on the last green in the final singles to ensure a 16–16 tie then, rather than chase outright victory, conceded Tony Jacklin's two-and-a-half footer. 'I knew you could make it,' said Nicklaus, draping an arm around Jacklin's shoulders, 'but under the circumstances, I wasn't about to make you try.'

Almost four decades after that historic act of sportsmanship, Nicklaus is surprised only by the fact that others might have been surprised at his generosity. 'I think that's what the spirit of golf, and the Ryder Cup in particular, is all about. I've asked every captain since what they would have done and each and every one agreed they would have done exactly the same. Tony was the first golf hero that Britain had produced in a long, long time and if he had missed that putt, he would have been the goat for a long, long time. I didn't think that would be right so I reached down and just picked up his coin.'

Even so, the Ryder Cup had become an uncomfortable mismatch for all concerned on both sides of the Atlantic. Of the fifteen contests between the War and 1975, the US won thirteen, frequently in a rout, drew one and lost one. It was during the 1977 event at Royal Lytham (GB and Ireland 7½, US 12½) that Nicklaus sought out Lord Derby, president of the PGA, and suggested – as gently as he could – that although the American players were honoured to represent their country, the Ryder Cup no longer set the competitive juices flowing, and perhaps the time had come to form a team representing all Europe. If President Jimmy Carter had proposed such a notion, he would have been rightly vilified but this was Jack Nicklaus talking and the British Isles listened.

In the thirteen matches since Nicklaus's suggestion was adopted, Europe have won on six occasions (including four out of the last five) and tied once as the Ryder Cup has developed into one of the most eagerly awaited events on the world's sporting calendar.

'You've either got or you haven't got style; if you've got it, it stands out a mile' runs the song, and Jack Nicklaus came dripping in the stuff. Famously gracious in victory, he was obviously a keen student of Kipling, and came across as equally sporting in defeat. Although Nicklaus won eighteen Majors and eighty-four tournaments across the world, he was the first to acknowledge that any golfer – no matter how dominant – will lose more events than he can ever possibly win, and he treated reversals accordingly. Going back to his famous 'Duel in the Sun' with Tom Watson, which Jack lost of course, I've always loved what he said to a friend with whom he had arranged to have dinner that evening. Not surprisingly, given the close nature of the defeat, Jack's friend ventured that he would fully understand if Jack wished to cancel. 'Why?' said Nicklaus, putting his arm around his pal's shoulder. 'Don't you want to eat? Don't forget, it's only a game.'

'Remember, it's only a game,' was something I had to keep reminding myself throughout the next rollercoaster twelve months during which I won four important titles – the Italian Open and Lancome Trophy in Europe, the Kapalua Invitation in Hawaii and Casio World Open in Japan. Yet again, however, but for a couple of poor rounds over the course of the entire season – why did I not have them in the same week and have done with it? Alas, golf is never that predictable – I might very well have walked away with at least two more glittering prizes.

In the Scandinavian Open in Stockholm, I held a three-stroke lead at the halfway stage, but ended up eight behind eventual winner Ian Woosnam after a miserable third round of 81. A closing 69 hoisted me into a share of fourth place but I never threatened Woosie's position at the top of the leaderboard. In the Celtic International at Galway, I decided to do things the other way around. After thirty-six holes, if you were looking for my name on the leaderboard, it was advisable to start at the bottom, down among the also-rans, a depressing ten shots behind Gordon Brand Junior. Eager to prove to the always-welcoming Irish galleries that I actually knew how to play this game, I completed the last two rounds in thirteen under par to haul myself within three shots of Gordon as joint runner-up.

The 113th Open was another disappointment, especially since it was played at St Andrews. The first-round scores rose in conjunction with the wind, as so often happens in that corner of the East Neuk of Fife. Joint ninety-fourth after an opening 75, I soared eighty places after a last round 67 and remain convinced that, had I been luckier with the weather on day one, I would have been out there jousting with Seve Ballesteros on the final afternoon.

Despite those irritations, 1984 was a highly lucrative adventure, which was just as well as things turned out. After winning the opening event of the season by beating Bobby Clampett (remember him?) by four shots to win the Italian Open in Monza, Christine announced that the arrival of Stuart suggested it was time to move to a larger house. We decided that the Wentworth Estate was the ideal situation, given its proximity to Heathrow, and so I took out a massive mortgage, which, to my mind, was a killer. On the plus side, Lyle Towers was situated a few yards from the fourteenth green on the East Course, so I did not have too far to travel whenever I wanted to practise far from the madding crowd.

My financial fortunes began taking an unexpected turn at the Lancome Trophy in Paris, where I came to the last round in joint fourth place alongside Johnny Miller but a less than encouraging five strokes behind Seve Ballesteros. With little genuine hope of victory, I shot a fine 67 to become the leader in the clubhouse at ten under par, which I thought might be good enough for fourth or even third place and a sizeable cheque towards our new home. With Seve, Eamonn Darcy and Bernhard Langer still out on the course and playing about an hour behind – Bernhard is renowned as one of the most meticulous players on the Tour – Mussie and I ordered a good four glasses of red wine by way of passing the time until the prize-giving ceremony.

At that point I belatedly noticed that all three were playing no better than strictly par golf, and ten under was suddenly the total to beat. On the seventeenth, Seve had a putt for a birdie to take him to eleven under. Eamonn, whose ball was pretty much in line, asked Seve if he would like it marked to which Seve shrugged carelessly. So Eamonn stuck down a 50p coin. Needless to say, Seve's putt collided with the coin and veered away from the hole. Delayed by Langer, upset by the coin incident, Seve was not now at his best and, with a face like thunder, he missed another birdie putt from twelve feet at the eighteenth and we found ourselves in a play-off.

Having never entertained the idea of such an eventuality and thereby dismissed any thought of heading for the practice ground in favour of guzzling red wine, Mussie and I rather tipsily made our way to the first tee. Seve duly arrived, all hot and bothered, the steam rising by the second, whereupon Mussie innocently enquired, 'Where have you been? We've been standing about here for an hour and a half.'

'What you mean where have I been? Langer's playing like a tortoise, there are coins all over the greens . . .' Seve was off and running, and clearly not giving any thought to our sudden-death session to come. I had a couple of practice swings in the near dark and swished off with a 1-iron over a tree, followed by a 9-iron to fifteen feet for a birdie three against Seve's par-four. We shook hands, patted each other on the back and I invited him to join us for another couple of glasses of wine. Aye, winning tournaments – even ones as prestigious as the Lancome Trophy – can be a deceptively simple operation.

Our day was far from over, however. After the prize-giving followed by press and TV interviews, Mussie and I were the last two in the clubhouse and, while we were awaiting our courtesy car to take us back to the hotel, a glamorous young woman strolled through the door. She had come to St Nom la Breteche from the centre of Paris, some twenty-five miles away, with a handful of complimentary tickets for that night's cabaret and dinner at the Lido Club in the Champs Elysées. Three hours later, a chauffeur-driven limo collected us at the Concorde Hotel and drove us to the Lido, where we had a VIP table. After a five-course meal and buckets of champagne, we were taken backstage to meet the famous Bluebell Girls. With their high heels and magnificent headdresses, they appeared to be over eight foot tall.

Mussie was grinning fit to burst – no doubt imagining the reaction in the caddies' hut when he produced the photographic evidence of this treat – when one of the Bluebells leaned over and said, 'By 'eck, luv, where d'you coom from?' in a broad Yorkshire accent. Thinking it such a Parisian institution, I was surprised to discover that the Bluebell Girls weren't all French, and their founder, Margaret Kelly, was born in Dublin and had a remarkable story to tell. Raised in dire poverty and abandoned by her parents, Margaret fled to Europe where, as a dancer, she performed in cabaret with Edith Piaf, Maurice Chevalier and Josephine Baker. She rescued her husband, Marcel Leibovici (a pianist/songwriter, who penned some of Piaf's greatest lyrics), from the grip of the Nazis in Paris during the Second World War, smoked several packs of cigarettes a day and could still dance the cancan when well into her 60s. She was awarded the OBE and the French Legion of Honour.

Margaret, who died at the age of 94 in 2004, looked after her girls like a mother hen. She was 74 when she finally retired, up until which time she directed and choreographed two shows a day, seven days a week, all the while serving as agony aunt and chaperone. An Arab sheikh once asked to buy the entire troupe, offering 16 Ferraris in exchange. Margaret sent him packing with a few choice words. Her physical demands were very strict. 'The Bluebell Girls must be very beautiful with long legs. They must be at least five foot eleven tall [see, I told you they were not really eight foot giants, Mussie], have high, well-formed derrieres and firm breasts, but not too large, because since the demise of the brassiere, dangling, voluminous breasts appear unpleasant, anti-aesthetic.' From our viewpoint in the middle of the chorus line, the Bluebell Girls were aesthetically pleasing in the extreme. What had started as just another day at the office turned out to be one of the most memorable Sundays of my life.

Having been fretting over funding the Lyle mortgage, within the space of six weeks I won £165,000 and had all but paid off the loan when I followed up my victory in the Lancome Trophy by winning the Casio World Open in Japan, beating American Gary Koch in another play-off. Then I added the Kapalua Invitation in the picturesque waterfront setting of the Bay Course at Maui. I regarded my wins in Japan and Hawaii as vitally important in establishing me as a force on the world stage. Now it was time to go win myself a Major . . .

The Open, 1985, Royal St George's

Third shot on the last.
A delicate sand-wedge to
trickle towards the hole.

But all it did was trickle
back to me. I thought
I'd blown it.

Fourth on the last.
Putter this time.
To within fifteen inches.

In for a par. Now all I had to do was wait. Langer and Graham needed a birdie down the last to force a play-off.

And neither of them got it.

Champion golfer of 1985 – Sandy Lyle.

I was so pleased Christine and Stuart (and James on the way) had made the mad dash to see me complete the round and share the moment.

Mussie, me and a certain Claret Jug.

The day after. Party time at home in Wentworth with Bernard Gallacher, Neil Coles, me, Ewen Murray, Tommy Horton, Nick Faldo, Queenie and about eighty others. Don't worry, lads, I'll be off soon to pick up the Chinese takeaway. But I'm not letting go of the trophy. No chance.

Past Champions. How many can you name? Answers below.

Back row, l-r: Tom Lehman, Bob Charles, Nick Price, me, Ian Baker-Finch, Nick Faldo, Tom Weiskopf, Bill Rogers; *middle row, l-r*: John Daly, Justin Leonard, Mark O'Meara, Mark Calcavecchia, Tom Watson, Lee Trevino, Seve Ballesteros, Tony Jacklin; *front row, l-r*: Gary Player, Peter Thomson, Paul Lawrie, Sir Michael Bonallack (captain of the R & A), Sam Snead, Roberto de Vincenzo, Jack Nicklaus.

The Masters, 1988, Augusta National

Of course the ball is in the pond on purpose. No one wants to win the par-three tournament on the Wednesday. It's cursed, don't you know …

Sunday afternoon. First tee. A two-stroke lead going into the last round, with six past champions hot on my heels. A kiss good luck and I'm off.

CORBIS

PHIL SHELDON

Seventy-second hole. Second shot. Needing a birdie to win.

PHIL SHELDON

PHIL SHELDON

... fifteen feet, maybe more, to win ... the blade of my putter bestowed
the merest kiss ... looking promising ... might even go in ... inches away
the ball turned slightly left ... and dropped.

This is going to fit nicely.
Thanks Larry.

Fits me too, boss.

A year on.
The champions'
dinner. 'Gie
them a haggis!'

The day after, Mussie
and the caddies throw
a hell of a do to
celebrate. There,
it suddenly sank in:
Sandy Lyle,
dual Major winner.

CHAPTER TEN

'AND THE CHAMPION GOLFER
FOR 1985 IS . . .'

Packing up baby Stuart, stuffing a suitcase with his favourite toys, wc decided to spend the first four months of 1985 in the United States, where I played with reasonable distinction in a couple of events, notably the Bing Crosby National and Greater Greensboro Open, in both of which I tied for fifteenth place. There was no hint of the glory that lay ahead at Royal St George's in the summer. Again, as had become my wont, if I had been able to string together four good rounds, I might have made an impression on the leaderboard, but an opening round of 76 destroyed my chances in the Bing Crosby while at the Greater Greensboro I began with a splendid 67 only to fade away as the tournament progressed.

However, my performance at the Masters probably best summed up my spring sojourn in America. My 65 in the second round was among the finest I have ever produced at Augusta, but unfortunately it was sandwiched between a 78 and a 76, and a last round of 73 left me tied for twenty-fifth place. At the halfway stage, I had held a three-stroke advantage over eventual Green Jacket winner Bernhard Langer. On the positive side, that seven-under-par second round reinforced my belief that Augusta was a course I could thrive upon, even if precious few Americans took any notice of my efforts for the simple reason that Curtis Strange, who had opened with an 80, matched my 65 on day two and, consequently, was being acclaimed the hero of the hour.

Returning to Europe with my family, I completed the Italian Open in eighteen under par but could still finish no better than third behind an inspired Manuel Pinero and Sam Torrance. I took third place again in the Car Care Plan International at Moortown, and was runner-up to Paul Way in the PGA Championship at Wentworth before my form vanished as if by black magic. I was joint twenty-fifth in the British Masters, and in the following week's Carroll's Irish Open at Royal Dublin I endured the most humiliating four or five hours of my entire professional career. Partnered by Mark James and David Feherty, my problems began on the third hole of the first round. I was safely on the green in two, about eight feet away from the pin, and ten feet away in three after the wind caught my putt. It took three more attempts for me to steer the damned ball into the hole.

After that, my form deteriorated with a pull here, a slice there, a hook over yonder, all the while negotiating the greens as though I was on a wacky crazy-putting course at the seaside. Coming to the last hole, I needed a par-four to break 90 but after unleashing the perfect drive, I struck a 5-iron and the ball caught the wind and proceeded to sail miles out of bounds. At that point I turned to Mark and David and said, 'That'll do it for me. I think someone's trying to tell me something.' I waited until they had putted out, tore up my card and left the course without passing 'Go', thus collecting a £200 fine, or whatever it was. According to the official European Tour records, my score was registered as a 99, after which I slunk off like an expelled schoolboy for a 'Right, Sandy, explain yourself' chat and coaching session with my dad at Hawkstone.

My rollercoaster season gained pace at the Monte Carlo Open (third) and French Open (second) where I scored eight successive sub-70s with rounds of 67, 69, 65, 68, 69, 64, 68, 64. The week before the Open, I should have enjoyed another morale-boosting high finish at one of my favourite events (I had won it twice after all), the Lawrence Batley Classic. I lay in fourth place going into the final round only to shoot a horrendous 80 and plummet to joint twenty-second, a dirty dozen strokes behind Australian Graham Marsh. The perfect way to prepare for Royal St George's, I don't think!

With the lively almost-two-year-old Stuart in tow, Christine and I decided it would be better to rent a house in Sandwich for the week of the 114th Open Championship rather than inflict ourselves upon fellow hotel guests, and found a suitable property about half a mile from Royal St George's. We shared it with Bernard Gallacher, his wife Lesley, the nine-year-old Kirsty, who is now a popular television personality, and their seven-year-old son, Jamie, our near neighbours and friends at Wentworth. This relaxed atmosphere was to prove invaluable as the tournament wore on and I found myself in contention. Coming home to assemble an electric train track or to play a game of Happy Families is the ideal way to push all thoughts of the Claret Jug to the back of your mind.

Although I had jettisoned the driver I used at Royal Dublin and the old man had tinkered with my swing here and there, I made no revolutionary changes, so there was no indication that this was the week I would become the first Briton to win the Open since Tony Jacklin in 1969, and the first Scot since Tommy Armour in 1931. Tommy Armour was born in Edinburgh in 1895, emigrating to the US at the age of 30. I certainly did not visit a fortune-teller who predicted great things, or stroll past an empty scoreboard to see a student, practising for the big event, randomly reaching into the bucket of names and placing the name 'Lyle' at the very top; neither did I dream of victory, nor experience a sudden premonition that 21 July 1985 would be my date with destiny.

I didn't really consider Royal St George's to be my kind of course. I had always believed that, given my notorious inconsistency, if I were to win an Open it would probably be at St Andrews, a far more forgiving course than the demanding Sandwich with its brutal par of 70. In fact, after one practice round I recall Philip Parkin asking me if I thought I could win and replying in all honesty, 'No, Phil, I don't think I can.'

After my last round shenanigans in the Lawrence Batley Classic, therefore, I felt a sense of relief more than anything else when, at the end of the first round, a curious-looking leaderboard showed that I was one of three Scots among the early pacemakers:

64 – Christy O'Connor Junior (Ireland)
68 – Sandy Lyle (Scotland)
     David Graham (Australia)
     Tony Johnstone (Zimbabwe)
     Philip Parkin (Wales)
     Robert Lee (England)
69 – D.A. Weibring (US)
     Bill McColl (Scotland)

Gordon Brand Junior (Scotland)
David Whelan (England)
Fuzzy Zoeller (US)

Among a chasing pack on 70, were a clutch of dangerous foes – Americans Mark O'Meara, Corey Pavin and Payne Stewart, South African David Frost, Australian Peter Senior, my Ryder Cup colleagues Ian Woosnam and Howard Clark and New Zealander Bob Charles, Open champion in 1963 and now 49 years old. A number of less familiar names were there, too – Luciano Bernardini of Switzerland and Kris Moe of the US to name but two. A job well done, it was back to the homestead for a game of Cluedo with the Gallachers, even if Bernie was less pleased with his opening gambit of 73.

By the end of the second round, a solid if unspectacular 71 left me tied for the lead with David Graham, Messrs Bernardini and Moe had been removed from the equation and, at the top, the scoreboard turned into a mad crush resembling the Harrod's sale with a mere two shots covering the leading dozen players:

139 – Graham (only alphabetically!)
      Lyle
140 – Johnstone
      O'Connor
      Weibring
141 – Clark
      Lee
      Woosnam
      Senior
      Bernhard Langer (Germany)
      Wayne Riley (Australia)
      Emilio Rodriguez (Spain)

Although I was not unduly fazed by being tied for the lead at the halfway stage – after all, I had won from the front on numerous occasions – any Major, and the Open in particular, can jangle the nerves and scramble the brain cells. Friday, 19 July being Stuart's birthday, I left the course as quickly as possible to start his party, complete with cake and jelly and, for the adults, a bottle or two of bubbly. By the Saturday evening, although I was less than enthused about my third-round 73, when I studied the runners and riders for the next day's climactic afternoon, I believed I was perfectly poised to mount a determined charge on the rails:

209 – Graham
      Langer
212 – Lyle
      O'Connor
      O'Meara
      Woosnam
213 – Peter Jacobsen (US)
      Tom Kite (US)
214 – Greg Norman (Australia)
      Weibring

I passed the morning until it was time to leave for the course for my 2.40 p.m. tee-off happily building Lego sets with Stuart on the lounge floor of our rented house. I felt no nerves, only a strange sense of calm, probably induced by the fact that in my heart of hearts, my sole ambition was not to ruin my first three day's work by blowing up in the wind, which had been a feature of the week. Of course, I knew I was in with an outside chance, but I felt none of the certainty displayed by one of Britain's previous Open heroes, Max Faulkner. On his way to the first tee for the final round at Royal Portrush in 1951, Max was approached by a young lad seeking his autograph. Renowned as the Clown Prince of Golf, as much for his Technicolor outfits in those days of grey and brown tweeds as for the constant banter he enjoyed with the crowds, he was deadly serious when he wrote: Max Faulkner, 1951 Open champion. Unlike me, however, Max began the final eighteen holes with a comfortable six-stroke lead over Argentinian Antonio Cerda, so he was being optimistic rather than cocky.

If I could have hand-picked any player in Europe to be my partner in the last round of an Open, it would have been Christy O'Connor Junior, an easy-going, no fuss character who could usually be relied upon to come up with an appropriately quiet wisecrack to ease the tension – but not this day when there was so much at stake for us both; even so, it was nice to have someone as decent as Christy at my side as I set out to – hopefully – keep my date with destiny. Perhaps it was the windy conditions but, on the outward nine, none of the leaders made any sort of early move to impose their authority on proceedings. Christy was playing quite beautifully from tee to green but could not buy a putt, while for all their battle-hardening experiences, reigning Masters champion Langer and 1981 US Open winner Graham, who had both started at one under par, were unexpectedly dropping shots all over the place. As the tension mounted, news came through that Tom Kite was on a charge and had burst clear up ahead of us with a birdie blitz on the outward nine holes, at which point the leaderboard had assumed an entirely unfamiliar look:

Kite	1 under
Graham	1 over
Lyle	2 over
Langer	3 over

High as he was flying, Kite's hopes were blown away at the tenth where he took a double-bogey six, after which he stumbled home in 40 to disappear from view. Of all the contenders as we turned for the final slog towards the clubhouse, Graham was producing the most clinical golf, nothing dynamic, just grinding out pars, whereas Langer was uncharacteristically out of sorts, visiting seven bunkers in the course of his round. Playing two groups ahead of the Australian-German combo, I slipped up at the thirteenth where I bunkered my tee-shot for a bogey five. I was in serious trouble again at the next when I drove into heavy rough on the left. I hacked the ball forward eighty yards, struck a 2-iron to the edge of the green, then holed from forty-five feet for the unlikeliest of birdie fours. As uplifting as this was, I knew I still faced three of the toughest closing holes in golf so I knew the trophy engraver wouldn't have my name in mind just yet. But when I rolled in another birdie from twelve feet at the fifteenth, I found myself in splendid isolation at the top of the scoreboard and almost burst into tears, not because of nerves, but through the sheer excitement of it all.

Langer matched my birdie on the fifteenth, but when I stood on the seventy-second tee of the 114th Open Championship, the gallery welcomed me like Caesar returning to Rome in triumph as the news filtered through that Graham and Langer had both bogeyed the sixteenth:

Lyle	1 over
Graham	3 over
Langer	3 over
Payne Stewart	3 over (Stewart had been sitting in the clubhouse for some hours after a fine 68.)

If this was a Hollywood movie, I would tell you that, as I

prepared to drive, my entire life flashed through my mind – striking my very first drive eighty yards as a three-year-old, the many, many days and nights spent honing my skills under the gaze of my dad, almost catching Tony Jacklin's ball after he won the Open at Royal Lytham in 1969 and vowing that I, too, would win the Claret Jug one day, Palmer, Player and Nicklaus, whom I was poised to join in the Open roll of honour. It didn't happen that way, of course – 458 yards away, a streaker, a brave soul on such a blustery afternoon, ran across the eighteenth green to be neatly intercepted by American Peter Jacobsen's flying rugby tackle. 'Can you see if it's a bloke or a lassie?' I asked Mussie. Pressure? What pressure?

After a prolonged delay until the commotion up ahead had died down, I finally struck the most important drive of my life. Understandably, given the occasion, it was not the best tee-shot I have ever produced but the result – the ball landed in light rough down the right-hand side of the fairway – left me in what would normally be a reasonable position to fly my approach into the heart of the green, 184 yards distant. However, this was anything but a normal situation. This was the shot that could win me the Open and I had a tricky downhill lie and wicked crosswind with which to contend. For the first time throughout the day, I was uncertain what to do. If I chose my 5-iron, I risked flying the green and bouncing out of bounds, but a 6-iron would bring the right-hand bunker – where a few golfing disasters have been enacted in the past – into play and I could see myself having to chip out sideways.

After much discussion with Mussie, I opted for the 6-iron. I struck the ball solidly, although it started to drift slightly towards the left, which I thought would be ideal until it struck the spine of the green and slowly rolled through the infamous 'Duncan's Hollow'. I could also not help thinking about another Scot, Eric Brown, who came to the eighteenth at Lytham in 1958 needing a four to win, a five to force a play-off against Australian Peter Thomson, and took a six.

My ball was barely visible, lying in about eight inches of grass, and I decided the only option was to play a delicate sand-wedge off the back foot in the hope of landing it on the crest of the ridge from where it should trickle down towards the flag. The instant I struck the shot I knew I had not made the right contact, and although the ball did, indeed, reach the crest, it hesitated as though trying to make up its mind, before rolling back down into the hollow. Never one to show my emotions, I could not help sinking to my knees, burying my face in the grass and slamming my club on the ground. I really thought I had blown it big time.

After a few calming words from Mussie, I putted up to fifteen inches. Christy knocked in his six-footer for a 72, which earned him a tie for third place and hushed the crowd, and I sank my 282nd shot of the championship before falling into the arms of Christine and Stuart. I had not expected to see my nearest and dearest standing by the eighteenth. Stuart tended to become overexcited whenever he saw me on a golf course, so Christine had decided to stay at home. She was actually washing up the lunch dishes when she heard on the television that I was in the lead. At that point, Howard Clark and his wife, Beverley, bundled Stuart and Christine into their car and made a mad dash to the course in time to see me complete my round.

Lyle	2 over
Graham	3 over
Langer	3 over

As the last pair hove into view on the eighteenth tee an agonising and stomach-churning thirty minutes later, both Graham and Langer needed a birdie three to force a play-off. Oh, yes, now I could feel the pressure all right. I watched the drama unfold on the TV in the European Tour bus with Stuart wriggling on my knee. I have often been asked to explain my true feelings at that point; after all, how could I not want Graham and Langer to screw up? But in all honesty, I didn't. Of course, I desperately yearned to be Open champion but I wanted to achieve that through my own efforts and not because the only two players who could deprive me of fulfilling my childhood fantasy drove out of bounds or lost a ball. In any case, I knew the eighteenth had yielded precious few birdies that afternoon, so I sat back and placed my fate in the hands of Lady Luck for safe keeping.

Unfortunately for them but blessedly for me, Graham found the bunker on the right-hand side of the green, from where he took three to get down, while Langer, who had sent his approach through the green, shaved the hole with his chip and missed his putt to match Graham's bogey five. After so many twists and turns over the final hours, I was the Open champion. Peter Alliss famously observed that I won the '85 Open 'playing in a cloud of unconscious competence' and I think what he meant – only *think* mind you – was that I performed without fear throughout that final afternoon by clearing my mind of any clutter. Following Woosie's philosophy of hit it, go find it, hit it again, go find it again, I had kept it simple (oh, how I wish I had continued playing 'in a cloud of unconscious competence' in the years ahead . . .).

But at that moment all I felt was a mixture of exaltation and relief as I phoned my parents at home in Shropshire. Dad admitted he had already indulged in a 'few wee drams' and fully intended to have a few more before the night was out. Apparently, the mother of all parties had already broken out in the hotel at Hawkstone, where they were in serious danger of running out of champagne.

As I took my place at the trophy presentation, waiting to hear the immortal words, 'And the champion golfer of 1985 – Sandy Lyle', I could see the Claret Jug, golf's Holy Grail, standing on the table in front of the clubhouse. The only thought running through my head was, 'It's mine – gimme, gimme, gimme.' After the dizzying round of TV, radio and newspaper interviews, during which Christine let out our secret that she was expecting the birth of our second child – James – the following January, it was home to Wentworth and an Indian takeaway with the Gallachers and Clarks – vegetable pakora and chicken tikka masala, if memory serves. Five hours' sleep later, I was out of the front door and on to the Wentworth course for a round of press photos and then on to Sunningdale to take part in a charity outing to raise funds for the family of the late Guy Wolstenholme. At the event, I met my first manager, Derrick Pillage, whom I had left two years previously to join Mark McCormack's International Management Group (IMG). He was overjoyed to see me, having invested a goodly sum on my winning the Open at odds of 33–1.

Meanwhile, back at Wentworth, Christine and John Simpson, who handled my affairs at IMG, had organised the erection of a huge marquee in our garden with a champagne and canape buffet for eighty by way of thanks to all our friends and the gentlemen of the press. As the day wore on and we fast ran out of food with no signs of the party ending, I had to phone the local Chinese restaurant in Sunninghill, the Jade Fountain, to ask if they could provide a takeaway.

'For how many, sir?'

'Oh, about forty should do it.'

'OK,' after a prolonged silence.

'How long will it take?'

'For forty? About two hours.'

Michael 'Queenie' King came with me to collect our mountain of food and, as the pair of us had obviously been quaffing too much champagne to take the wheel, Nick Faldo kindly offered to drive (I told you there was a nice lad in there somewhere). It was pandemonium in the restaurant. Diners had been waiting an eternity for their meals while the chefs had been fully employed putting together our order, so Queenie, being Queenie, took it upon himself not only to apologise on our behalf, but to take me round every table introducing me, 'Meet Sandy Lyle, the 1985 Open champion, who has forty hungry hacks to feed back at the ranch.'

Day two of being Open champion dawned with a number of serious hangovers, the arrival of Bruce Forsyth's chauffeur bearing a bottle of champers (just what we needed) and an invitation to appear on the 'Terry Wogan Show', which I had to turn down in order to spend a few days quietly reading through the mound of letters and telegrams that had arrived from friends, acquaintances and complete strangers:

'Well done! You showed real guts but don't be in too much of a hurry. You will win it again – OFTEN. Once you know you can do it, next time it could be by a street. Much love to you all, Christine, the baby and the old folks.' Henry Cotton.

'As a tribute to your outstanding achievement, I wrote and

recorded the enclosed tape that may give you and your family a smile (Max, who I did not know from Adam Faith, had penned a special song in my honour). Everybody in this household is very proud of you. May you go on and on and . . .' Max Bygraves.

'We were so pleased for you and it couldn't have happened to a nicer person. Obviously playing with you in the Pro-Celebrity event at Fulford last year set you on your way. You were such a popular winner.' Jane and Bill Roach (Ken Barlow of 'Coronation Street').

'Always knew you could do it.' Nick Price.

'Please accept from an ancient writer this small present for your son, Stuart, to be kept until he is old enough to read it – about six. You gave me so much pride and pleasure watching you win the Open that I feel I must give you something back.' Roald Dahl. Enclosed was a signed first edition of *Charlie and the Chocolate Factory*.

'Just a few lines to congratulate you on your wonderful win. You must be absolutely thrilled at winning that great champ-ionship, especially in the adverse weather conditions you had to cope with over the four days.' Bobby Locke.

'It was a great thrill to see you take the Open title while lying in my hospital bed. It almost made me burst my stitches with excitement.' Dickie Henderson.

From Hawkstone Park and Clober, from Lindrick and Carnoustie, from the Ladies' Section of Wentworth and from the members of Stratford-on-Avon they arrived, plus the following telegram from Santander in Spain:

'Many ignored your talent but I knew you are a great cham-pion. Your Open victory is instrumental for British and European golf and I could not be any happier. Savour your deserved victory but please be very cautious with commitments that might derive from particularly being British. Bear in mind that you cannot please everybody. Congratulations to all the family, your friend Seve.'

I took Seve's warning very much to heart because I was aware that Bill Rogers, who had won the Open at Sandwich four years earlier, had all but burned himself out within a few months of that triumph as he criss-crossed the globe 'trying to please everybody'. I knew that with IMG's connections, my victory would be highly lucrative in terms of sponsorship deals and endorsements and had no intention of traipsing all over the world to cash in on my title, which is why I had no hesitation in rejecting – and in so doing upsetting a number of Americans – an invitation to compete in the US PGA Championship at Cherry Hills, Colorado. Instead, I played slightly nearer home in the Glasgow Open at Haggs Castle, where I lost a play-off to my buddy, Howard Clark.

I'd fulfilled my boyhood dream of becoming Open champion and preferred to postpone renewing my acquaintance with the Americans until they arrived on these shores for the forthcoming Ryder Cup at The Belfry.

CHAPTER ELEVEN

FLYING THE EUROPEAN FLAG

'Each and every one of us knows what we have to do over the coming days.' So began captain Tony Jacklin's team talk on the eve of the twenty-sixth Ryder Cup contest at The Belfry in 1985. 'I don't need to emphasise precisely how tough it's going to be, so I want to tell you two things. Something changed at Palm Beach Gardens two years ago. Up until then, the Americans went in to the Ryder Cup wondering how many points they were about to win by. Tonight, they will actually be considering the possibility of defeat. For the first time since Lindrick in 1957 – when Dwight D. Eisenhower was President and Harold Macmillan the Prime Minister – they've accepted that losing is a possibility. Secondly, they may look impressive on paper, but I have a team full of passion and determination. Who wants to win the Ryder Cup more? The United States or Europe? We do.'

As usual, the Americans had, indeed, assembled a mighty twelve but for once no one in the European camp felt intimidated in any way. From the Order of Merit, our team comprised: Sandy Lyle, Bernhard Langer, Seve Ballesteros, Ian Woosnam, Sam Torrance, Howard Clark, Manuel Pinero, Jose-Maria Canizares and Paul Way. Jacklin had insisted upon three captain's 'wild card picks', and he added Nick Faldo, Ken Brown and Jose Rivero. That made four Spaniards, a German, three Scots, three Englishmen and a Welshman. Margaret Thatcher may have snapped her handbag shut and fumed at the notion of a European Union, but the golfers of Great Britain and Ireland had warmly embraced the European Ryder Cup community. In later years, Sweden, Denmark, Finland, Italy and France would also come to be represented. Furthermore, judging by the number of golf courses currently operating or being built in and around Moscow, the day cannot be too far off when a Russian helps to lower the Stars and Stripes.

Although I took deep pride in representing Scotland in the World Cup and the Dunhill Cup – just as I had in playing for England Schoolboys in my youth – nothing compares to standing under the flag of Europe at the opening of a Ryder Cup. To line up shoulder-to-shoulder with eleven men who, week in week out, are your arch rivals but are there beside you as your team-mates is a feeling like no other. You can 'feel' the sense of comradeship and I can't for the life of me understand those who think they should be paid for playing in the contest. Competing in a Ryder Cup is a privilege granted to a chosen few and the notion that, as well as receiving top-of-the-range golf bags, blazers, sweaters, trousers (even if they sometimes split), shirts etc., they should be financially rewarded strikes me as obscene.

I will now step down from my soap box and return to The Belfry. As we surveyed Lee Trevino's side at the opening ceremony

– during which rookie Rivero insisted the Americans sang a song that included a line starting 'Jose, can you see . . .? – we took in the quality of the opposition. Yes, they had brought with them the reigning US Open champion, Andy North, and the soon-to-be US PGA title winner Hubert Green, but I was *the* Open champion, Langer was the current wearer of the Masters' Green Jacket and we had something they did not in the shape of Seve, a man on a mission who had never hidden his dislike of all things American. If Jacklin was the captain, Seve was our spiritual leader, intent on coming out with all guns blazing like the Spanish armada in full sail.

Seve and Pinero launched into Curtis Strange and Mark O'Meara in the morning foursomes, winning 2 and 1 to put the first European point on the board, but thereafter the Americans assumed early control by inflicting three heavy defeats upon us. Bernhard Langer and Nick Faldo, who had won three points out of four in tandem two years previously, were cuffed 3 and 2 by Calvin Peete and Tom Kite. Ken Brown and I were sunk 4 and 3 by Lanny Wadkins and Raymond Floyd, after which Howard Clark and Sam Torrance went down 3 and 2 to Craig Stadler and Hal Sutton. A lunchtime menu reading Europe 1, US 3 did not make for hearty appetites.

Jacklin made some inspired changes for the afternoon four-balls, introducing Paul Way and Ian Woosnam, two bonny fighters in any scrap, into the fray at the top of the order. They responded magnificently, beating Fuzzy Zoeller and Hubert Green by one hole. With Seve and Pinero seeing off Andy North and Peter Jacobsen, followed by Langer and Jose-Maria Canizares's half against Stadler and Sutton, as the sun set over The Belfry that first evening, we had trimmed the Americans' lead to 4½–3½. Having been stood down after the loss to Wadkins and Floyd, I was eager to rejoin hostilities the following morning, and my spirits lifted when Jacklin took me aside to give me the news that I would partner Langer against Stadler and Curtis Strange in the fourth and final match of the fourballs.

By the time we arrived on the seventeenth tee we were two down with two to play, but the overall score stood at 5½–5½. If we could win the last two holes, we would end the session at six points apiece. Should we lose, the Americans would take what could be a crucial 6½–5½ lead. Jacklin and Woosie – who had earlier combined with Way to produce a magnificent 4 and 3 trouncing of Green and Zoeller – were chewing their fingernails at the side of the green as Stadler rolled his long approach putt up to the flag for a sure-fire birdie. That left me to hole an eighteen-footer for an eagle to prolong the contest. To an almighty roar, which must have been heard in every corner of the course, I managed to do just that and off to the eighteenth we trooped, followed by a massive gallery who fully appreciated the importance of this particular 474 yard stretch of the Midlands.

Again, things looked grim. Langer and I both left our second shots some distance from the pin from where we took two putts for matching par-fours. Stadler faced no more than an eighteen-inch 'gimme' for par and a one-hole victory. That length of putt was cheerfully conceded by countless golfers all over the country every day of the week, but this was not a friendly for a couple of quid. This was for a point in the Ryder Cup and when Stadler turned to us as if expecting us to say, 'Take it away,' Langer and I pretended to be studying some far-off spot in the distance. To be honest, we were mortally embarrassed to inflict such an indignity upon a former Masters champion but, 'Hey, putt out, chum,' was our unspoken message and I knew from the nod that Bernhard and I exchanged that we were in complete agreement.

We may have felt embarrassed but no way did I feel guilty about asking Stadler to putt again; Dad may have ingrained the etiquette of golf into me from a young age but every half point in a Ryder Cup can be crucial and, given the tension of the moment, it was a putt that was eminently missable. We were fully aware that had it been Bernhard or myself standing over the self-same eighteen-incher, then Stadler and Strange would have had no compunction in inflicting the same trial of nerves upon us; come the end of the match when we shook hands there was certainly no animosity on their part although I imagine the air might have turned a nice shade of blue when they eventually reached the American locker-room. For reasons that will forever be a mystery – perhaps he was guilty of being over-casual – the Walrus sent his tap-in sliding past the hole. Never has a half in any golf match inspired such a mixture of jubilation and dejection. In the clubhouse, Henry Cotton, wise old owl that he is, who had first played in the Ryder Cup way back in 1937, was heard to comment, 'That's going to cost America the Ryder Cup.' That notion is flatly rejected by Stadler, who rightly points out, 'Every time the Ryder Cup comes round, I've got to watch that all over again on telecast. What they don't show is my partner whipping it into the water, leaving me alone with a driver and 1-iron to the hole. Up ahead, Andy North had also hit it in the water, so did Hubert Green. I was just about the only guy to finish the hole. I'll never understand the reaction – like I never three-putted before in my entire life? The putt that lost the Ryder Cup? Yeah, I've heard that a lot over the years, but I've never bought into that particular story. What was it, the Saturday morning? There was still a lot of golf to be played. I made a lot of putts in my life, I missed a lot of putts in my life, and I have to say the Ryder Cup consists of twenty-eight matches. A single putt can't determine the outcome if everyone else has done their job.'

The Saturday afternoon was one of almost unremitting joy, and when I again sat out the foursomes, which has never been my favourite brand of golf, I tore around the course like any excited spectator, although I had the advantage of being on the action side of the ropes. Canizares and Rivero whipped Kite and Peete 7 and 5 – an extraordinary outcome over eighteen holes. Seve and Pinero added a second all-Spanish triumph with a comfortable 5 and 4 defeat of Stadler and Sutton, and Langer and Brown soundly defeated the previously unbeaten Floyd and Wadkins 3 and 2. So even allowing for Way and Woosie's 4 and 2 reverse against Strange and Jacobsen, we would enter the climactic twelve singles with a precious 9–7 advantage, requiring us to win 5½ points to prise the Ryder Cup from America's grasp for only the fourth time since 1927.

As Jacklin called us together to draw up the battle plan, otherwise known as the order of play, Manuel Pinero's quiet but intense voice was heard from the corner of our suite in The Belfry Hotel. 'Give me, Wadkins. Please, I want Wadkins.' I have to confess my first thought was, 'Have him. Go right ahead, Manuel,' because Wadkins is one of the toughest matchplay opponents you could wish – or not wish – to meet. It was his outrageous chip against Canizares at Palm Beach Gardens in '83 that was instrumental in America's victory two years earlier. Wadkins was renowned as golf's most ferocious bar-room brawler, a lionheart to be approached only with a chair and a whip. Convinced Trevino would place Wadkins, a high-speed player guaranteed to race round any course, at the top of his starting list, Jacklin duly pencilled in Pinero's name at number one. After the captain's meeting, skipper Tony almost skipped back into our midst to impart the news, 'Manuel Pinero will play . . .' long pause for effect, '. . . Lanny Wadkins.'

Whether Pinero harboured a long-held grudge against Wadkins I cannot say, but his 3 and 1 victory reinforced the European momentum built up the day before, especially so when Paul Way followed the Spaniard into the clubhouse as the two-hole conqueror of Floyd: Europe 11, United States 7.

Although Woosie lost to Stadler, who displayed true grit in recovering from our Saturday morning drama on the eighteenth, Seve secured a half against Kite after recovering from three down with five to play. I enjoyed a relatively stress-free 3 and 2 win over Jacobsen, and Langer was never in trouble against Sutton, winning 5 and 4: Europe 13½, US 8½.

Then, as cheer after cheer went up from every corner of The Belfry, along came Sam, who, as a boy, had fantasised about growing up to be 'The Man Who Holed The Putt That Won The Ryder Cup'. Actually, that honour might have gone to Howard Clark, who had a four-foot putt on the seventeenth green to beat O'Meara 2 and 1, but destiny had decreed it was Sam Torrance who was to be granted sporting immortality upon this day and in this corner of Sutton Coldfield.

Three down after ten holes, Sam was not playing well (in fact, he completed his round in 76) but he had finally drawn level on the seventeenth with a majestic approach to within eight feet of the pin for a birdie four. From the moment North's ball landed with a delicious *plop!* in the water on the eighteenth on his way to a double-bogey six, Sam had the luxury of three putts from eighteen feet to win the Ryder Cup. He did it in one before, as the Scots say, 'greetin' like a wean'. For the record, Howard Clark went on to defeat O'Meara, Rivero lost to Peete, Faldo went down against Green, Canizares defeated Zoeller, and Brown, already relishing the party to come, lost to Strange in the final match: Europe 16½, United States 11½.

For my part, life did not come any sweeter – Open champion and Ryder Cup winner in the space of two months – and the subsequent celebrations were long and hard. We stood on the roof of the clubhouse spraying champagne upon the ecstatic crowds, we sang, we danced, we laughed, we cried and generally behaved outrageously. If there had been jelly to spoon at one another, we would have done it – all except Nick Faldo, who, miffed at having failed to contribute a single point to our success, was conspicuous by his absence. Faldo explained his reaction thus:

I could not find it in my heart to join in all those joyous celebrations. As far as I was concerned, the other 11 fellas had won the trophy. I simply did not feel part of the team, having failed to do my bit. And so, while Tony Jacklin and the lads stood on the balcony spraying the jubilant spectators with champagne and Concorde flew overhead dipping its wings, I sat alone at a corner table in the clubhouse. One of the greatest moments in European golf and there was I, Little Jack Horner sulking in the corner. It would have been nice if Tony or someone had come looking for me, put his arm around my shoulders and said, 'C'mon, my son, get your ass out there, you're as much a part of the team as anyone.' That was when my tendency to be a loner came back to haunt me with a vengeance.

Those words sadden me even now because Nick Faldo *was* one of our team and had more than pulled his weight in 1977, 1979, 1981 and 1983 by winning 11 points out of 15 while remaining unbeaten in singles. Perhaps one of us should have sought him out but whenever Nick adopted his Greta Garbo 'I want to be alone' pose, it would have taken a very brave man to pour a bottle of champers over his head and invite him to join the fun and games. In the middle of his complete rebuild under coaching guru David Leadbetter, he had finished forty-third in the Order of Merit and I sincerely believe that when Jacklin offered him a Ryder Cup 'wild card' he should probably have replied, 'Thanks, Tony, but I think it better if I sit this one out.' Not an easy thing for Nick to do, I accept that, but at least I can talk from a position of some understanding of his plight. I was there myself four years later.

I opted out of the frolics around midnight, many hours before Sam, Woosie and their fellow serial-party animals were diving fully clothed into the hotel swimming pool as the festivities continued until dawn. Ah well, work hard, play hard – doubly so when we knew that, having won the Ryder Cup, our next task, two years hence, was to retain it and to do that we would have to beat the Americans on their own soil for the first time. Not only that but the competition was to be held in Jack Nicklaus's back garden at Muirfield Village, the course he designed and christened in honour of its Scottish namesake where he won his maiden Open in 1966.

We flew to Columbus, Ohio with nine survivors from the victorious 1985 team – Ian Woosnam (the world number six), Howard Clark, Sam Torrance, Nick Faldo, the new Open champion from, appropriately, Muirfield, Jose Rivero, Bernhard Langer (world number three), Seve Ballesteros, Ken Brown and myself (world number four). Jose-Maria Olazabal, Gordon Brand Junior and Eamonn Darcy replaced Paul Way, Manuel Pinero and Jose-Maria Canizares. During the flight, the celebrations from The Belfry had threatened to break out all over again in mid-Atlantic when Slammin' Sam and his actress girl-friend Suzanne Danielle announced their engagement, but Tony Jacklin was there to supervise us like the head teacher on a school outing.

Although it is regarded as being one of the hardest courses in championship golf, I liked Nicklaus's design. He had incorporated lookalikes of his favourite eighteen holes across America. The sixteenth par-three, for instance, is a dead-ringer for the sixteenth at Augusta, but thirty-four yards longer. As I had finished joint sixth in eleven under par at Nicklaus's Memorial Tournament at the end of May, it held no fears for me. When we arrived, the Golden Bear was in the clubhouse, captain for the second time in three contests, ready to greet us, with the band of the Ohio State University launching into 'Three Cheers for the Red, White and Blue' as a musical accompaniment.

After sharing the points in the opening foursomes, we made our decisive move in the afternoon fourballs, during which Nicklaus approached Dave Musgrove at one stage to comment, 'I can't believe the scores your guys are doing out here. I designed this to be a hard course.' Oh, it was hard, all right, but the Europeans were in irresistible mood:

Brand and Rivero beat Ben Crenshaw and Scott Simpson
3 and 2

Langer and Lyle beat Andy Bean and Mark Calcavecchia
1 hole

Faldo and Woosnam beat Hal Sutton and Dan Pohl 2
and 1

Ballesteros and Olazabal beat Curtis Strange and Tom
Kite 2 and 1

Europe 6, United States 2

I was delighted to renew my alliance with Bernhard Langer forged at The Belfry in '85 because Bernie is my kind of guy – straightforward, no affectations and blessed with a dry sense of humour. I think a lot of people labour under the misapprehension that because he is a committed Christian, Bernhard is a bit of a stuffed shirt and, consequently, not much fun to be around, but that is only because they do not know him.

Honest, gracious and modest, Bernhard is everyone on the Tour's kind of guy. When he missed that fateful putt against Hale Irwin on the final green of the last match of the 1991 Ryder Cup at Kiawah Island, South Carolina, Seve, already a Ryder Cup captain-in-waiting although still a supposedly humble footsoldier serving under Bernard Gallacher, was first to comfort the distraught German. Bernhard's miss had given America victory by a single point. 'Nobody in the world could have made that putt,' whispered Ballesteros as Langer stood alone amid a veritable Mardi Gras of whooping and hollering Americans, 'nobody.'

Langer never forgot that kindness and six years on at Valderrama, as Seve stood alone on the clubhouse terrace on the Saturday morning before the final round of singles and gazed across the still-deserted velvet fairways to a far-off spot on the horizon, where the departing raindrops shimmered brilliantly in the sun's rays, he felt the fall of a strong hand on his shoulder. 'Whatever happens this day,' smiled Bernhard, 'always remember that nobody in the world could have done more for this team. Nobody.' It was Seve and Bernie's turn to win by a single point.

Back in 1987, in day two's foursomes Bernie and I – I did play foursomes sometimes – were pitted against America's toughest combination, Lanny Wadkins and Larry Nelson. They boasted a 100 per cent Ryder Cup career record of played nine, won nine from 1979 (during which Nelson beat Seve four times) and 1981. They were the opponents from hell, golfing twin brothers of Sylvester Stallone's Rocky Balbao.

At the first hole, a 446 yard dogleg par-four, we discovered that, on the fastest greens imaginable, the pin had been placed in the most diabolical position, but a bogey five (I had opened proceedings by hooking my drive into the trees) was sufficient to give Bernie and me a morale-boosting early lead. The Americans, safely on the green in two, could do no better than a double-bogey six after Wadkins sent their second putt through the putting surface. That's how fast Nicklaus had ordered the greens to be prepared. We hung on thereafter and eventually finished the match at the seventeenth with a 2 and 1 victory, bringing Nelson's long unbeaten run to an end. That must have hurt him dearly but not as much, I suspect, as never being granted the Ryder Cup captaincy he so craved. If one player ever deserved to lead his country, it was surely Larry Nelson.

With Seve and Olly beating Ben Crenshaw and Payne Stewart, and Faldo and Woosie snaffling a half point against Hal Sutton and Larry Mize after having been four down after ten holes, we had nudged another notch in front: Europe 8½, US 3½.

It was almost an inevitability that, when the draw for the afternoon fourballs was announced, Bernie and I were once again lined up opposite a fired up Wadkins and Nelson, still smarting from their earlier defeat. The match swung one way and then the other as the 'Barmy Army' – about two thousand of whom were at Muirfield Village – engaged in a battle of noise with ten times that number bedecked in various weird and wonderful costumes fashioned from the Stars and Stripes. It was an epic struggle. Wadkins birdied the fifteenth only to see me rattle in a long putt for an eagle, and all the while Bernhard was nipping away at them like a rabid terrier. 'Anything you can do, I can do better,' you could almost hear him mutter.

To give you some idea of the quality of golf our quartet produced, Wadkins covered the last five holes of Nicklaus's devilish masterpiece in four under par yet he and Nelson could make no impression on our lead, and so, approaching the eighteenth green, we still held a tenuous one-hole advantage. To raucous cheers from the Europeans in the gallery, I took an 8-iron and landed the ball six feet from the pin. Given the lightning quick greens and the fast-dwindling light, it was a putt I did not relish having to hole for what could prove a priceless point. My misgivings were confirmed when Wadkins put his ball a yard away. 'USA! USA! USA!' chanted the American legions. 'Get inside that and I'll kiss you,' I told Bernhard. Majestically, magnificently, miraculously, his 8-iron rolled the ball to within inches of the cup. 'Anything you can do, I can do better.' With the eyes of the world upon me, I made do with blowing him a kiss instead.

Woosie and Faldo also played their part to perfection that Saturday afternoon, reaching a better-ball ten under par for the fourteen holes it took them to annihilate Curtis Strange and Tom Kite 5 and 4: Europe 10½, US 5½.

We required 3½ points to retain possession of the Ryder Cup and four to win the trophy outright for the second successive time. We knew it would be hard because the Americans would come out snarling, but never in our worst imaginings did we appreciate just how hard as a succession of US victories went up on the board:

Match one: Woosie, after surrendering a mere half point in his four outings with Faldo, lost by one hole on the final green against Andy Bean: Europe 10½, US 6½.

Match two: Howard Clark brazened it out against Dan Pohl, again on the eighteenth: Europe 11½, US 6½.

Match three: Sam Torrance, one down on the eighteenth tee, won the final hole for a half against Larry Mize: Europe 12, US 7.

Match four: for the fourth time, the match went all the way to the eighteenth where Faldo missed an eight-foot putt to hand victory to Mark Calcavecchia: Europe 12, US 8.

Match five: Payne Stewart beat Jose-Maria Olazabal at the seventeenth: Europe 12, US 9.

Match six: Scott Simpson beat Rivero 2 and 1: Europe 12, US 10.

Match seven: Tom Kite thrashed Sandy Lyle (sorry, fellas) 3 and 2: Europe 12, US 11.

Match eight: enter Eamonn Darcy and Ben Crenshaw, who, normally the most unflappable of characters, had been using his 3-iron on the green after snapping his putter clean in two in a rage after losing the sixth. Body shaking, knees trembling, face ashen, Eamonn had a six-footer on the eighteenth for victory. With the adrenaline flowing, Eamonn gave the ball an almighty wallop and it would have been travelling still had it not hit the centre of the hole at full steam and disappeared from view: Europe 13, US 11.

Match nine: predictably, Langer and Nelson were involved in a titanic struggle in which they shared the spoils on the eighteenth: Europe 13½, US 11½.

Match ten: ridiculed by the American press, who had been suggesting he was past it (well, he had finished a lowly third in the US Open behind Scott Simpson earlier that summer), Seve had a two-footer on the seventeenth against Curtis Strange and succeeded Sam Torrance as 'The Man Who Holed The Putt That Won The Ryder Cup'. The ball rolled into the hole and Seve, bless 'im, celebrated as only he can by dancing round the green. On the golf course he is the King of Europe, on the dance floor? Well, he is no John Travolta: Europe 14½, US 11½.

Match eleven: Wadkins cuffed Ken Brown (again already thinking about the celebrations to come) 3 and 2: Europe 14½, US 12½.

Match twelve: Gordon Brand Junior secured an honourable 'away draw' with Hal Sutton: Europe 15, US 13.

We had done it. For the first time in fourteen attempts Uncle Sam's golfing nephews had been humbled in their own backyard and, boy, did we let them know about it. Seve and Olly led us in a Spanish flamenco, we drowned Tony Jacklin in champagne, we sang, Bernhard unfurled the flag of Germany, Sam produced the Scottish Lion Rampant, and then we all trooped off to the beer tent to join our wonderful supporters for a drink or five. As the carnival raged, over in the American locker-room Jack Nicklaus, the first US captain to suffer defeat on American territory, was embarking on an emotional speech, which reduced Ben Crenshaw to tears.

As we returned to Heathrow to scenes reminiscent of The Beatles in their heyday, I was not to know that the sixteenth at Muirfield Village, where I had lost to Tom Kite, would be the last hole I would ever play in the Ryder Cup. By the time of the 1989 contest, back at The Belfry, my game was in terrible decline. I knew that Tony Jacklin was considering offering me a 'wild card' and, quite frankly, the prospect of it was tying my stomach in knots. I had given myself the task of trying to regain my form in a number of post-Open tournaments in Europe and the States. I needed to prove to myself that I would be able to perform in the matches – and not be the weakest link in the team. My attempt failed and I knew what I had to do. Picking up that phone to Tony wasn't the easiest of decisions and not one I envy anyone else having to make. When we spoke Tony still felt I would be a good asset to the team but I knew that pulling out was the correct decision – never more so than when I saw Christy O'Connor Junior (who took my 'place') win against Fred Couples. I cheered as loudly as any other spectator in the land when he edged out Fred in an eighteenth green thriller in the final day's singles. That win secured a point beyond value in the 14–14 draw that kept the Ryder Cup on this side of the Atlantic.

CHAPTER TWELVE

CONQUERING AMERICA
AND THE 'FIFTH MAJOR'

Although 1986 was a fairly humdrum year in Europe where I failed to win a single title for the first time since my 'rookie' year of 1978 (in fact, I had only five top ten finishes from my thirteen appearances), I did have the immense satisfaction of savouring my first American tournament success. The famed Greater Greensboro Open at Forest Oaks, North Carolina, is an important event whose past champions include Sam Snead, Billy Casper, Gary Player, Tom Weiskopf, Bob Charles, Raymond Floyd and Seve Ballesteros.

After opening rounds of 68, 64 I was flying high at the top of the leaderboard before, as only A.W.B Lyle can do, I allowed the chasing pack to close the gap after a lacklustre 73. A final round of 70 was enough to earn me a two-stroke victory over American Ryder Cup stalwart, Andy Bean, and announce my arrival on the US Tour. Even though I far preferred playing in Europe, it was a pampered life for golfers in the States. Everything was laid on from cars, either chauffeur-driven or self-drive, to fine dining in the clubhouse restaurants, to magnificent practice facilities with bucket upon bucket of brand new balls delivered to your feet.

The European Tour has made great strides forward in the intervening years but two decades ago everything was fairly primitive in comparison to America; it was like going from the Football Conference to the Champions League. The 1985 Benson & Hedges Open, for instance, one of Europe's most prestigious tournaments, was played at Fulford where, as impressive as the course was, the practice ground was a cricket-cum-hockey-cum-football pitch, comprising mostly clay and clover and precious little grass. The caddies were still catching balls out there in those days, which was a very dangerous task when you had twenty players firing off the tee. It was anything but ideal and I found I was hitting the ball so badly, I would have about two dozen swings then make my way to the first tee.

(What can I say? Whatever I was doing wrong I left on that wretched practice ground and after rounds of 70, 69, 71 I went into the final day at Fulford in 1985 just three shots behind the pace-setting Rodger Davis of Australia. Then Ian Woosnam, who had appeared well out of contention in twenty-second place, blazed round in an astonishing 62, becoming the first player to shoot eight successive birdies in the process so I had to produce a 64 to pip my old adversary by a single stroke.)

The importance of that first tournament win in America in the 1986 Greater Greensboro, against the very best players preparing for the following week's Masters at Augusta, can be gauged by the fact that when my parents moved house at Hawkstone, my dad called their new home 'Greensboro'. I was to celebrate an even more momentous victory in the US twelve months later by capturing the Tournament Players' Championship (TPC) at Sawgrass. Dubbed the 'fifth Major' by the Americans, the TPC was worth $180,000 – $18,000 more than Larry Mize would bank for winning the Masters seven days later. I had arrived at Sawgrass fresh from a coaching session with Jimmy Ballard, having recently shot 81, 75 to miss the cut in the Doral Open then 77, 83 to suffer the same fate at the Honda Classic.

I had heard great things about Jimmy from a number of the American pros, notably Hubert Green, Curtis Strange and Peter Jacobsen, although I had my doubts when he strapped me into a harness called a 'Swing Connector'. It felt incredibly restrictive but corrected a minor flaw in my stance. According to Jimmy, the origins of the Swing Connector could be traced all the way back to Babe Ruth, the baseball legend of the 1920s, who used to encourage his young New York Yankees team-mates to practise their swings with a towel tucked under their left arms, the theory being if the towel dropped to the ground, then their back-swing was wrong. One of those who benefited from Ruth's advice was Sam Byrd, who, as a gifted golfer, subsequently quit baseball to join the Tour, winning over twenty tournaments and coming runner-up in the 1945 US PGA Championship, which was then a matchplay event. Byrd later turned to coaching and employed Jimmy Ballard as an instructor, thereby passing on Babe Ruth's towel secret out of which grew the Swing Connector.

Sawgrass is a terrifying place with water, water everywhere, island greens, tight pin positions, narrow fairways, high-speed greens – exactly the type of course on which I never felt entirely comfortable, but I felt renewed enthusiasm after visiting Jimmy. At some point during my first three rounds of 67, 71, 66 – and I cannot remember exactly when because my mind was in such a turmoil (I only know my scores from the tournament records) – Christine decided that our marriage, which had been deteriorating since the birth of our second son, James, fifteen months earlier, was over and that we should initiate divorce proceedings. Being a professional who is constantly traipsing around the world can put a strain on even the most solid of marriages but although Christine and I had been suffering problems in the marital home, the suddenness of her decision still came as an almighty shock. I suppose I thought we would work things out in the fullness of time when we had the chance to sit down and thrash out the crisis but it wasn't to be.

While Christine packed Stuart's and James's suitcases and departed for England, I was left with my thoughts and a round of golf to play. Right to the wire, there were six players in contention – Greg Norman, Mark O'Meara, Ben Crenshaw, Scott Simpson, Jeff Sluman and A.W.B. Lyle. And then there were two. When I rammed home a forty-foot birdie putt on the seventy-second green for a closing 70, I barged my way into a play-off with Sluman. At the second extra hole, I enjoyed a moment of good fortune when, just as Sluman was lining up a six-foot birdie attempt for victory, a spectator took it upon himself to dive into the lake surrounding the green. Sluman backed away from the putt, took aim again, missed, and I capitalised by securing the title at the third play-off hole which happened to be the eighteenth.

The closing hole at Sawgrass is just about the last place on earth you want to be on a dark evening when the sun has long since set. With water running all the way down the left-hand side of the fairway – where Alistair the 500lb alligator awaits any unsuspecting ankle – I drilled a 1-iron off the tee even though

I couldn't see where the ball had landed in the gloom. When I arrived at my ball it was as though someone had drawn a black velvet curtain over the green, so having no idea where the flag was, I aimed for the lights of the TV commentary box.

There was no loud sigh from the gallery so I knew I hadn't dropped my approach shot into the water. Nor was there any loud cheering which suggested I was some distance away from the pin. Sluman generated the same muted reaction when he followed me into the pitch dark and we arrived in the green to find both balls sitting about ten feet apart just over the putting surface. I opted for a good old-fashioned Scottish links chip-and-run with my wedge struck – imparting a bit of top-spin for good measure – and the ball scooted on past the pin by eight feet. I think that played tricks with Sluman's mind because it made the green look faster than it really was so he went for a high, flop shot which landed and died fifteen feet short. When he missed, I managed to coax ball into hole for my most important victory on the US Tour to date and one which brought the added bonus of a ten-year exemption from having to qualify for the US Tour.

The question of whether the Players' Championship, as it is known, should be granted 'fifth Major' status is one that has caused great controversy on both sides of the Atlantic since it was founded in 1974. If time be the only criteria, then the TPC has little right to be granted admittance, something to which I referred in a throwaway remark after my victory in '87. 'What's the difference between the TPC and the British Open, Sandy?' demanded an American reporter. 'Oh,' replied I, 'about one hundred years.'

I was being unfairly flippant because, in many ways, the TPC is a better tournament than the US PGA. The field is chosen entirely on merit over the preceding twelve months plus a couple of 'wild card' invitations, so there are no amateurs or American club pros, and the list of winners is as impressive as the PGA's – perhaps even more so. It includes Jack Nicklaus, Lee Trevino, Raymond Floyd, Lanny Wadkins, Fred Couples, Jerry Pate, Greg Norman, Davis Love, Nick Price, David Duval and Tiger Woods. Traditionalists will argue that golf – like tennis with Wimbledon and the US, French and Australian Opens – should comprise just four Majors, but all sports are continually evolving and I am willing to be persuaded that the TPC is worthy of elevation, and not just because I am a past winner.

Although my 1987 victory was something of a hollow triumph because I did not have my family around me to celebrate with, it showed me how tough the mind can be. Christine and my separation had come as no great shock. The pressures of playing golf around the world can eventually have a devastating effect on the most rock-like relationships, but being away from the boys hurt like hell and I found it incredibly difficult to put a brave face on it during the prize-giving ceremony.

Perhaps not surprisingly, given my personal circumstances, the week after the TPC, I missed the cut in the Greater Greensboro Open and with the Masters looming, decided to head back to Jacksonville for some sunshine golf in a private plane thoughtfully provided by my good friend Neil MacPherson. Doughnuts and car magazines on a private jet – the way to go!

After hacking round Augusta in 77, 74, 68, 72 to finish joint seventeenth behind Larry Mize – who holed an outrageous 140-yard on the eleventh to defeat Greg Norman at the second play-off hole – I returned home to the heartbreaking prospect of living in an empty and silent house where I was used to the rooms reverberating to the laughter of my two boisterous and beloved laddies.

Christine readily agreed that I could see the boys as often as I wanted, which dulled the ache, and I threw myself into playing golf, frequently not very well. I travelled to Monticello for the Italian Open and finished well down the field in a tie for forty-first place, fifteen shots behind Sam Torrance. What I didn't realise at the time, however, was that I was about to win a far greater prize in Jolande Huurman. I had seen Jolande, a young Dutchwoman who operated as a freelance sports masseuse on the European Tour, helping the likes of Seve and Nick Faldo with their aches and pains, at many tournaments but we had only chatted in passing. For reasons I cannot explain – I certainly was not in a jubilant mood at Monticello – when I spotted her talking to South African Gavin Levenson I walked up from behind and enveloped the unsuspecting lass in a huge bear hug before giving her a hearty smack on the cheek; a most un-Sandy-Lyle-like rush of blood to the head (or maybe heart).

Although Jolande had worked on the Tour for some time, she only had the vaguest idea of who I was. However, during the Spanish Open at Estepona the following week, I plucked up the courage to invite her round to my hotel suite for a light supper, complete with suitably romantic views of the sun setting over the Mediterranean from the balcony. I must have been smitten because I even went shopping for smoked salmon, Spanish ham, crusty bread and, knowing how the Dutch love cheese, consider-able blocks of Edam and Gouda. I also traipsed half a mile down a country road to a *bodega* in search of an impressive bottle of wine. Not being a wine buff – I know what I like and like what I know – I chose the fanciest-looking bottle which also happened to be the most expensive. Sufficient recommendation, I thought.

Feeling very satisfied with myself, I greeted Jolande's arrival by producing the bottle and two glasses – at which point she burst out laughing.

'And what is that you are giving me to drink?' she managed between giggles.

'This,' I replied, proudly brandishing the label, 'is the best bottle of wine to be found in the whole of Spain.'

'Oh, no it's not, Sandy – it's genever . . .' Instead of a bottle of rioja, Sandy the Sophisticate had been about to serve a potent Dutch gin which, to my palate, could have doubled up as a paint remover.

Over dinner I explained that Christine and I had broken up but Jolande was suitably horrified to discover she was sitting in a hotel suite with a married man. It was only with great perseverance that, a few weeks later, I persuaded her to accompany me to Dave Musgrove's legendary barbecue before the Scottish Open at Gleneagles when love blossomed. The following week we stayed together at the Greywalls Hotel during the 116th Open Championship at Muirfield won by Nick Faldo (and well done to him), a week in which we found it incredibly difficult being together while pretending *not* to be together.

On the Sunday afternoon (when I would finish joint seventeenth) Jolande caught a taxi to Edinburgh Airport en route for Holland via Heathrow before I teed off but, luckily for me, her flight was delayed for some hours and, even more luckily for me, by chance we bumped into each other at Heathrow where Jolande's massage table was held up coming through the baggage carousel causing her to miss her connecting flight. Given the prices of hotel rooms around Heathrow, I invited her to spend the night with me (my invitation was far from being the act of a Good Samaritan I have to confess) and she has been at my side ever since.

My sole European victory in Europe of a brightly chequered 1987 came at the German Masters in Stuttgart. The brainchild of Bernhard Langer and his brother, Erwin, it seemed pre-ordained that Bernie would win this inaugural event. He issued his statement of intent in the opening round when he shot a 68 to trail Tommy Armour III by two strokes while yours truly ambled round in a lacklustre 73 to lie seven off the pace. In round two Bernhard was joined by Christy O'Connor Junior at the top of the leaderboard on 137, while I moved to within five shots with a 69. Our host was out in front after the third round, but with a slender one-shot advantage over Seve Ballesteros, a steady 70 lifted me to within four shots. Better late than never, I belatedly made my move in the last round, scoring 66 against Bernie's 70 to find myself in yet another play-off.

We halved the first extra hole – the seventeenth – in regulations fours, then on the par-five eighteenth, Langer chose to hit a 3-wood off the tee which left him with another long 3-wood to the green. Uncharacteristically, he struck a low, squirty second shot off a hazardous downhill lie, which flew straight out of bounds despite the best efforts of the German spectators to keep their local hero's ball in play. I was not the most popular visitor Stuttgart has ever greeted.

Alas, 1987 was to end with four defeats; first I lost to Ian Woosnam in the final of the World Matchplay at Wentworth, then was beaten by Nick Faldo as England pipped Scotland in the final of the Dunhill Cup at St Andrews. Even worse in the eyes of my fellow Scots, I committed a major *faux pas* before the Dunhill when Sam Torrance, Gordon Brand Junior and myself decided to attend the opening ceremony in hired kilts. I was proudly surveying myself in the mirror of our room of the Old Course Hotel when Jolande piped up, 'Sandy, I think you're wearing it the wrong way round.'

Being a mere man, I followed Jolande's fashion tip and sashayed down the main staircase into the reception area where Sam's mum, June, took one look at me and burst into hysterical laughter; thanks to Jolande (and what do the Dutch know about the wearing of kilts, I ask you?) now I really did have the damn thing on back to front!

After St Andrews, it was off to Japan for the Kirin Cup, a six-man team event involving Europe, Australasia, the US and the host nation. After beating the Americans in the qualifying round-robin section, we proceeded to surrender to them when we met again in the final, my third loss at the end of the year.

While St Andrews will forever remain the spiritual home of golf, Tokyo is now home to the ancient game's most passionate practitioners, the *kichigai* (golf nuts). For those able to afford the prohibitive membership fees of a club near the centre of the city – before the economic slump, membership of the ultra-exclusive Koganei Country Club cost £2.75 million with an annual subscription of £50,000 – untold luxury awaits, even if you have to arrive on the first tee before 6 a.m. to be certain of beating the crowds.

Velvet fairways, flawless greens, an open-air spa bath by the ninth green, computerised mini-monorail systems to whisk your clubs along the edge of the fairways, moving walkways to speed those weary limbs on to the next elevated tee, and the finest food and *sake* – such is life for your pampered Japanese club member.

Funnily enough, it is estimated that fewer than one in six of Japan's 15 million regular golfers has ever set foot on an actual course. How very wise . . . The three-tiered Shiba range in central Tokyo has space for 240 golfers, an Olympic-sized pool, a sushi bar, two restaurants, massage parlour, sauna, beer garden, wine bar, ten-pin bowling and a professional's shop. Ranges are even constructed on the roofs of department stores and surrounded by 150-foot-high netting. But why venture outdoors on a dank morning? Among the table lamps and coffee tables on the sixth floor at Seibu – Selfridges with *sukiyaki* – *kichigai* can while away the hours on a glass-enclosed practice green complete with real grass and real sand bunkers. (I am reliably informed there is even a brothel in the Shinjuku area called the Hole-In-One, with a putting green in the waiting room.)

But the one thing you must never, ever do is shoot a hole in one out on the course. For as well as the traditional round of drinks for everyone in the clubhouse (a small beer costs a large fortune by our standards and there might be 200 members in attendance at any given time), the lucky golfer is also expected to complete the following rigmarole: give engraved clocks noting the course, hole and date for close friends and relatives and cigarette lighters similarly embossed to workmates, provide a generous tip for the caddie, not to mention a new cherry blossom tree for the club. Aye, success comes at a high price in Japan.

Following the triple disappointments of the World Matchplay, Dunhill Cup and Kirin Cup, a fourth frustration came along in the World Cup at one of my favourite venues, Kapaula, even if the weather – gale-force winds and driving rain – was more reminiscent of Helensburgh in November than Hawaii. With Sam

Torrance wearing the other Scotland sweater, we issued a joint declaration of intent by winning the Pro-Am and were always in contention once the tournament proper was under way. After seventy-two holes, we were tied with Wales – Woosie and David Llewellyn – on a two-under-par aggregate of 574, only to lose the title in a play-off at the second extra hole. Woosie undoubtedly deserved to win the individual title, though, having completed his four rounds in the heaviest rain seen in Maui in a quarter of a century, in a remarkable fourteen under par. He won by five shots from that seemingly perpetual runner-up, Sandy from Scotland.

As 1987 drew to a close, my New Year's resolution was to add a few more titles to my CV and on 10 January I flew to America with Jolande for the opening event of the US Tour, the Tournament of Champions at La Costa in Carlsbad, California. There I birdied the first hole of my first round. Was that an omen for my fortunes in 1988? California was struck by hurricane winds during the fourth round, so the event was decided over fifty-four holes, at which time I lay joint sixteenth. Steve Pate was declared the winner. After tying for twenty-fifth place in the Bob Hope Classic in Palm Springs on eleven under par (aye, it's a tough life in America) with an average of thirty-one putts per round, which the Americans regard as pathetic, it was on to the Arizona desert for the Phoenix Open at Scottsdale.

I repeat, it's a tough life in America, and despite compiling three successive 68s at Scottsdale, I entered the final round some seven shots behind Davis Love III. Before leaving for the course, I told my friend Richie Alamo, with whom I always stayed when in the area, that I felt if I shot a 64, I thought I could still be in with a chance. Richie, who sported the most luxuriant beard, promised to shave off his whiskers if I did, indeed, return a 64.

Perhaps it was because I thought I was due off at 11.05 a.m. rather than 11.01 a.m. and, consequently, did not have time to think, but I leapt from the first tee like a voracious greyhound sniffing rabbit stew, holing a fifteen-foot putt for a birdie on the opening hole.

The pin position on the second was clearly the work of a devious mind, the flag lying only a few feet from a deep bunker. The sensible approach was to aim for the green some way from the flag. Was it the image of Richie's shiny chin? My 6-iron landed the ball six inches from the cup for a second successive birdie. After squandering further birdie opportunities on the fifth and sixth, I clawed back another shot on the ninth with an 8-iron to fifteen feet to reach the turn in a three-under-par 32. Start sharpening that razor, Richie, I thought as I made my way to the tenth, where another golden birdie opportunity passed me by.

The eleventh at Scottsdale has been the graveyard of many. The fairway curls along a lake with the green sitting like a little peninsula in the water. With the flag on the left of the green, I drew the ball towards both bin and water and heaved a sigh of relief when it came to rest twenty feet past the hole. When I holed my fourth birdie putt of the day, I found myself punching the air in jubilation, which is not like the Sandy Lyle I know at all. When I moved to five under par for the day on the thirteenth, I discovered that the electronic leaderboards had gone on the blink and, consequently, I had no idea where I was lying in relation to the leaders. Spotting former pro turned TV commentator Steve Melnyk standing high above us on a scaffold, Mussie asked for the latest information. 'Sandy's one behind Freddie Couples,' was the encouraging answer.

Having begun the final round seven shots off the pace, I drew level with a birdie at the fifteenth and stood on the seventeenth tee, a short par-four where it is possible to drive the front of the green 324 yards away, providing you avoid the various water and bunker hazards. I opted to do just that – much to Mussie's amazement I have to say – and two putts from thirty yards took me to seven under par for the round, sixteen under par for the tournament, and needing a par on the last hole for a 64. I could not wait to see the look on Richie's whiskerless face. As Rabbie Burns so wisely put it, 'the best laid schemes of mice and men gang aft a'gley'. Thinking more about getting to work on Richie's chin with the shears rather than winning the damn tournament, I dumped my 7-iron approach into a greenside bunker to drop my only shot of the afternoon and allow Richie to make his great escape. He was standing ashen-faced (or what we could see of his face) at greenside and thought it was all over – but it wasn't. I enjoyed something of an escape myself when Couples, requiring a four on the last to beat me by one shot, snap-hooked his drive across the 180-yard-wide stretch of water bordering the fairway, his ball bouncing off towards the tented village, before hitting a little old lady on the calf, and rebounding into the lake.

Come the play-off, Freddie and I shared the first two extra holes – the sixteenth and seventeenth – and found ourselves back on the eighteenth tee with me thinking, 'Well, lightning won't strike twice – he's bound to aim down the right this time away from danger.' But lightning did, indeed, strike twice. Freddie fired his drive slap bang into the middle of the lake, allowing me the luxury of two putts from six feet for my third victory in America.

I might also have won again in the Honda Classic at Eagle Trace, Florida, but drove into a bunker on the seventy-second.

The ball came to rest right up against the lip, requiring me to play with one foot on the sand and the other on the bank. The resultant bogey handed Joey Sindelar the title by a single stroke. Typically Lyle, after my defence of the TPC came to a premature end when I missed the halfway cut with rounds of 79, 72, the following week I regained the Greater Greensboro Open title that I had won two years previously. After an opening 68, I made my charge on the Friday afternoon when I had twenty-seven putts in a round of 63, striking the ball so far and so straight that Mussie – never one for flowery praise – admitted that he had enjoyed watching me so much he would happily have paid for the privilege.

Adding a third-round 68, by the turn on the final Sunday afternoon, I held a three-shot lead over Jeff Sluman, with Ken Green another stroke behind and the rest of the field nowhere. I was sauntering along on cruise-control when Green exploded into action with birdies on the tenth, eleventh and thirteenth, which I bogeyed. Having held a comfortable advantage forty-five minutes or so earlier, I was suddenly in a tie for the lead with the charging Green. Even worse was to follow on the seventeenth where Green holed a monster putt for a birdie, and the championship, which had looked to be mine, appeared to be slipping inexorably away. Through the back of the green with my approach to the eighteenth, I hit the hole with my chip – had the flag been in place the ball might well have struck it and dropped instead of remaining above ground – leaving Green a three-footer for the title. Whether he was guilty of complacency I cannot say, but the ball spun out and, having been granted this last-minute reprieve, I set off for the sixteenth tee to begin our play-off with a renewed jauntiness in my step.

A perfect drive left me with a simple wedge to six feet whereas Green needed a 6-iron for his approach, which he dumped into a greenside bunker and from where he did well to land the ball within four feet of the flag. When my birdie putt dropped, my first prize of $180,000, added to my winning cheque in Phoenix ($118,000), plus my runners-up cash from the Honda Classic ($52,266), made me the first ever European to head the US money list. The only negative aspect was that the Masters was due to begin in four days' time and the last player to triumph at Augusta after winning the previous week was Sam Snead back in 1949. History was against me but, what was it Oscar Wilde said? 'The one duty we have to history is to rewrite it' – or as Henry Ford so memorably put it, 'History is bunk . . .'

Ryder Cup

The Greenbrier, West Virginia, 1979. Bernard Gallacher, me, Brian Barnes and Ken Brown (wearing team colours you note) ready to take on the Americans.

Tony Jacklin was a constant source of encouragement and advice for a terrified rookie.

Walton Heath, Surrey, 1981. The 'Dream Team'. No wait, this is us. Trousers still fully intact … but not for long.

PGA National, 1983, Florida. Flying out in great style. And on Concorde.

GETTY IMAGES

PETER DAZELEY

EMPICS

The Belfry, Warwickshire, 1985. 'Each and every one of us knows what we have to do over the coming days,' so began Tony Jacklin's team talk on the eve of the tournament.

And boy did we do it.

POPPERFOTO

PETER DAZELEY

Muirfield Village, Ohio, 1987. Preparing to retain the trophy. 'Head steady Seve. Ollie, watch his stance.'

Langer and Lyle. What a pairing.
He chips in against Nelson and Wadkins …
I help him up. Teamwork.

Played three, won three.

POPPERFOTO

We'd done it. For the first time in fourteen attempts we'd beaten the Americans in their own backyard. Cue wild party. Well, Sam and Woosie were there after all …

I didn't realise at that special moment that I'd never play Ryder Cup golf again.

A Wonderful Life

'Don't look, Shandy. That guy's packing a piece. His jammy piece I think.'

'The grip's fine, and with a nice pastel sweater, you'll be the complete golfer.'

'I thought I was teaching you how to drive, Nigel.'

Special Agent Lyle. With my good friend Neville Cramer; I was aiming for the target on the left.

'I'm fine, honestly. If someone could just find my stomach …'

EMPICS

Alfred Dunhill Cup, 1992. It was always an honour to play for my country. Diddymen bunnets were all the rage at the time, I promise.

Three past champions practising at Augusta.

My great friend Seve.

Some Players Do Have Them!!

PETER DAZELEY

Mussie riveted by the action.

The best caddie of them all.

('That's what you told me to say, right Jolande?')

PHIL SHELDON

PETER DAZELEY

'Thank goodness you mentioned it darling. I would have looked a prat if I'd worn the kilt back to front ...'

World Cup in Hawaii, 1987. The weather was more like Helensburgh in November but Sam insisted on wearing his shades to look cool.

The Old Course in June. Or is it St Moritz? Hard to tell.

GETTY IMAGES

The Open, 2005, St Andrews. I proved I can still mix it with the best.

August 2006. At home in Balquidder. Peaceful and happy with my kids James, Quintin, Lonneke and Stuart.

CHAPTER THIRTEEN

FIFTEEN FEET, MAYBE
MORE, TO WIN . . .

Our arrival into Georgia from North Carolina was delayed. Well, when I say 'our' arrival, I actually mean all the players and their families who had been with us at the Greater Greensboro Open. Those heading for the Masters were on a charter flight which Jolande and I were responsible for keeping on the tarmac for quite some time as I first negotiated the play-off with Ken Green and then the press scrum that followed. It was late on the Sunday by the time we arrived at the Holiday Inn and we just bunkered down (pun entirely intended given what was to happen the following Sunday) on the Monday, trying to relax. Oh, and obviously getting a haircut on the balcony of the hotel was part of that plan, in full view of anyone interested in the business of the leader of the US money list. You'd have thought I could afford a decent barber at least, but Jolande had done the job earlier in the year so we had to keep the luck going – not that we are superstitious you understand . . .

I'd been entranced by Augusta National ever since my first visit in 1980 and although feeling physically and emotionally drained from my efforts at Greensboro, I *knew* that this was a championship I could win. After all, if I extracted the four best rounds from my six previous appearances in the tournament – 70, 68, 68, 65 – that 271 total would have been good enough to win the Green Jacket every year for the last decade.

A 65 on my final round in 1988? That would have done me. It would have saved me from some of the most nerve-racking moments of my career, although shooting a score like that would also perhaps have robbed me of the distinction of playing one of the most talked-about shots in Masters, perhaps golfing, history. But as things worked out, my appearance in various 'Golf's Greatest Moments' videos and DVDs was to be safe. I was to be well short of seven under for the final eighteen, even though I knew it was possible – I'd done it in the past and only two years previously perhaps the greatest champion of them all had matched that score in astonishing fashion. I should know, I watched every shot.

In 1986, I had gone into the final round tied with Jack Nicklaus in ninth place on 214, only four strokes behind overnight leader Greg Norman but facing what might have been the strongest last-day leaderboard ever assembled in a Major championship. As Jack and I teed off and I pondered the quality of the players who would follow us up the first fairway, I was reminded of his comment the previous evening when he was asked what it would take to win. 'Sixty-six will tie and a sixty-five will win it,' he prophesied. To my ears, however, it sounded like an impossible dream for either of us when you considered the players we would have to overhaul:

Greg Norman	-6
Seve Ballesteros	-5
Bernhard Langer	-5
Nick Price	-5
Donnie Hammond	-5
Tom Watson	-4
Tom Kite	-4
Tommy Nakajima	-4
Jack Nicklaus	-2
Sandy Lyle	-2

For six holes, Jack's prediction appeared beyond the capabilities of either of us as we amiably chatted our way round the course without picking up any early birdies, which might have inspired a charge. I was happy to be part of what I thought would be our two-man support cast and I think Jack – who had been dismissed as 'done, washed-up and through' in a newspaper article before the tournament – was simply content to be playing in the fifth-last pairing of a Major again after several barren years. At the par-four seventh, Jack struck a pretty poor tee-shot into the rough down the right from where he could only hack it on about a hundred yards. He now faced a treacherous 7-iron off a downhill lie to a flag situated in the back left corner of a baked-hard green, meaning the landing area was about the size of a coffee table. It was a near impossible shot but Jack put the ball within a foot of the hole to save par, a timely reminder that here was a guy who could play a bit.

At the eighth, the 535 yard par-five, Jack's driver again let him down and his ball sailed into the trees. Standing in the middle of the fairway, I could see him pluck his 3-wood from the bag, so I imagined that he had not only found a good lie but had been doubly fortunate to have a relatively easy escape route. To the accompaniment of the loud clatter of club hitting branches, his ball sailed 220 yards towards the green as the crowd went ballistic. When Jack finally emerged from the undergrowth, he was sporting a sheepish smile. 'I was aiming at a gap of about ten feet, didn't connect properly, but the ball found a gap of less than ten inches.' From a position where he might have dropped one or even two shots, he again saved par, which suggested the golfing gods might just be with him on this day.

That gut feeling intensified when the Golden Bear drilled home birdie putts from eleven feet on the ninth and twenty-five feet at the tenth but, even so, he was still four shots adrift of Seve, who had moved on to eight under par by holing out from forty yards for an eagle on the eighth. All this time I was playing well if not spectacularly (I eventually went round in 71 to finish joint eleventh) but as the mixture of excited roars and sympathetic sighs went up from different parts of the course, I felt privileged to have the best seat in the house throughout the unfolding drama.

When Seve bogeyed the ninth behind us and Jack claimed his third successive birdie on the eleventh, the gap had shrunk to just two shots, only for the advantage to swing Seve's way yet again when the Golden Bear dropped a shot on the short twelfth to fall three behind. On the par-five thirteenth, he crashed his drive so close to the trees that Jack Junior, who was caddying for his dad, complained, 'This is too much for my twenty-four-year-old heart, Pop.'

'What about mine? I'm forty-six,' grinned Pop, striking an imperious 3-iron to thirty feet from the hole for yet another birdie and yet another crescendo of noise from his adoring following. Seve, determined to win a third Green Jacket following his victories in 1980 and 1983, surpassed Jack's feat when it was his turn to play the thirteenth with a sumptuous 6-iron to eight feet for his second eagle of the round. That took him into a seemingly unassailable four-stroke lead. It had become the clash of two titans. On the par-five fifteenth, Jack launched a humungous drive of 298 yards, leaving him 202 yards to the green. 'Do you think this would be a good time for an eagle, son?' he asked Jack Junior, before unleashing a mighty 3-iron to eight feet from the hole, thus reducing the deficit to two as the crowds whooped and hollered.

The noise each and every one of Jack's shots generated was deafening, never more so than on the par-three sixteenth, where his 5-iron split the pin, coming to rest six feet behind the hole before rolling ever so slowly to within three feet. I steered a nice 6-iron to twenty feet for a birdie – as if anyone noticed! Whether he was unnerved by the cacophony of cheers that greeted Jack's latest birdie, back on the fifteenth Seve dumped his approach into the water whereas his playing partner, Tom Kite, made his move with a birdie. Although still trying to concentrate on my own golf, even I could not fail to experience a tingle of excitement as I glanced at the leaderboard on our way to the seventeenth tee:

Ballesteros	-8
Kite	-8
Nicklaus	-8
Norman	-6

I cannot overemphasise the level of noise. It was quite unlike anything I have ever experienced on a golf course before or since. The so-called washed-up old has-been could have made a comfort stop and even this simple call of nature would have been cheered to the rafters. On the seventeenth, Jack drove into the rough on the left and was swallowed up by the swarm of spectators. If I could not see him, I certainly had a clear sight of his ball as it emerged from the throng to land eleven feet from the hole. He was still faced with a wicked double-borrow putt, the type of putt that if you attempted it thirty times, you might – with luck – hole once. After racking his brains, trying to gauge the right line, when Jack hit it, he appeared to know that it was going nowhere but straight into the middle of the hole. He stalked the ball every inch of the way with the eye of a tiger. Cue new outbreak of pandemonium. The Golden Bear was now in sole possession of the lead, and the impossible dream had become a distinct possibility. Poor Seve, it was somehow inevitable that minutes later he would three putt the same green, but Kite, still only one shot back on eight under par, had been joined by Greg Norman after the Australian's back-to-back birdies on the fifteenth and sixteenth.

Not surprisingly, we (well, Jack, to be strictly accurate) were cheered every step of the 405 yard eighteenth, which, disappointingly perhaps, Jack failed to birdie, tapping in for a par-four and the 65 that he had predicted would 'win it'. Now, all he had to do was wait.

Kite had a twelve-foot birdie putt on the eighteenth to force a play-off but the ball lipped the hole. Then Norman, having birdied the seventeenth, arrived on the seventy-second and last hole of the fiftieth Masters requiring a birdie to snatch the Green Jacket from the Golden Bear's hungry claws. The Australian sliced his approach into the gallery, chipped on to sixteen feet, missed the putt and, at the venerable age of 46, Jack Nicklaus had won his eighteenth Major championship. For the record, from the ninth tee that climactic afternoon at Augusta, Jack scored birdie, birdie, birdie, bogey, birdie, par, eagle, birdie, birdie, par – seven under par through ten of the toughest holes in golf. That is the play of a true master.

In *New Yorker* magazine, writer and golf historian Herbert Warren Wind described this victory as '. . . nothing less than the most important accomplishment in golf since Bobby Jones's Grand Slam in 1930', while in his telegram of good wishes to his old friend, Arnold Palmer wrote, 'Congratulations. That was fantastic! Do you think there's any hope for a fifty-six-year-old?'

For my part, Jack had been one of my earliest heroes, so to be chief witness of his extraordinary triumph remains a highlight of my career, and having savoured the atmosphere around the eighteenth green as an onlooker, it intensified my desire to experience it again in the future – but next time as the centre of attention.

And so it proved to be two years later, even if I was full of nagging doubts as myself, Jolande, Mum and Dad (who had flown in from the UK) and Dave Musgrove sat in a McDonald's eating our breakfast and relishing the only decent cup of tea we could find (it was all down to the water not being hot enough in other places, Mum explained, in that way mothers do). We had stopped off on our way to the Tuesday practice session, driving there in a head-turning Cadillac the organisers had kindly supplied. Although it was a nice feeling to arrive for the Masters as the leading money-winner on the US Tour, did that suggest I had peaked too soon by winning in Greensboro forty-eight hours earlier, or was I in the best form of my life and destined for even greater things over the coming six days? The Monday of Masters week had been taken up with press and TV interviews – when

you are number one in America, everyone wants to talk to you
– so I was eager to shake off any cobwebs and teamed up with
Ian Woosnam against Seve Ballesteros and Greg Norman, or
'Shropshire versus the Rest of the World' as we billed it. The
contest ended honours even, although Woosie and I lost twenty
bucks apiece in side-bets.

By habit, I do not normally like playing practice rounds at
Augusta where, before they tightened up on such things, you
could be constantly interrupted by radio reporters, photographers
or autograph-hunters even in the middle of the fairway. It took
an age to fight your way through the throng to every tee and,
of course, if you stop to sign ninety-nine autographs, the one-
hundredth person in line would complain that you 'snubbed'
them. So because practice can be very tiring at the Masters, I
usually preferred to go out early with Mussie before most of the
crowds piled through the gates, simply noting any subtle changes.
Augusta is an exhausting course – it may not look like it on television but the drop from the tenth tee to the twelfth green is
over a hundred feet, for example – so I always thought it made
far more sense to tee-off at 7.30 a.m., say, and stroll round at
your own pace, familiarising yourself with the smells and sights,
just getting a 'feel' for the place, if you like. It also goes without
saying that the Augusta of a Tuesday practice round bears no
resemblance whatsoever to the Augusta of a Thursday when you
tee-off with the Green Jacket at stake.

By tradition, Wednesday is the date of the annual par-three
tournament, an event few want to win because of a supposed
curse. While it is an undeniable fact that no player has ever won
the par-three and the Masters in the same year, it is my continuing belief that hoodoos, like records, are made to be broken,

and I later became the first European to win this fun day out in two successive years in the early 90s.

So that was it, one practice round and an outing in the par-three contest and I was ready to meet Raymond Floyd on the first tee at 2 p.m. on a cold and windy Thursday afternoon, just about my least favourite time to set off for two important reasons. One, as the day wears on and the greens become firmer, so Augusta becomes ever more difficult, and two, when you are among the last to go, as Floyd and I were, you cannot help but monitor the leaderboard. If player after player is coming in with sub-par rounds, the pressure becomes all the greater. If the scores are in the middle to high 70s, you know Augusta is in unfor-giving mood.

With a 30mph wind wreaking havoc, only six players broke par in what Jack Nicklaus called 'the most difficult conditions at the Masters in thirty years'. All in all, therefore, I was highly satisfied with my opening eighteen holes, five birdies and four bogeys adding up to a 71. That was nine strokes better than my playing partner, Floyd, and, sadly, ten less than my wee pal Woosie, who shot an 81 on his Masters debut, but he returned in triumph three years later. The first round leaderboard read:

Larry Nelson	-3
Robert Wren	-3
Bernhard Langer	-1
Mark Calcavecchia	-1
Don Pooley	-1
Sandy Lyle	-1

It is hard not to feel paranoid when you are handed your second late starting time in as many days – 2.25 p.m. on the Friday – and although the cold wind had given way to a searing sun, my mood was not helped when I promptly bogeyed the first hole to drop back to level par. Fortunately, I responded with three swift birdies and faced a three-footer on the ninth green to assume the outright lead in the fifty-second Masters. A thirty-six-inch putt may not sound that onerous a task but this one was as vicious as a rattlesnake on a green made virtually unplayable by the heat and lack of watering. I gave the ball the tiniest nudge with the blade of my putter and to my relief it disappeared down the hole. Such was the speed and slope of the ninth green that, had I missed, the ball would undoubtedly have gathered pace and rolled right off the putting surface. Three putts were considered the norm at the ninth, nine of the ninety players in the field staggered off to the tenth tee having four-putted it.

Further birdies on the thirteenth and fifteenth lifted me to six under, a position I maintained despite driving on to the lip of a sprinkler-head on the eighteenth fairway, from where I sent my approach racing through the green and had to sink a testing ten-footer to save par. My score of 67 was bettered only by Fuzzy Zoeller, who soared up the leaderboard with a magnificent 66 then caused consternation among Augusta members by claiming the greens had been 'tricked up'. 'If you've got a downhill putt, you're just touching the ball and hoping you can make the ten-footer coming back,' bemoaned Fuzzy, as though he had shot an 86 rather than 66. 'If that's golf, I'm in the wrong damn league. Golf is supposed to be fun. This wasn't fun. It's a joke out there. You don't hear the roars from the crowds at Augusta any more. It's like a morgue. If they don't start listening to the players, they're going to be sitting around here looking at themselves and saying, "Where did we go wrong?" '

Fuzzy was not alone in his vehement criticism. Ben Crenshaw

agreed saying, 'There may not be anything living on the eleventh green. They need to call the Augusta fire department,' while Fred Couples said, 'You just can't hit your putts soft enough.' Charles Coody, the 1971 Masters champion, called it 'goony golf'.

It was hard not to have sympathy with that sentiment but whereas Fuzzy generated hostility, I inspired hilarity during my press conference when I let slip that one of the reasons behind my leading the Masters was because Jolande had been 'tickling my feet' at night.

To explain, I had suffered an allergic reaction to the Georgia pollen and was having difficulty breathing through my nose during the night, which was interfering with my sleep. Jolande, being something of an expert in reflexology, massaged the pressure points on the soles of my feet and – hey presto! – I was cured. The headline writers, as you can imagine, made merry with the tale of Sandy and Jolande's hotel bedroom secrets: 'Why Sandy Likes a Tickle in Bed'; 'Big Sandy's Foot Fetish' and all that kind of thing.

Tickling feet notwithstanding, after a day of high scores – first round joint leader Larry Nelson had nine bogeys in his 79 – I could but look forward to the weekend shoot-out with renewed confidence:

Sandy Lyle	-6
Mark Calcavecchia	-4
Gary Hallberg	-2
Fuzzy Zoeller	-2
Don Pooley	-1

As Chi Chi Rodriguez famously observed, 'that Green Jacket plays castanets with your knees', but I could hear no such warning noise on the outward nine holes of the third round as I collected birdies on the second and eighth to move into a four-stroke lead over the pursuing posse. Augusta exacted retribution at the thirteenth, where I struck my one poor shot of the day, and on the sixteenth when dame fortune turned her heartless back on me. The thirteenth, the fragrant sounding Azalea, features a sharp, almost 90 degree dogleg to the left and, frustrated by the long delays on that and the previous three tees, I foolishly hammered my drive into the creek bordering the fairway, from where I was relieved to escape with a bogey six.

The 170 yard sixteenth, with a 'fairway' comprised almost entirely of water, has been the ruination of many Masters' hopes over the years. If my tee-shot had pitched just six inches to the left, the ball would have rolled down the slope towards the hole, instead of which it bounced through the green into the thick stuff on the apron. With the ball nestling in grass that I can only liken to wire wool, I was a mere foot or so off the putting surface but I knew that if I tried to chip the ball out, there was a risk it might run all the way down and off the green at the other side. The putter represented my only option but even that was fraught with danger. I had to hit the ball with sufficient force to clear the apron, but then almost draw to a halt before trickling down to the pin. One revolution more and the ball would have done just that but it remained defiantly on the very edge of the green for my second bogey.

By Saturday evening, the top of the leaderboard had become as crowded as Oxford Street on Christmas Eve. Six Green Jacket owners – Seve Ballesteros, Bernhard Langer, Craig Stadler, Ben Crenshaw, Fuzzy Zoeller and Tom Watson – were among those in close attendance. Watson, champion in 1977 and 1981, had been among the very few to defend the speed and contours of the greens saying, 'It's like what my friend Sandy Tatum [a former president of the US Golf Association] once said. "We're not trying to embarrass the best players in the world. We're trying to identify them." ' So when he four-putted the sixteenth, missing three times from as many feet, Fuzzy Zoeller was heard to mutter darkly, 'I hope he enjoyed every stroke.'

Sandy Lyle	-6
Ben Crenshaw	-4
Mark Calcavecchia	-4
Bernhard Langer	-2
Fred Couples	-2
Fuzzy Zoeller	-2
Seve Ballesteros	-1
Craig Stadler	-1
Don Pooley	-1
Tom Watson	level

I did not sleep well, waking up at 2 a.m. in need of Jolande's gentle ministrations before drifting off again. With the dawn came the same sheer gut-wrenching panic I used to feel as a child while sitting in the dentist's waiting-room contemplating the pain to come and fully aware that it might be even more intense than my worst imaginings. I was not due to tee off with Ben Crenshaw in the final group until 2.55 p.m. so I was stuck in that mental waiting-room for many hours, my mind spinning like a tumble dryer at full speed. I felt so many emotions and so many different thoughts filtering through my head – that the difference between sporting triumph and disaster, always a very, very thin dividing line, is even more slender at Augusta; that I could feel the breaths of the greatest players in the world on the back of my neck; that this could be the last time I would ever be in contention on the final day of the Masters, so I might as well make the most if it, enjoy it, in fact; that I was better being two shots in front than ten strokes behind; that there would be frustrations, putts that would not drop, shots that would land in bunkers or in water, long delays, so always remember Dad's mantra, 'tempo before temper'; that I was nearing the end of my physical reserves, given my efforts at Greensboro the weekend before; that I had now led the fifty-second Masters for twenty-seven holes and had never been renowned as a front-runner; that with the temperature in the high 80s, the next few hours would test mind and body to the absolute limit; that any tension and pressure I had felt during the previous seventy-two holes was nothing in comparison to what lay ahead; that I had proved I could win a Major in the Open Championship at Royal St George's in 1985, and now I had a glorious opportunity to double my collection; and what I would not give for a 65 like Jack Nicklaus's two years earlier. All that apart, I was quite calm.

If I could have selected the perfect companion for my round of destiny, it would have been Ben Crenshaw, or 'Gentle Ben' as he is known. His air of relaxed composure evidently rubbed off on me as I smacked a perfect drive up over the hill to run down the first fairway. I breathed a huge sigh of relief even though the leaderboard showed that Greg Norman, eleven adrift at the start of his final round, had gone out in an astonishing 30 to soar from five over to one under, Don Pooley had birdied the first three holes to move to four under, and Mark Calcavecchia had reduced my advantage to a single shot with a long putt on the opening green. I needed to react swiftly to the various dangers and a drive and 7-iron to the second green set me up for a birdie four.

On the par-three fourth, my 5-iron fizzer not only cleared the green (where is the swirling breeze at Augusta when you need it?) but came to rest in a nasty, little valley twenty yards from the flagstick. Faced with a downhill lie on to a sloping green as hard as ice, it was a situation that had 'bogey!' emblazoned across it. My preferred shot would have been a modified pitch and run but with so little green to work with, there was every chance the ball would squirt past the pin and disappear into the front bunker, so I had to take my sand-iron and play a high floater fifteen yards through the air. Miraculously, the ball landed as softly as I could have wished on a projected landing area no bigger than a dinner-plate, and rolled straight into the centre of the hole, transforming a potential bogey four into the unlikeliest of birdie twos. Ben Crenshaw later said that although it was my bunker shot on the eighteenth that would go down in golfing folklore, that chip on the fourth was ten times more difficult.

If that chip carried a measure of luck about it, there was also an element of justice because, according to Nick Royds of the R & A, my ball was the first one for which the crowd ringed around the edge of the green had parted and allowed to run through all day. That fourth hole was crucial to my momentum, especially when I three-putted the sixth from forty feet after the breeze had sent my approach far left of the green. On the seventh, I pulled a 1-iron into the trees a hundred yards from the green and although I managed to fashion an escape route through the branches, the ball came up short and rolled into a bunker, from where I splashed out to twelve feet and sank the putt for a morale-boosting par.

As Mussie and I made our way to the eighth tee, news came that up in front, Craig Stadler had just eagled the hole and was now two behind in second place on five under. 'Don't worry about it, Sandy,' Mussie told me. 'They're going to be making charges all afternoon and you'll just have to live with it. There are six former Masters champions snapping at your heels and they'll all be thinking they can catch you.'

Well, catch me if you can, I thought, firing a terrific 7-iron off a downhill lie on to the green of the boomerang-shaped ninth, where the pin was situated at its most teasing on the front left. The ball pitched ten feet beyond the flag, then spun back to about thirty-six inches from the hole to give me an outward half of two-under-par 34 and a three-stroke cushion, which, when you are about to run the gauntlet of Amen Corner, is not nearly as comfortable at it may seem. Officially, Augusta's Amen Corner does not exist. You will certainly not find the name on any map of the course. It was invented by American writer Herbert Warren Wind in honour of the miraculous manner in which Arnold Palmer covered the eleventh, twelfth and thirteenth holes on his way to victory in 1958. Thirty years later, this little corner of Augusta was almost 'Amen and rest in peace' to my Masters ambitions.

Although I struck an ideal drive down the eleventh, the ball picked up a clump of red, Georgian clay slap bang on the contact area. I had aimed right of the green to avoid the water down the left, but because of the mud – and you could see the ball performing all sorts of weird and wonderful aerial manoeuvres in mid-flight – it drifted farther right than I intended into the fringe. I was not actually on the green, so Mussie was prohibited from lifting my ball to clean it, and concerned about what effect the mud would have on the ball's speed and line, I left my first putt eight feet short and missed the next for a bogey five, which was extremely annoying having started the hole flawlessly only fifteen minutes before.

While standing on the eleventh green waiting for Crenshaw to putt, I looked over to the par-three twelfth where Bernhard Langer – who hits his short irons roughly the same distance as me – was about to tee-off. He struck an 8-iron to the rear, right-hand side of the green. I thought, 'Thanks, Bernie, an eight-iron it is.'

The twelfth – Golden Bell by name, Living Hell by nature – is the shortest hole on the course at 155 yards, and one of the most treacherous. In the first round of the 1980 Masters, Tom Weiskopf needed six attempts to clear Rae's Creek, which bites into the front of the green, before two-putting for a thirteen. As his wife Jeanne choked back the tears, a friend of Tom's leaned over and lightened the mood of despair by asking, 'Tom's not using new balls, is he?' If you clear the water, more trouble lies ahead on the green. The wind can spring up in an instant and whistle around the trees, creating a vortex. On a gusty after-noon, the wind can dump the ball short or carry it twenty yards over the green, according to whimsy, so I was relieved to step on to the twelfth tee and discover not a single leaf moving. It was so still, it was almost eerie.

The pressure was beginning to build – I now led Calcavecchia by two strokes with Stadler another shot away in third place, but two par-fives were coming up and I knew that, if I could emerge at the other end of Amen Corner with my advantage intact, I would be in a very strong position to ward off any challengers. The clubface of my 8-iron struck the ball maybe one millimetre too low (such can be the margin between victory and defeat) but directly on line, which raised hopes it would land within five feet of the hole. Another birdie and it would surely be game, set and match, as we say in golf. Agonisingly, the ball cleared the creek by four yards but landed a few inches short of the green, paused as if trying to make up its mind whether to stay there or not, then rolled at gathering speed back down into the water. It was a truly sinking feeling.

'That was a shit shot, shit, shit, shit,' I berated myself, while Mussie, as usual, was the voice of reason. 'Aye, but it's done. That's ancient history now. Let's play the next shot and just make sure you don't take a five.' I took a drop at about seventy yards from the pin but although it was an A-plus chip shot – a foot or so less and it would have trickled into Rae's Creek for a second time – I was unable to hold the ball on the green, which was becoming harder by the minute in the pizza-oven temperature of the Georgian sun, and it rolled on through the back. Each successive shot was becoming that little bit harder. I was now confronted by six feet of fringe followed by a sloping green – a mite too hard and the water awaited, so when I finally trudged away having signed for a two-over-par five, it was almost with a sense of relief. The bogey and double-bogey on the eleventh and twelfth meant that, having led the Masters for thirty-eight holes since midway through the second round, I had now been joined on five under by Calcavecchia and Stadler. Bernhard Langer was hovering one shot behind, but even before I had made my way to the thirteenth tee, the leaderboard had been altered again to reflect the latest news from farther up the course:

Stadler	-6
Calcavecchia	-6
Lyle	-5
Langer	-4

At 465 yards, however, the par-five thirteenth represented a relatively straightforward birdie opportunity. I hit a huge drive across trees to bypass the dogleg, leaving me a 7-iron of just 170 yards to the flag. Whether I had subconsciously spotted the creek on the right in my mind's eye, I slightly pulled my approach shot and the ball bounced on to the so-called hog's back, which divides the green. Six inches either side of the ridge and I would have had a putt for an eagle but, with luck against me of late, the ball took a hard sideways bounce through Nicklaus's Valley – a marshy, swampy furrow which Mussie helpfully informed me had been added by the Golden Bear in a moment of heartlessness during one of Augusta's frequent redesigns – and into a greenside bunker. When I surveyed the lie, my spirits sank even lower. The ball was resting in a small hole on a downward slope to the rear of the sand-trap, preventing me from imparting the clubhead speed I would need to generate any spin on the ball, which would behave as though badly plugged. Ideally, I would have opted to play a high, floating shot but, to all intents and purposes, I might have been handcuffed so restricted was my swing. I had to play out almost sideways. To have aimed at the pin would have been to risk another visit to the water and then I would have been contemplating a seven or even worse. That left me a fifteen-foot putt for a birdie, which, unsurprisingly given my recent adventures, I missed. Although a par five went down on my scorecard, I knew it was a shot dropped rather than saved.

Augusta was also making mischief for those around me. Having negotiated Amen Corner, Bernhard Langer bogeyed the fourteenth, fifteenth and sixteenth to fall away, then Stadler bogeyed the sixteenth to join me on five under, leaving Calcavecchia in sole possession of the lead. Reassuringly, I still felt I was playing well and in control of both my swing and nerves, a belief reinforced by the 7-iron second shot I landed inside eight feet of the pin on the fourteenth. Neither Mussie nor I were entirely confident about the right line and my birdie putt missed by a hair's-breadth. While waiting to hit my approach to the fifteenth, Mussie became unusually loquacious. 'What a lovely view you get from up here,' he said, surveying the water, green, crowds and flowers beyond. The he turned serious. 'OK, you've lost the lead and now it's you doing the chasing, but think of it as a weight that's been taken off your shoulders. Use that to your advantage. Let Calcavecchia do the work for a change.'

Conscious that it was on this exact spot that Seve Ballesteros's lingering hopes vanished in 1986 when he went for the flag and watched in horror as his ball sank without trace in the water guarding the green, allowing Jack Nicklaus to snatch the Green Jacket, I aimed for the middle of the target. My 5-iron approach landed on the rock-hard surface and kicked twelve feet or so into the back fringe. Under the pressurised circumstances, I manufactured a glorious chip that looked like dropping but teased the hole and slid past. That left me a difficult right-to-left five-footer, which I misread. It was a crushing blow because it meant that I had covered the thirteenth and fifteenth holes in regulation par fives, two holes where, with my length off the tee, a brace of birdies should have been well within my capabilities – and I was still one stroke behind Calcavecchia.

With the flag tucked mischievously just behind the bunker on the lower tier of the par-three sixteenth green, the game plan was to keep the ball below the hole, instead of which I sent my 7-iron shot a good fifteen feet past the flag – precisely the place I did not want to be. It was the type of putt I would not have relished in a practice round, let alone the seventieth hole of the Masters, when there are no easy shots and the momentum appears to be swinging away from you. I was confronted by a putt fraught with dangers down a steep slope and with a thirty-six-inch borrow that could easily result in my having another six-footer coming back to save par. 'If it goes in, it goes in,' I told Mussie as we studied the line from every angle. 'And if it doesn't, then I'll have to face the music.' Now I could hear and feel that Green Jacket playing castanets with my knees.

Fortunately, my line and pace were absolutely perfect and although the ball was travelling at a fair old rate of knots, it dropped right in the middle of the hole. Having been faced with the prospect of a bogey four and falling two shots behind with two holes to play, I was now level with Calcavecchia and even punched the air half a dozen times in – for me – a rare outburst of jubilation. The crowd reaction may not have been quite as ecstatic as when Nicklaus was performing his miracles two years earlier, but the cheers for a Scot closing in on an American were an uplifting sound. I suppose there is nothing any sporting audience likes better than two gladiators going nose-to-nose and members of the audience were probably readying themselves for the Russian-roulette drama of a play-off.

I matched Calcavecchia's par four on the seventeenth but only after a scramble. First I hit a spectator with my drive down the left-hand side. Then, although my ball ended up in light rough, I had a wedge to the green, and a crucial birdie was a distinct possibility. I repeat, at this stage in the Masters there are no easy shots. My pitch came down two yards short of my intended landing area and the ball spun back off the green, from where I finally holed a nervy little three-footer for par.

Mark Calcavecchia, my lone rival for the Green Jacket, was not particularly well known in Europe at the time, although he had proved what a fierce competitor he was by beating Nick Faldo in the singles during the 1987 Ryder Cup at Muirfield Village. Nevertheless, he was a rising star and it was only due to illness that he never rose quite as high as his fellow professionals expected.

He was not one to crack under pressure, however, as he would show at Royal Troon in 1989 when he beat Australian duo Greg Norman and Wayne Grady in a play-off to win the Open Championship. He was also a bit of a character. Twelve months later he and some friends swigged champagne from the Claret Jug in a St Andrews' hotel, then rinsed out the telltale dregs before handing the trophy back into the safe keeping of the R & A. Calcavecchia was accused of turning up to the official dinner tipsy, late and dishevelled. 'We'd had a few drinks, yes, but drunk? Heck, no,' he explained in outrage. 'They claimed I wore jeans. Unfair again. I looked about as good as I can in a suit. The invitation said seven thirty for eight. I had to ask what that meant and was told cocktails at seven thirty, dinner at eight. My car was late arriving, so I got to the clubhouse at seven fifty-five – five minutes before dinner.'

In his fourth Ryder Cup appearance, at The Belfry in 2002, Calcavecchia was thrashed 5 and 4 by Padraig Harrington in the final afternoon's singles. After that, he was diagnosed as suffering from apnoea – a potentially fatal condition that causes brief interruptions to breathing during sleep, leading to daytime exhaustion, severe headaches and possible depression – and took to wearing an oxygen mask in bed. He had won fifteen tournaments worldwide at the time, but it is not surprising that

Calcavecchia's career went into something of a decline and I guarantee there has never been a happier winner than when he ended his four-year title drought by winning the 2005 Canadian Open. Back in the spring of 1988, he was young, lean and hungry and I was fully aware that if I wanted to slip my arms into the Green Jacket, I would have to win that right and not depend upon Calcavecchia making a mistake on the closing hole.

Standing on the eighteenth tee I knew that Calcavecchia was short of the green – just – in two. His second had actually landed on the putting surface and had rolled off, leaving a delicate chip to follow. Mark pitching in was unlikely but a par was all too possible, which would leave me with a birdie for victory and four for a play-off. And so I pondered the single most important tee-shot of my career, trying to decide what was the best way to achieve the birdie. If I opted for the kamikaze approach with my driver, that would leave me with only a 9-iron or pitching-wedge to the green, but it was a long carry over the bunker down the left side – 270 yards all uphill – and with my natural fade it was probably a risk too far. So the preferred option was to hit a 1-iron 250 yards, just short of the bunker. That should give me exactly the right angle to the pin, which was farther forward than it had been earlier in the week. Lee Trevino once advised that if you are ever caught out on the course in a lightning storm, then reach for your 1-iron 'because even God can't hit a one-iron', but it was a club I knew and trusted so the shot held no fears.

From the moment I struck the ball it looked promising in the air but the instant I saw it bounce left I thought, 'Oh no, please, *please* don't go left.' The ball was not listening and my heart missed a few beats because I knew from the way it had gone into the sand that it would probably end up flush against the face of the bunker. Although it may look like one, massive sand-trap on TV, there are actually two bunkers on the eighteenth with a grassy spine running between them. Depending on my lie, I realised it might prove very difficult to get the ball high enough quickly enough to clear the lip but also with sufficient distance to reach the green. To make matters worse, as Mussie and I walked down towards the bunker we heard an almighty cheer from up ahead. Calcavecchia had played his third and from the noise there was every chance it had gone in. Did I now need a birdie just to tie? I tried my best to look nonchalant as I approached the sand pit while inside my stomach was doing somersaults. Intense relief hit me on reaching the bunker. We discovered that the ball had come to rest on the face of the trap, giving me the advantage of an uphill rather than flat lie and bringing the green easily within range of a 7-iron. And the news had filtered back that Calcavecchia's pitch had been a delight – and had just missed the hole. He made his par. Now all I needed to win was to be down in two from here.

Crenshaw, meanwhile, had driven well left off the tee and it took him an eternity to persuade the massive crowd now following us, being the last match, to move back out of his line of sight. That delay was beneficial because it allowed me plenty of time to visualise the shot to come, to rehearse the flight of the ball in my mind over and over again. If I had not been allowed that pause for reflection, who knows what the outcome might have been? A sudden rush of blood and the ball might have caught the lip and moved forward only a hundred yards or so, or even ended up in the second bunker a few feet in front of me. As Crenshaw's ball finally emerged from the trees, I was suffused with a peculiar sense of calm. I could not see the flag from my position in the bunker, so had taken my line from a cloud behind the clubhouse, giving thanks that Augusta was windless that evening, and when the ball came out I knew instantly in my soul that it was the perfect height and on the perfect line.

Sprinting from the bunker, I watched my ball descend directly behind the pin and was disheartened not to hear a massive roar from behind the eighteenth green. Gradually, the noise began to swell as I almost jogged up the fairway telling Mussie, 'It's coming back to the pin, the ball's coming back to the pin.' By the time the cheers had reached the peak of their crescendo, I was convinced I was less than a foot from the hole. 'Tap it in, doff my cap to acknowledge the applause, sign my card, then slip my arms into the Green Jacket, thank you very much,' I thought to myself. To my dismay, when I walked on to the green I discovered I had a fifteen-foot putt to win the Masters. I know from the television footage I have seen that it appeared much shorter but, believe me, it was all of fifteen feet and maybe even more.

Again Crenshaw had gone left, into the middle of the crowd surrounding the green, from where he took ages (and ages . . . and ages . . .) to prepare to play his chip-cum-putt, while I was prowling around the green considering the grain, spike marks, speed and line, never once thinking about holing out, but merely preparing myself for a play-off against Calcavecchia. Still the delay went on as Crenshaw agonised over the six-footer he needed for par to finish in fourth place and a difference of $13,000 in prize money compared to joint fifth, which, even to a multi-millionaire, made it a putt well worth considering.

By this stage, it seemed to me as though many hours had

passed since we stepped on to the eighteenth tee just over 400 yards distant. My efforts both at Augusta and in winning the previous week at Greensboro had taken their debilitating toll. My legs felt weak and I could feel my concentration wavering – both symptoms the result of tiredness rather than nerves – and while I had been sucking up the dregs of my reserve tank for the past few holes, I was now running on empty with the red warning light flashing away. Somehow, I had managed to free-wheel my way in but the last thing I needed was an extra-time shoot-out with Calcavecchia, although I consoled myself with the thought that if a play-off was necessary, at least it would begin at the tenth, which was downhill all the way. I was so weary I could not face the prospect of an ascent up one of Augusta's exhausting slopes. It was a Sunday evening, the shadows were lengthening, it was time to pour a nice malt and put your feet up, not be hovering over a fifteen-foot putt in the near-dark to win the Masters on a crusty green.

It is funny how the mind works. As Crenshaw's ball finally dropped – thank you, Ben, now kindly leave the stage – I suddenly remembered a long-ago conversation with Lee Trevino during which he told me he would always prefer a fifteen-foot down-hill rather than a thirty-foot uphill putt to win a tournament. Trevino's reasoning was that with a downhill putt, all you have to do is set the damn thing in motion, whereas when you are feeling a bit numb, it is easy to leave an uphill putt well short. In view of the slope, I had to imagine I was aiming at a target two feet away on a line on which all the little borrows cancelled one another out, making my target the right lip.

The blade of my putter bestowed the merest kiss upon the ball and halfway to journey's end I was thinking, 'This is looking quite promising.' Four feet from the hole it looked as though it might just tickle the right edge. Two feet from the hole it was as though the ball was being operated by remote control – 'Oh, there's the hole over there, sniff, sniff, sniff' – while I was thinking, 'Crikey, it might even go in!' A couple of inches out, the ball turned slightly left as if under orders, and disappeared right down the centre of the cup. Mussie's arms went up and I performed a brief highland fling, before all the emotions of the past seven days hit me like a locomotive and I stood in a daze with a beatific smile on my face. I had joined the company of Hogan, Sarazan, Snead, Palmer, Nicklaus and Player by adding the 1988 Masters title to my 1985 Open Championship. I was a dual Major winner and the overriding emotion as I hugged Jolande was simply one of the most intense relief. Now all I had to do was compose myself sufficiently – and it is no easy matter to start doing mental arithmetic sums when you are human jelly and you have a lump in your throat the size of a tennis ball – to check my card and sign it before heading off to Butlers Cabin for the official Green Jacket presentation conducted by 1987 winner Larry Mize and Augusta chairman Hord Hardin.

Just before the presentation I had been reunited with Mum and Dad – who by then had consumed at least one large whisky to steady his nerves – on the verandah of the clubhouse. They, together with the commentary team of Steve Rider, Tony Jacklin and Nick Faldo – was it just my imagination or was dear, old Nick smiling through gritted teeth? – were waiting to greet me. 'Many congratulations, Sandy,' said Steve, 'but are you aware that you have kept the people of Britain up until two o'clock in the morning back home?' (Among them was Russ Abbott, ensconced in a hotel room in Bournemouth. Well into a bottle of champagne, he leapt into the air at the moment of triumph and almost brought down a very expensive chandelier on his head.) 'I'm sorry, the people of Britain,' was all I could come up with by way of reply as my dad thrust a reviving paper cup of Scottish golden nectar into my grateful paw.

Dad and I did not say much to each other – we had no need to. Both of us were fully aware of what the other was feeling. This was the fulfilment of a dream spanning a quarter of a century. If winning my first Major at the 1985 Open was a memorable experience, to become a double winner was to have all my wildest fantasies come true, so Dad and I just smiled at one another and if, as they say, a picture can paint a thousand words, then those smiles represented one million and more. I would have liked nothing better than to disappear into the night with my parents, Jolande and Mussie but first I had to deal with all the press and attend the official Augusta members' dinner in the clubhouse grill. Jolande took Mum and Dad back to the hotel for a wash and change while I recapped a very emotional round of golf to the world press. By the time we did all meet up again (even back in 1988 there seemed to be a hell of a lot of TV stations around the globe) Dad was certainly ready for something non-liquid in his stomach. Mum had to reprimand him – 'Alex!!!' – as he started to chat up Hord Hardin's wife at dinner and it wasn't long until he was ready for his one and only fireman's lift up to his bed.

The Holiday Inn had been the social centre of the Masters throughout the week but when Jolande and I hit the disco dance floor around midnight, all the party animals had already departed for the airport or car-hire offices. Here I was, the new Masters champion, all dressed up and nowhere to go. Instead of the rave

242

I had expected to join, I'm sorry to report that my celebrations were a bit of an anti-climax, which was probably a blessing, given that I was expected back on the course at 6.30 the following morning for an interview with CBS television.

Mussie and a group of his fellow caddies, bless 'em, more than made up for that disappointment when we arrived at Hilton Head, South Carolina for the following week's Heritage Classic by laying on a magnificent barbecue in my honour with mountains of steak, lobster and prawns. The one thing the caddies do like is a good nosh-up! After all the drama, emotion and excitement of the previous few days, I think it was there, surrounded by family, friends and well-wishers from Fleet Street, that it finally sank in: Sandy Lyle, 1985 Open champion, 1988 Masters champion, and number one on the US money-winners' list. I was standing on the pinnacle of world golf, fondly imagining there might be even better things to come . . .

CHAPTER FOURTEEN

THE GREAT SANDY LYLE MYSTERY

In the immediate aftermath of Augusta, I had no inkling of the dark days that lay ahead. Although a Scot had just sauntered off with the greatest prize of all in American eyes, the natives could not have been friendlier. Lanny Wadkins, Hubert Green, Curtis Strange, Paul Azinger and Andy North were just a few of the many who took time out to congratulate me personally when I arrived at Hilton Head as the new Masters champion. I played well throughout the Heritage Classic without setting the South Carolina heather on fire, finishing joint thirteenth behind Greg Norman.

Curiously, I did not perform nearly as impressively in the Dunhill British Masters at Woburn when I returned to Europe in June but found myself going into the last day with a four-stroke lead over Nick Faldo after rounds of 66, 68, 68. Aye, who was it said that golf is a funny old game? Faldo and I both played miserably but I sneaked home with two strokes to spare by playing slightly better awful golf than he did. It was, without doubt, the worst I have ever played to win a tournament, but as everyone was preoccupied with fussing over my Green Jacket, no one seemed to notice that I just might have been the least deserving victor in golfing history.

As in any sport, you take a win however it is achieved, especially when it comes two weeks before the US Open. This year the tournament was played at Brookline, Massachusetts. I began promisingly and led the field by two strokes midway through the second round only to fade away, trailing in joint twenty-fifth as the title went to Curtis Strange. To Seve Ballesteros went the 117th Open Championship at Royal Lytham where, just to be different, I started and finished poorly, otherwise I might well have won my second Major of '88. I was one of sixteen players tied for thirty-fifth place after an opening two-over-par 73, six shots behind Seve, but leapt up to joint sixth after a second round 69. Then, after play was suspended because of an incessant downpour on the Saturday, I found myself right in contention with a splendid 67 on the Sunday, sitting close behind three of my oldest rivals:

Nick Price	-7
Seve Ballesteros	-5
Nick Faldo	-5
Sandy Lyle	-4

For eight holes I throttled Lytham, putting for birdies or eagles on every green without sinking a single effort. My challenge disintegrated when I bogeyed the ninth and eleventh. Seve won his third Open with a remarkable 65 – surely one of the most brilliant final rounds of Major championship golf – while my closing 74 was sufficient for equal seventh.

All in all, however, 1988 had been the most memorable year of my career with victories in the Phoenix Open, the Greater Greensboro Open, the Masters, the Dunhill British Masters and the World Matchplay Championship. I was 30 years of age and physically in my prime – who could have imagined that three long years would pass before I won another tournament?

The one drawback of being the Masters champion is that everyone wants you to play in their tournament – the Japanese, in particular, are just crazy about that Green Jacket with its funny little badge in the shape of Augusta National. Consequently, I had just two weeks in my own bed around Christmas before heading back across the Atlantic for the Tournament of Champions, an unofficial 'world championship' at La Costa in San Diego, beginning on 8 January. After finishing tenth, I decided to stay on the west coast for the Bob Hope Classic, played over five rounds, and reached a three-man play-off with Paul Azinger and eventual winner Steve Jones. That was swiftly followed by the Phoenix Open, the AT & T at Pebble Beach and the Los Angeles Open – a landmark of sorts because I now look back upon the week of the LA Open as the start of my decline.

After opening rounds of 68, 66, 68, I was leading my old Masters rival Mark Calcavecchia by two shots late on the final afternoon when my game mysteriously deteriorated over the last three or four holes. I did not know exactly what was wrong but suddenly I was uncomfortable with my hand position, my rhythm and even the previously simple matter of keeping my head still. I finished runner-up to Calcavecchia and promptly made an appointment to see Jimmy Ballard whose diagnosis was that I was merely in need of some fine-tuning. Wise man though Jimmy undoubtedly is, my troubles continued to mount, and after languishing in joint forty-third place in the Doral Open and twenty-seventh equal in the Honda Classic, I reached a new low in the Nestle Invitational. I shot a miserable first round 78, then when chasing a few birdies down the stretch merely to make the halfway cut, I hooked my approach to the eighteenth into the water. Enough is enough, I thought to myself, shaking hands with my two playing partners, walking off the course and incurring a $500 fine.

Having made all manner of wrong decisions concerning my golf, I managed to get one thing right in 1989 when I proposed to Jolande on her birthday – 26 March – by fashioning an engagement ring from one of those little metal tie-up strips used to secure bin-liners. The real thing arrived a few days later when John Bowles, who was once entrusted with the care of the Crown Jewels (no cheapskate I!), brought round a selection of diamond rings from which we made our choice. We didn't make a big thing of it – I really couldn't imagine anyone being that interested. We sat chatting with the press corps flying out to Augusta for my defence of the Masters with Jolande making no effort to hide the rock on her finger.

It was Mark Calcavecchia's wife at the time, Sheryl, who twigged first when she caught sight of the ring in the clubhouse bar and asked, 'Have you two got something to tell us?' The press lads were upset – in the nicest possible way – that we hadn't told them but we sincerely didn't believe our engagement merited a public announcement. Anyway, aren't they supposed to be *investigative* reporters?

But with a club in my hands I no longer knew what I was doing. I missed the cut in seven of my next eight tournaments including, embarrassingly for the defending champion, at the Masters, where I shot 77, 76. I could not even slink off to hide my shame, having to stay on in Augusta until the final afternoon so I could be on hand in Butlers Cabin to present Nick Faldo with the prize that had been mine twelve months earlier. It seemed like a lifetime ago. The one highlight of my return to the Masters was introducing all the former winners to the delights of that unique Scottish delicacy haggis, neeps and mash at the champions' dinner.

The haggis was piped in with due solemnity at which point the faces of Sam Snead, Gene Sarazen, Byron Nelson and the rest of the old fellas were a picture as I plunged my trusty dirk (English translation: knife) through the sheep's stomach and launched into Rabbie Burns:

> Fair fa' your honest, sonsie face,
> Great chieftain o' the pudding-race!
> Aboon them a' ye tak your place,
> Painch, tripe, or thairm:
> Weel are ye wordy o'a grace
> As lang's my arm.
> Ye Pow'rs, wha mak mankind your care,
> And dish them out their bill o' fare,
> Auld Scotland wants nae skinking ware,
> That jaups in luggies;
> But, if ye wish her gratefu' prayer,
> Gie her a haggis!

It is safe to say that the Augusta National Golf Club has never witnessed a scene quite like it and when his turn came to act as host, Nick Faldo responded to my culinary challenge with fish 'n' chips and mushy peas. By far the most popular Masters feast, however, has been the Thai banquet laid on by Vijay Singh in 2001.

If I hoped that a return to Europe would conjure up the magic of the year before, I was swiftly disabused of the notion. Results were bad – the PGA Championship sixty-fifth, British Masters missed the cut, Irish Open joint fifteenth, Scottish Open joint tenth, the Open at Royal Troon joint forty-sixth, the Benson & Hedges missed the cut, European Masters joint twenty-eighth, Lancome Trophy joint fifty-first. 'Why is this happening to me?' I screamed silently.

I was trapped in a whirlpool spinning down, down and farther down. Seventeen years on, I regret to say that I am still searching for the answer. I have talked to everyone, the Nicklauses and Palmers, trying to feed off their knowledge, and consulted a tribe of gurus, anyone and everyone who might be able to put their finger on exactly what had gone wrong. With the benefit of 20/20 hindsight, I should probably have taken a three-month sabbatical and gone home to my father, instead of which I listened to every conflicting opinion. My timing had gone, my ball striking was not as clean as before, I was not concentrating and I was putting for pars and bogeys from six feet where I had been putting for birdies or eagles previously. The harder I worked – day after day, week after week, month after month – the worse I played and so the more frustrated I became.

Bernard Gallacher mischievously sent me a Nick Faldo instructional video through the post, which was as welcome as the rock that arrived unsolicited at the home of Ian Baker-Finch after the 1991 Open champion's career had entered a similar freefall. 'Sleep for six weeks with this rock under the left side of your pillow,' explained the accompanying letter, 'then put it under the right side of your pillow. During the day, keep it in your pocket at all times. This has worked for me and is my gift to you.' Ian sensibly ignored this piece of crazy paving.

Among the many coaches whose assistance I enlisted was David Leadbetter, who had remodelled Nick Faldo's swing and transformed him into the most successful golfer in the world. When you have a problem with your health, I reasoned, you consult the best available doctor and Leadbetter, according to informed opinion, was the very best golfing physician around. Whereas I had fondly imagined that Leadbetter might have a little pill to cure my ailments, he decided we had to embark upon major surgery. We virtually started from scratch with my posture, grip, knee position, stance, balance, backswing, follow through, all of which seemed to be exactly the opposite of what I had done before. I am not nearly as supple as Faldo – being naturally knock-kneed for a start – so I felt incredibly uncomfortable performing these drills until my body ached.

No matter how much effort I put into it – and I worked off and on with Leadbetter for the best part of two years – I remained ensnared in a downward spiral and became embarrassed to step on the first tee never knowing where the ball would fly or if I would embed the club in the ground before making contact. Tactically, I could have coped if I had developed a simple fade or draw by adjusting my approach to any given hole, but here was a former winner of two Majors topping his drives and watching the ball scuttle along the ground like a nervy six handicapper in a tense finish to a club medal.

As a keen student of the game, I saw no harm in complying with Leadbetter's scientific experiments as opposed to my dad's simpler approach. Even when I became Masters champion I was always eager to pick up any little nugget of information that might make me an even better player. As you would expect, whenever I talked with Dad on the phone his reaction was, 'I hope you know what you're doing, son.' I had no idea what I was doing, as it happens. I genuinely believed that given the many hours of advice and tuition I was receiving, within three or four months I would be flying again. I was guilty of blithely ignoring the fact that my swing had been honed between the ages of 12 and 14 and that Leadbetter's teachings, however well they may have worked for others, went against all my natural instincts.

That was why I subsequently embraced 'Natural Golf', a concept promoted by the incomparable Moe Norman. Of all the remarkable characters I have met in over thirty years of tournament play as both an amateur and professional, I have no hesitation in saying that Moe was the most extraordinary of them all. When he died at the age of 75 in September 2004, his many obituaries referred to him as 'golf's unknown legend'. You may never have heard of him – few have – but it is an undeniable fact that whenever Moe ambled on to the practice ground, Sam Snead, Jack Nicklaus and Arnold Palmer went out to watch, because for all his eccentricities, here was a man who rivalled Ben Hogan as the purest striker of a golf ball the world has ever known.

Blessed with a natural talent that ought to have brought him any number of Majors, he won 'only' fifty-four tournaments, notably two Canadian Amateur championships, and set thirty-three course records, including three sub 60s and four 61s. His failure to win the big tournaments was the abiding tragedy of a life like no other. I had the privilege of meeting Moe on three or four occasions and on hearing his story I couldn't help but wonder what a Hollywood scriptwriter would have made of it. Probably no one would have believed the tale was possible.

One of six children born in humble surroundings in Kitchener, Ontario, it is entirely probable that the defining moment of Moe's life occurred at the age of five when he suffered head injuries after being struck by a car while sledging in the snow. His parents being too poor to afford medical treatment, Moe never received hospital care and grew into a curious child, adept at working out the most complicated mathematical problems but otherwise an educational failure. It was only in later years that those who knew and loved him realised he might have been autistic, and after the release of the famous movie starring Dustin Hoffman and Tom Cruise, Moe affectionately became known as 'the Rain Man' in the locker-room.

Like many great players – Seve Ballesteros for one – Moe was introduced to golf as a caddie. He got a job at Rockway Golf Club when he left school at 14, and quietly honed his own skills when the day's work was done, routinely swiping upwards of fifteen hundred balls in a single session before plunging his bloodied hands into a bucket of ice. With professional lessons beyond his means, Moe invented a style all of his own, a stance and swing stripped bare of all unnecessary fripperies as he saw it. Ripping every coaching manual to shreds, Moe gripped the club in his palms rather than his fingers, adopted what looked like a ridiculously exaggerated stance with his feet planted wide apart, and with his left arm and shaft forming a single axis, grounded the club a foot behind the ball and let fly, and all this in the blink of an eye. The results of this unique action were astonishing. Moe seldom, if ever, took a divot and each and every ball flew unerringly straight down the middle. If ever there was a golfing genius it was Moe Norman and had he ever bothered to develop his putting skills, there is no knowing what he might have achieved.

When he first descended upon the Canadian amateur circuit, neither his fellow competitors nor the crowds knew what to make of him. To be frank, Moe did not look or live like an athlete. His 'diet' consisted mainly of chocolate bars, he hitch-hiked to tournaments and slept in bunkers to save money, and he wore ill-matching second-hand clothes. It was not unusual for Moe to shuffle on to the first tee resplendent in washed-out lime green shirt and ill-fitting yellow trousers. He frequently played barefoot when he could not afford golf shoes, his hair resembled a burst couch, his teeth were like crooked tombstones and he spoke to himself in a curious high-pitched sing-song voice throughout his swing.

After winning his first Canadian Amateur championship in 1955, Moe was invited to compete in the following year's Masters, where the field included Ben Hogan, Walter Hagen, Sam Snead, Byron Nelson and Gene Sarazan. He caused apoplexy among Augusta members by insisting upon carrying his own bag during practice. Indeed, it was only with some persuasion that he reluctantly agreed to avail himself of the services of a local caddie for the first round proper. From tee to green, Moe produced golf of the gods but three-putted six greens on his way to a highly respectable 75. It does not require his remarkable talent for figures to work out that if he had two-putted those six greens, he would have begun his Augusta adventure with a 69. Round two was the same story – flawless golf followed by frantic putting added up to 78 and, there being no halfway cut at the time, Moe took himself off to the practice ground to work on a tip provided by Sam Snead. After smacking 800 balls, Moe's hands were in a ruinous state and he walked off after the ninth hole of the third round, drove home to Canada and was never seen at Augusta again.

When the mood was upon him, Moe's anger was a thing to behold; when his putter let him down – as it was frequently wont to do – he would tie the offending implement to the back bumper of his car and 'drag it screamin' through the streets to teach it a goddam lesson it will never forget'. With any other club in his brawny hands, he was the complete master. As the late golf writer Peter Dobereiner described it: 'Moe Norman can not only get the ball up and down from the ball-washer, he could, if sufficiently motivated, play it out of the cup and back into the ball-washer.' Such a manoeuvre would have held great appeal for Moe, who was never one to take the easy option. Competing in a professional tournament in Quebec, on the eighteenth tee a kindly spectator informed Moe that a par four on the final hole would constitute a new course record. 'What is it?' he asked his caddie. 'A driver and nine-iron,' came the reply, whereupon Moe hit a 9-iron off the tee, pulled his driver from the bag, smacked a beauty on to the green and sank the putt for a three – birdie golf the Moe Norman way.

Even when he embarked upon a brief flirtation with the US Tour, Moe could not resist hamming it up for the gallery, either by using a Coca-Cola bottle as a tee on the first hole, or by asking his caddie to roll the ball towards him and unleashing an inch-perfect 260 yard drive while the ball was still in motion. Moe's style was anything but text-book and although under my current coach, Ken Martin, who was one of the disciples of 'Natural Golf', I have discarded many of Moe's theories, to a great extent they have much in common with my dad's original philosophy of 'keep it simple'.

I first met Ken after making contact with 'Natural Golf' to ask whether I could tag along to their next clinic in Jacksonville. They kindly emailed me saying, 'Stay where you are, we'll come to you.' I did not meet Moe in person until some time later but Ken and I struck up an immediate rapport and he even caddies for me from time to time in America so he can study my game in close-up.

Another whose help I hope will become invaluable in the years ahead is Australian sports psychologist Noel Blundell, who worked with Paul Annacone when he was serving as Pete Sampras's coach. What's good enough for Sampras is certainly good enough for me, especially when I discovered he had been advising Rodger Davis who, in the space of a month, went from no-hoper to winning the first million-dollar tournament Down Under. It may seem strange, but the first thing Noel taught me was how to breathe correctly (and there was I thinking I'd been breathing properly since birth) by using my abdominal muscles to relieve any anxiety. Tiger Woods has been using a sports psychologist since his youth but, of course, when I was starting out if I'd consulted a shrink everyone would have thought I was barking!

The competitive fires within me still burn with the intensity of old, so I could not have slept at nights had I walked away at any time in all these long years of inner turmoil. It has been no consolation to know that I was not first to conquer the world only to forget everything I had ever known – Bill Rogers, Johnny Miller, Tom Watson and Seve Ballesteros have all suffered similar experiences for various reasons. Maddeningly, whenever it does come all right, my touch inevitably disappears again.

After three seasons without a tournament victory, I won the 1991 BMW International Open in Munich with rounds of 65, 65, 71, 67. The following year I won the Italian Open, heading a powerful leaderboard that included Colin Montgomerie, Vijay Singh, Mark O'Meara and Eduardo Romero, and then added the prestigious Volvo Masters title at Valderrama, where I beat Monty in an all-Scottish play-off. Typically, I did not make things easy for myself. After birdying the fifteenth to earn a share of the lead, I flew my 4-iron approach to the sixteenth into the rough behind the green with very little room to manoeuvre because I was so near the flag. Although there was a lot of grass around the ball it had been trampled down by the crowd, so to make things even more hazardous I had a bare lie off rock-hard ground. The only way to play my third was as a bunker shot, using the clubhead speed and a wide swing in the hope of launching the ball high into the air. The shot was fraught with danger because there was every chance I would scull the ball right through the green as though hit by a 1-iron, and I was mightily relieved when it dropped from the clouds to within six feet of the hole to salvage a par.

On the seventeenth I struck a woeful drive down the left-hand side. It ran over a bank bordering the fairway from where, with the ball lying about two feet above my navel, I proceeded to semi-shank a 5-iron into the rough ninety yards short of the green. Blessed, or possibly cursed, with the unhappy knack of being adept at making a bad thing worse, I shanked my third shot straight out of bounds, only for the ball to hit a tree and bounce back into play. This was the stuff of golfing nightmares because I now had no angle into the pin on to a landing spot no wider than the rim of a wine glass if I was to have any chance of even getting close to the hole. Against all laws of probability, my chip finished within five feet and I escaped with a par where I ought to have been looking at a double-bogey or worse.

After a routine par four on the eighteenth, which made a nice change, and with Monty unable to prise a single birdie from Valderrama's notoriously tough finishing stretch, it was off to the dogleg tenth to begin our shoot-out. I won the toss to play first and knew that, if I hit a good drive, it could put additional pressure on Monty who, with his inherent cut, would be concerned about the huge tree overhanging the left-hand side of the fairway about a hundred yards distant. I could not have written the script better. My tee-shot landed in perfect position in the middle of the fairway about 130 yards from the green, while the luckless Monty blasted his ball straight into the tree. He then topped a 3-iron through the branches followed by a 4-wood, which stopped just short of the bunker guarding the green. I flew my approach to twenty-five feet from the flag to be on in two, following which Monty's fourth shot finished outside my ball. Assuming Monty would miss, I was cheerfully thinking I had three putts for the title when he defiantly sank his monster putt for what was, under the circumstances, a phenomenal bogey five. What I did not know was that after the last group had cleared each hole, they had cut the green, so the tenth was far faster than I expected and my first putt ran all of four feet past. I managed to steer home the second, despite my beating heart.

At the time, I thought the Volvo Masters would act as the springboard to relaunch my career but, alas, it is now fourteen years since that last tournament victory. I came close in the 2002

Dunhill Links Championship played over Carnoustie, Kingsbarns and St Andrews, where my rounds of 69, 67, 67, 68, the first time I had posted four good scores in many a long day, left me in a tie for third place behind Padraig Harrington – the cheque of around £175,000 represented my biggest ever pay day, incidentally. More importantly, that result guaranteed my European Tour Card for another season. Twelve months later and after twenty-five years on the circuit, I lost my card when I dropped out of the European Tour all-time top forty money-winners' list for the simple reason that all my tournament victories had been achieved long before the advent of massive prizes.

Obviously I have a vested interest in this situation, but I really feel that a points system would be a far fairer way to calculate the top forty rather than money. Annual inflation has obviously weakened my standing. As a former Open and Masters champion, plus three-time winner of the European Order of Merit, I find it embarrassing – no, make it 'hurtful' – that my manager, Robert Duck of Hambric Stellar Golf, has to sit down at the start of each new season and pen a series of begging letters along the lines of, 'Dear Sir, Our client Sandy Lyle is very interested in playing in your tournament if you would be interested in having him . . .' To give you some idea of how prize money has risen, when I won the Open in 1985 I received a cheque for £65,000; when Tiger Woods was crowned champion twenty years later, he received £720,000. Fortunately, most sponsors tend to look on my request sympathetically – plus the fact that I am exempt from having to qualify for a number of events as a past winner – or I would be faced with the prospect of returning to the qualifying school, from which I graduated in 1977.

I like to think I can still play a bit, as I proved to myself and,

I hope, to a few others in the 2005 Open Championship at St Andrews. Going into the fourth round of the 134th Open, I was joint ninth on six under par, and delighted to be playing in one of the last pairings on the final day of a Major after what seemed an eternity. Ken Martin and I had worked on my left-to-right fade in practice in an attempt to eliminate any pull-hook, and I struck the ball well throughout the week, hitting a succession of perfect long shots at the right time. If I had started the last afternoon better and developed some early momentum, who knows what I might have achieved?

As I teed off in front of the clubhouse windows, the leaderboard read:

Tiger Woods	-12
Jose-Maria Olazabal	-10
Retief Goosen	-9
Colin Montgomerie	-9
Brad Faxon	-8
Sergio Garcia	-8
Vijay Singh	-7
Michael Campbell	-7

In a large group on six under par, which included John Daly, Bernhard Langer and Darren Clarke, it was nice to find myself back in the midst of such elevated company. According to Bob Ferrier's *World Atlas of Golf Courses*, 'Nowhere is there an easier start to a championship course than the first hole at St Andrews.' Hmmm, not when you hook your drive nearly on to the second tee just five feet short of the Swilcan Burn, which snakes around the first green before winding away to cross the eighteenth fairway. I had a clean lie but although I was only 103 yards from the flag, my chip was into the face of a strong wind, which came and went in capricious gusts. I struck a three-quarter power pitching wedge at the precise second the wind came howling back and the ball hovered around in the air before coming down on such a good line that I thought I might have holed it for an eagle two. Given the silence around the green, the spectators must have somehow lost sight of the ball in mid-flight. In reality, the ball had disappeared all right, straight into the burn. Confronted by a treacherous fourth shot over the burn to a flag on the very front of the green, I charmed the ball to within twenty-four inches of the hole, not knowing whether to be relieved I had salvaged a five from a possible double-bogey six or infuriated that I had not launched an immediate charge at Tiger and the rest with a birdie, or even what would have been an admittedly flukey eagle.

I parred the second, third and fourth – which is always a stern challenge – birdied the 564 yard par-five fifth to return to six under, then promptly three-putted the sixth on the huge double-green as a result of a misjudged pitch. By way of making amends, I holed a thirty-footer for a birdie on the seventh and put my tee-shot on the par-three eighth – where it was mightily diffi-cult to get the ball close – to five feet only to miss my birdie putt. That was the turning point of my round. If I had moved to seven under at that point, I would have been on a high. Instead, my shoulders drooped when my drive on the ninth smacked into the lip of the fairway bunker, bounced into the air and thought about hopping over, but opted to roll back into the sand for another shot dropped.

Now five under and fast losing touch with the leaders, I missed from eight feet on the tenth for a second successive bogey, salvaged a par three on the eleventh despite a wayward tee-shot that landed way to the right, misread a birdie putt on the twelfth, and fluffed a five-footer for par on the thirteenth after two splendid shots to the green. I'd slumped to three under. After that the rest of the round, which I had begun with such high hopes, became an exercise in damage limitation. I was eventually round in 75 for a three-under-par total of 285 and joint thirty-second whereas a 70, which should have been well within my capabilities on a course I knew and loved, would have earned me a share of third place behind Tiger and Monty. In the 134th Open Championship, that would have been a massive boost to my morale.

I was so angry with myself that it took me many weeks to recover from the crushing disappointment of what might have been, and I subsequently missed the cut in six of the last seven tournaments of the European season. To have come so close to making a serious impact at St Andrews only to be let down by poor putting was infuriating. On the plus side, for three and a half rounds I had not looked out of place in the presence of the current greatest golfers in the world, even at the venerable age of 47.

After all these years I am still no nearer to solving the great 'Sandy Lyle Mystery' of why all the king's horses and all the king's men have been unable to put my game back together again, but I remain stubbornly convinced that I am capable of ending that fourteen-year wait to win another tournament. I have to accept, however, that I do not have time on my side, especially against the new breed of golfing 'super-athletes'. The circuit is a very different world from the one I knew when I began life as a professional in 1978. Not only have the equipment manufacturers made great strides in club and golf-ball technology, but the Tiger Woods generation comes equipped with a vast team of personal fitness trainers, dietitians, sports psychologists, physiotherapists and lap-top computer coaching aids.

I have nothing to prove and will continue playing for my own satisfaction but, given my talent, I must admit to being something of an under-achiever. I am proud to have won two Majors but there will always be a lingering sense of regret that my career came to such an abrupt halt when, instead of adding to my victories in the Open and Masters, I entered a kamikaze dive from which I was unable to pull out. It has been a great adventure, I have travelled the world and visited many exotic places but, if I am honest with myself, I should have won more tournaments and played in more Ryder Cup contests. If I had gone off the rails a bit and started smoking pot or hitting the bottle, at least I would have had no one to blame but myself whereas I have increased my efforts only to remain becalmed.

Reading again the lovely telegram Seve Ballesteros sent me after my Open triumph – 'Savour your deserved victory but please be very cautious with commitments that might derive . . . bear in mind that you cannot please everybody' – I realise I should have remembered those words at the beginning of 1989 and spent the first few months relaxing at home with my family (and checking out my Green Jacket in the mirror) rather than playing week in week out in America.

A couple of years ago now, when Colin Montgomerie was struggling with his game, he asked me whether I thought he should visit David Leadbetter or someone of that ilk to change his swing. I replied unhesitatingly, 'Don't even think about it. You've grown up with your swing and that's what has brought you to where you are today, leading money winner in Europe for seven successive years. You'll work it out for yourself.' That's why I was delighted for Monty when he won the Order of Merit for a record eighth time in 2005. *Don't even think about it* – oh, how I wish I had heeded my own advice.

CHAPTER FIFTEEN

A WONDERFUL LIFE

But like Clarence, the angel without wings, reminded James Stewart's character George Bailey when they met on the bridge in Bedford Falls, it is a wonderful life and I am fortunate to have so many special memories from both on and off the golf course to look back upon with a warm glow.

On 20 October 1989, Jolande and I were married in Gibraltar, in the same registry office where John Lennon and Yoko Ono had been wed twenty years earlier. The former Beatle selected a crumpled cream jacket and polo neck from his wardrobe for the occasion whereas I opted for a kilt (having belatedly and shamefully worked out exactly how it should be worn) in the Sinclair tartan that the Lyles are eligible to wear and which I had taken possession of before the Masters champions' dinner at Augusta earlier that spring. My splendid tartan arrived courtesy of Kinloch Anderson (kilt-makers by appointment to the Royal family no less!) who generously offered to kit me out when they heard that I was planning a Scottish theme night at Augusta. At my final fitting, the tailor opened up his battered leather case to reveal a second kilt which, I have to say, did not look nearly as smart as my Sinclair.

'What's that?' I enquired snootily. 'Who'd want to wear an old thing like that?'

'Her Majesty the Queen would want to,' came the reply. 'She's had it forty years and sent it back to us to have it dry-cleaned . . .' Sorry, ma'am . . .

Stuart and James were in attendance in Gibraltar but, at six and three years old respectively, were way too young to act as best men, a duty which passed to twice former English Amateur champion, Terry Shingler. Terry had been a Busby Babe in his youth but never made the first-team squad at Manchester United and so, consequently, was not on the fateful flight from Munich in 1958. Jolande drove us from her mother's house across the Spanish border in Sotogrande where we had been staying and, old romantic that I am, with the sun blazing through the windscreen, I nodded off in the heat which earned me a sharp dig in the ribs from the elbow of my wife-to-be.

The ceremony was a private, unpublicised affair attended only by my mum and dad, Jolande's divorced parents (Evelien and Bas) and their respective partners plus her three brothers, after which we returned to Sotogrande for a barbecue in the garden of my new mother-in-law's home overlooking the Mediterranean. Normally painfully shy at any such function, my dad was so relaxed he broke the habit of a lifetime by making a speech, an unheard-of phenomenon.

While we were enjoying an idyllic wedding day, further along the coast Tony and Astrid Jacklin had been forced to take their phone off the hook when Fleet Street caught whiff of our nuptials and began bombarding them with calls. So secret had our arrangements been that although Jolande had spoken to Astrid that very morning to arrange a dinner date the following week, she did not even let the Jacklins in on our plans.

We delayed our post-nuptial holiday until the week after the Sun City Golf Challenge in South Africa, following which we had arranged to stay in the honeymoon suite of a five-star hotel on the beach in Cape Town. It all sounded perfect but the reality would have been sorely disappointing if it had not been so amusing. For a start, our promised 'sea view' was only viable if you hung out the bedroom window at a precarious angle, the bathroom was so small you scraped your knees on the walls when you sat on the loo (also scuppering any notion of a romantic bath for two!) and, whereas John and Yoko retired to a king-sized mattress in Amsterdam for their famous 'Give Peace A Chance' protest, Jolande and I were surprised to discover that here was one honeymoon suite that came equipped with twin beds. We stayed one night before checking out and moving into a genuinely luxurious hotel based on the design of an ocean liner along the coast.

The crystal clear waters of the Atlantic looked so inviting that the following morning after breakfast, I changed into my beach shorts, ran down the sand like an excited five-year-old (all the while thinking to myself, 'Hmmm, the beach is strangely quiet . . .') and plunged into the sea. The Atlantic? The Arctic more like; thank goodness for the future success of our honeymoon that I had only gone in up to my knees before realising why the beach was all but deserted and retired hurt to the pool bar for a cocktail!

Whenever I read an article headlined *Sandy Lyle: What Went Wrong?* I could point to a five-year spell in the 1990s when the answer would have been 'just about everything'. Although it has been a blessed life in many respects – as a 12-year-old if anyone had offered me an Open Championship and a Masters Green Jacket plus the chance to travel the world and savour so many experiences, I would have replied, 'That'll do for me, pal' – like everyone I have had my share of heartbreak.

From a young girl, Jolande had endured a series of 'women's problems' involving a series of operations culminating in the removal of an ovarian cyst, so you could imagine our joy when we discovered she was pregnant during the 1991 Volvo Masters at Valderrama. One night shortly before Christmas at home in Wentworth, she collapsed in agony and later miscarried while undergoing an internal scan in hospital. Emotionally, it was a cruel blow but physically Jolande felt there was still something amiss and, with that uncanny knack that only women possess, bought a pregnancy testing kit that suggested she was still pregnant.

When Jolande phoned her gynaecologist he told her that unbeknown to anyone she must have been expecting twins in the first place. Any relief we might have felt that at least one of our twins had survived vanished when another scan showed it to be an ectopic pregnancy and our second baby was lost. We were subsequently advised that, if we wanted to have children, Jolande should consider IVF treatment but she was reluctant to risk multiple-births given her medical history. However, the day she was due to talk it over with the specialist, Jolande discovered she was pregnant again and our lovely Lonneke was born on 1 April 1993, weighing in at a healthy 10lb 11oz. I didn't cry when I won at Sandwich or Augusta, but there were tears in my eyes when I first held my beautiful daughter. When our son, Quintin, arrived two years later, our family was complete.

Tragically, Quintin was less than two months old when we received the traumatic news that Jolande's mum had committed suicide in Spain.

There was further anguish the following year when my parents died within six months of one another. By then, Jolande, Lonneke, Quintin and I were living in a sprawling home which had formerly been a country house hotel in Dolphinton in the Scottish borders. Dad loved being back in Scotland when he came to visit, just sitting in a garden chair surveying the rolling hills beyond. He was taken into hospital just after we had drawn up plans to build a self-contained flat on the top floor should my parents ever feel the need to move in with us.

Again, being February, we were thousands of miles away in America where I was competing in the AT & T event at Pebble Beach. I immediately withdrew to fly home to Scotland, pick up the car and drive through deep snow to Hawkstone. Dad was unconscious and, after a brief visit, I raced back up the A1 to pack my bags in preparation for a longer stay in Shropshire, but had only walked through the door at home when we received the phone call that Dad had died.

My mind went back to that day when I witnessed Tiger Woods breaking down in tears at his moment of triumph in this year's Open at Hoylake where he was grieving over the loss of his father to cancer a few months earlier. I knew exactly how he felt because the loss of my dad left a deep scar that I feel to this day. He had been at my side since childhood, gently encouraging me on the golf course and quietly instilling his sense of decency and honesty. He had been there at my Open and Masters victories and he had always been there for me during my years of despair, offering guidance and words of wisdom. Even now, each time I pick up a club I can hear his voice in my ear repeating the mantra, 'Tempo not temper . . .'

Mum, bless her, was totally lost without him, which is why I will always remain convinced that she died so soon after of a broken heart. She was taken into hospital after suffering a mild heart-attack on the Saturday night of the Open at Royal Lytham, insisting that Jolande did not tell me until the tournament was over. Quite rightly, Jolande did inform me and immediately after I holed out in the final round, we dashed from Lancashire to Shropshire to be at her bedside. I had a business meeting on the Monday but Jolande popped in to see Mum again when she was sitting up happily in bed studying all the latest photographs of her four grandchildren which Jolande had brought.

When Jolande left, Mum was utterly contented, surrounded by photographs and having seen everyone she wanted to see – my sisters Anne and Alison, her grandchildren and Jolande. By the time I arrived in the evening there was even talk of her being moved out of intensive care into a normal ward. Jolande and I returned to Scotland at 1 a.m. on the Tuesday morning and had just climbed into bed when the hospital phoned to say she had suffered another heart-attack; half an hour later she passed away.

For a variety of reasons, we had to wait two weeks before holding Mum's funeral and on the night of her cremation, when I was due to leave for America to prepare for the US PGA Championship, we heard from Holland that Jolande's father was in hospital in a coma.

Instead of flying across the Atlantic it was over the English Channel to Holland where Jolande was able to sit beside her dad for a few hours before the doctors unplugged the machinery keeping him alive. In the space of eighteen months we had lost both sets of parents, three within six months and two within a few weeks. Just to complete an unremitting spell of misery, Jolande then underwent a hysterectomy meaning it would be a long, long time before I could focus my mind fully on golf again.

But everyone, whether they are a golfer, prince or plumber, has to suffer such depths of woe and, as I said earlier, all in all it has been a wonderful life because golf has not only brought me titles and financial security – 'My wife made me a millionaire,' I like to jest, 'before her I used to be called "multi"' – but has taken me to the most exotic places and introduced me to so many fabulous experiences and fascinating people.

One of the great perks of being an Open or Masters champion is that I've had the opportunity of experiencing all kinds of adventures and meeting all manner of people that would have been denied me had I become a green-keeper, say; like the Queen, for instance, who I am disappointed to relate did not wear her ancient kilt on the two occasions our paths crossed, the first time being shortly before our Ryder Cup victory in 1987 when my mum and dad accompanied me to receive my MBE. After arriving at the front gates of Buckingham Palace, we were escorted into a magnificent room – all chandeliers and liveried flunkies – where my tummy immediately began to rumble with nerves. I was idly wondering what were the chances of a cup of tea and maybe a cucumber sandwich when Her Majesty entered and it was my time to be called forward. She had obviously done her homework on me because we had quite a lengthy chat about golf and my 1985 victory at Royal St George's as Mum and Dad stood there beaming proudly.

I was invited back to the palace later that same year for lunch with the Queen; I had seen television pictures of her garden parties and I naturally assumed I would be one anonymous face amid a cast of thousands so I was somewhat surprised to find there was not a huge swarm piling past the guards at the gates. 'I must be a bit early,' I thought as I was shown up the steps into a reception room where I expected to see a huge notice board with the various seating plans with the name A.W.B. Lyle hidden away in the furthest recess on table 67 or whatever. But there was only one sheet of paper bearing ten names plus the Queen at the top. My fellow guests included business tycoons, scientists, people with what I call 'real' jobs, with me being the sole sportsman.

We were given a glass of champagne then the Queen entered with two corgis at her feet following which we had a relaxed natter before being taken into another room where an army of twenty waiters hovered around us. It was all very informal and I discovered the Queen was a bit of a golf fan on the quiet and enjoyed watching all the big tournaments on television. It was a wonderful afternoon but we knew it was time to go when the corgis – who had obviously been well trained – rose to their paws and padded over to the door. The Queen is too polite to say, 'It's been nice to have you, now clear off . . .' but that was clearly her cue to depart.

My Open success also brought an invitation to join the Red Arrows air display team at RAF Scampton in Lincolnshire for two days, an experience which has to be one of the biggest thrills of my life. It was not without some trepidation I reported for duty but, like meeting Muhammad Ali face to face at an awards ceremony, these kind of things do not happen every day and the chance to fly in a Hawk jet fighter was too good an opportunity to turn down. Probably the best known Bomber Command station, it was from Scampton that No. 617 Squadron took off on their famous 'Dam Busters' mission on 16 May 1943 and one of the Lancasters used on the raid sits in pride of place on the runway.

I was introduced to the nine pilots in the officers' mess where they were knocking back pints of beer – which cost about 30p in today's money – as if they were on a stag night. When I asked, 'Which of you guys is flying me tomorrow?' they all pointed at one another to gales of laughter. The following morning I underwent a full medical followed by instruction on how to use the ejector seat which I had no plans to do. 'If the pilot says eject,' I was told, 'pull this lever and don't stop to ask why . . .' Once fitted into my flying suit and helmet we took off, whereupon Squadron Leader Richard Thomas went straight into a series of steep 360-degree turns around the airfield.

'I'm looking for a cooling tower,' he told me through the earphones.

'Well, find it quick,' I managed to mumble with my head twisted grotesquely to one side by the G-forces.

We finally levelled off and were gently following a river when the voice in my ear interrupted my reverie.

'So, do you want to have a go at flying a plane?'

'Eh?'

I took the controls for about five minutes without mishap before handing back to the pilot as we approached Scarborough through the clouds. 'Doesn't it look lovely?' I thought before the pilot flipped us over and I was looking at Scarborough upside down by which time I had turned a less than lovely colour of green. Right side up and after an hour of feeling six times my body weight on top of my shoulders I was in agony. Once on the ground I slithered off the wing tips and made my way on legs of jelly to the sanctuary of the mess. Although mugs of tea and platefuls of bacon rolls had been laid out for my return, my usually indomitable appetite had mysteriously vanished. It was at that point I discovered that my morning jaunt had been but a 'pleasure flight' designed to gauge how my mind and body would stand up to being part of a full-blown aerial display after lunch.

The names of the manoeuvres says it all: Tango Bend to Big Battle . . . Cyclone . . . Goose to Steep Climb . . . Corkscrew . . . Vixen Loop . . . Opposition Barrel Rolls . . . For seventeen minutes I had no idea where I was in relation to the world; I was looking down at the clouds, up at the hangars along the runway, there were planes behind me, beside me, in front of me, and all the while the pilots were chatting away over the intercom.

'This is better than the Ryder Cup any day, isn't it Sandy?'

'Not right now, it's not. At least the Ryder Cup is played on the ground.'

The climax was the Vixen Loop in which the nine planes joined up in close formation – with wing tips almost touching – then zoomed off in every direction like a giant firework exploding. I am proud to say I completed my spell of duty with the Red Arrows without being sick which, to a landlubber like me, was a major achievement.

I took to the 'air' again in rather more exotic surroundings when I was one of a group of professionals invited to Brunei to coach the Sultan's golf-mad nephew, Prince Hakim, who had formed a friendship with Bernard Gallacher after meeting him at Wentworth during his education in England. At 21, Prince Hakim had every 'big boy's toy' known to man, including his private eighteen-hole floodlit course so he could play at night after the searing sun had gone down. The Brunei royals did everything in style – Michael Jackson had been flown out to perform at the Sultan's 50th birthday celebrations while Stevie Wonder and Whitney Houston were regular entertainers at family weddings – and Prince Hakim's 'games room' came equipped with two F18 fighter jet simulators, as close to the real thing in every detail except for the absence of an ejector seat, as used by the US Navy to train their 'Top Guns'.

'Chocks away, Ginger!' as Biggles used to say. I fired the engines, taxied out to the end of the runway and soared into the wide blue yonder at the controls of my F18; I headed out over the South China Sea and all was going well until I came in to land feeling well pleased with myself that I had the speed right, the angle of descent and the wing level correct when I heard this ungodly eruption of noise – I had forgotten to lower the undercarriage thereby writing off $30 million of 'plane'. Being a simulator, of course, I was able to walk away from the wreckage with a sheepish grin but I didn't half feel a prat.

Although his father, Prince Jefri, preferred boats – his fifty-metre super-yacht named *Tits* boasted two lifeboats in *Nipple 1* and *Nipple 2* – Prince Hakim's major hobby was cars, around 1,200 of them according to estimates: Ferraris, Maseratis, Aston Martins, Lamborghinis, Rolls-Royces, custom-built Bentleys which have only recently appeared on the roads of Britain but which were a common sight in Brunei a decade or more ago, all in every shade on the colour chart and housed in his multi-storey car park within the palace grounds.

His pride and joy, however, were the three McLaren F1s, the world's most expensive (at $1 million each) and the world's fastest (top speed 240mph) road cars. One morning the Prince's personal test-driver invited me out for a spin in one of the McLarens which had been suffering clutch problems. The idea was to accelerate, brake hard, accelerate quicker, brake harder, accelerate even quicker and so on in the hope that when the clutch was completely warmed up, then the shuddering would be cured. 'Please bring it back in one piece,' beseeched the Prince as we shot out on to the streets of Brunei (when you're a member of the Royal Family, speed limits do not exist). We had reached 150mph when Bang! the clutch disintegrated and we had to phone the equivalent of the Brunei AA to transport us back to the palace behind a tow-truck. After my escapade with his F18 fighter, all I could mutter was, 'Don't blame me, your Royal Highness . . .'

But my most memorable high-speed adventure has to be the day I spent at Silverstone shortly after my '88 Masters victory in the company of Nigel Mansell who was testing his latest Williams Formula One racing car. I was allowed to sit behind the wheel with Nigel standing beside me in his racing suit stripped to the waist, smiling fit to burst in my Augusta Green Jacket.

'Right, you've had a shot in my car, so it's only fair I have a shot of yours,' said Nigel, pointing at my Porsche 944 Turbo. It took Nigel less than a lap to assume complete mastery of the Porsche by which time he was making the car perform in ways I never knew possible. Closing fast on a mechanic testing a Ford Escort RS1600, Nigel growled, 'Watch this . . .' Changing down a gear, he overtook the unsuspecting Escort driver in a blur, leaving him behind in a cloud of smoke. Thanks, Nigel, that was one white-knuckle, brown-trousers ride I will never forget.

I also endured one white-knuckle arrival in America when my good friend Neville Cramer – a US Immigration agent – played a wicked trick on me by arranging for one of his fellow officers to meet me as I walked down the steps of the plane. While Neville stood hidden from view laughing like a hyena – and the British press saw their former Open champion standing with his hands behind his head while the official was menacingly muttering something about 'a full body strip-search' – I knew what real fear was like until Agent Cramer came to my rescue.

On another occasion, Neville took Jolande and me to a shooting range where we were photographed using a vast array of firearms. These pictures came in unexpectedly useful for a prank on Michael Bonnalack's daughter, Sarah, on honeymoon with her new husband. After much plotting and planning, Neville turned up at the happy couple's hotel room door in full uniform.

'I am Special Immigration Officer Cramer and I would like to ask you a few questions.' After demanding their passports, Neville went on: 'We have reason to believe you are connected to some very dangerous people.' And so saying, Neville whipped out the photographs of Jolande and me with machine guns slung round our necks. 'And they asked me to give you these,' he finally grinned, producing a bottle of champagne and a box of chocolates. Being the gent he is, Neville also took Sarah and her new husband out for dinner.

Only recently I sampled another unique experience when I played golf on a course carved out of the snow in St Moritz in the Swiss Alps. This picture-postcard resort in the Engadine Valley may have hosted two Winter Olympics and entertained the most glittering of the world's glitterati at its various après-ski venues, but it also stages a little-known golf annual tournament. The 'fairways' on the frozen lake consisted of compact powdery snow, we played with red balls and were given three different coloured plastic cups to use as tees for our drives, approaches and pitches on to greens – which were Augusta pace – about the size of a family kitchen. The nice thing about golf in the snow from my point of view is that the hole is about a foot in diameter.

Before the sun came up, turning the whole scene into a winter wonderland, it was absolutely freezing so, consequently, we were bundled up under layers of thermal ski jackets and trousers, woolly hats, gloves, dark glasses for the glare and heavy walking boots instead of golf shoes. I shot 33 over the nine holes to finish joint second but as the sponsors, Chivas Regal, had thoughtfully provided hot toddies and whisky 'soup' on every tee, it was a right merry band which made its way back down the mountainside.

Buckingham Palace ... the Red Arrows ... fun and games in Brunei ... whizzing round Silverstone at 140mph with Nigel Mansell ... at the risk of repeating myself, it *has* been wonderful, none of which would have been remotely possible had I not become a champion golfer. I began my career in the era of Tom Watson and Jack Nicklaus, enjoyed a brief (all too brief, I have to confess) spell when many judges regarded me as the best player in the world, and still love the feeling on the first tee even though in my heart of hearts I know I can never hope to threaten the reign of Tiger Woods. We have no way of knowing whether Tiger will overhaul Jack Nicklaus's total of eighteen Majors but now that he has passed the age of 30 (and with twelve Grand

Slam titles in his possession) I am constantly asked where I would place him in the game's All-Time Greats list. It is, needless to say, an impossible question to answer given that the equipment Tiger is using bears no resemblance to that used by Sam Snead; then there is Nicklaus to be considered and Byron Nelson, who won eighteen tournaments in 1945. But what we can say is that Tiger is the outstanding player of his era. He is an extraordinary athlete – his dad always maintained that he had the physique to be an Olympic sprinter – rising at five in the morning for an hour of gym work before heading for the practice ground.

And what of my own future ambitions? During the Major-title barren years of 1980–86, Jack Nicklaus would happily tell the following joke at his own expense: 'A guy goes into a bar with his dog and orders a beer. The barman switches channels on the TV and on comes the latest golf tournament. I make a birdie and the dog does a back-flip on the bar. On the next hole, I sink another putt for a birdie and the dog repeats his back-flip. "Your dog must be a real Nicklaus fan", says the barman. "What does he do when Nicklaus wins a tournament?" To which the guy replies, "I don't know, he's only six years old . . ."'

Since it is fourteen years since I enjoyed my last tournament success, I would obviously relish another victory in Europe before joining the seniors when I reach the 50 milestone in 2008. As a former Major winner, I will be granted automatic exemption for the Champions Tour in the US where, around that time, I expect to be joined by Seve Ballesteros, Nick Faldo, Bernhard Langer (and the way he's playing, Bernie could take America by storm) and Ian Woosnam, which could also bring the long-mooted notion of a Seniors Ryder Cup one step closer. I do not intend playing on until my sixties because at my age I now prefer to spend as much time at home as possible, but the prospect of spending three or four years competing in seniors golf both in Europe and the United States holds great appeal. Despite the absence of a tournament victory in what seems an eternity, I still love playing the game with all the passion of my boyhood and will probably still be playing for fun in my eighties and beyond.

Before then, I would also like to become involved in golf architecture, not just putting my name to a 'signature' course but, rather like granddad almost ninety years ago, by rolling up my sleeves and getting my hands dirty. I have already designed two courses, in Tokyo and Berlin, and I'm pleased to say the Berlin one has won a couple of awards. The design business is a very crowded market and I would be vying for contracts with established names like Jack Nicklaus, Tom Weiskopf and Pete Dye but unlike Jack, who has countless projects under construction around the world at any time, I would be more interested in building one or two courses a year to which I could devote my full attention. Having been born on the land, I think I have a good eye for what constitutes a fantastic golf course such as Kingsbarns outside St Andrews, where Mark Parsinen and Kyle Phillips combined to produce a natural masterpiece.

I have recently become an ambassador for the Macdonald luxury hotel group – and been appointed a non-executive member of the golf board – for whom I will play exhibitions, hold coaching clinics, make personal appearances and the like and, given their interest in the sport, hopefully I will be able to design a course for them in the years to come.

Although I still love travelling and visiting new places, my greatest joy is simply spending time with my family in Balquhidder where, I am delighted to say, my older sons Stuart and James are regular visitors. I also own houses in Florida and Wentworth but Balquhidder is now 'home' and despite its remote setting – the only people who find us are bewildered tourists seeking directions – it lies close to both Glasgow and Edinburgh airports so I can be in Europe just as quickly as when I lived in Surrey. With 700 acres of 'garden' comprising rugged hills, forests, streams and shoreline, I can indulge all my hobbies of fishing, shooting (I even shot the deer which provided us with the venison for last year's Christmas lunch), quad biking – the perfect retreat.

Because golf involves so much travelling, I treasure every moment I can spend with the children where sitting round the kitchen table laughing and joking over dinner more than compensates for all those lonely nights of hotel room service. Just as Hawkstone provided the ultimate adventure playground when I was growing up, Balquhidder is a wonderland to Lonneke (who shows all the passion and determination to succeed on stage and in musical theatre as I did at her age in golf) and Quintin, who is a real 'outdoor' type; together we sail, canoe, water-ski, cycle and throw ourselves into all manner of pursuits.

My main hobby is what we Scots call 'footerin' (English translation: 'messing about'); having always been interested in all things mechanical since childhood, I can happily spend hours dismantling and cleaning my quad bike then putting it all back together again or simply mending the guttering. It may not be everyone's idea of relaxation but to my mind it represents absolute bliss. Unlike the vast majority of husbands, since being at home is something of a treat for me I'm an avid DIY fan, be it painting and decorating or rebuilding one of the tumbledown wash-houses on our land as a home for our housekeeper of ten years, the blessed Carol Cowan, who is as important in the Lyle home as any caddie out on the course, with the invaluable assistance of our good friend, Peter Brennan, who has masterminded the conversions of our various homes over the years. Jolande, who does all the plumbing and electrical work, will tell you that I'm *not* an 'avid DIY fan', that what I do, in effect, is take lots of things to pieces then leave it to Stuart and James to put them back together.

To the fairway born, I consider myself one very lucky man to have achieved so much, and to have been surrounded by love throughout my life. Yes, I could and should have won more Major titles but just like the American President is forever referred to as 'Mr President' even after he has surrendered the keys to the White House, I will always be an Open and Masters champion.

I am proud of having become the first Briton since Tony Jacklin sixteen years earlier to win the Open ... I am proud of being the first Briton to win the Masters ... I am proud to have been one of what was termed the 'Big Five of European Golf' alongside Seve, Faldo, Langer and Woosie ... I am proud of helping Europe win the Ryder Cup in 1985 after so many years of crushing defeats before retaining the trophy in '87 when the Americans were defeated in their own back yard for the first time ... I am proud that I remain the only European to have won the TPC in the States ... and I am proud that I might have inspired the next generation of European golfers by my achievements ...

My dad always used to say, 'Sandy, I don't care what you might or might not achieve over the rest of your life. You've *won* the Open, you've *won* the Masters, if I die tomorrow then I will die a very happy man.' I miss Dad more than I can say, but console myself with the thought that he did just that.

POSTSCRIPT

2006: RETURN TO RYDER CUP DUTY

A s the European team sang, danced and sprayed champagne over our joyous supporters in front of the clubhouse after inflicting the first ever defeat upon the United States in their own backyard at Muirfield Village in 1987, I had no reason to believe that it would be nineteen years before I would be involved in the Ryder Cup again.

And so, when captain Ian Woosnam invited me to become one of his lieutenants at the 2006 contest at the K Club, County Kildare, it was as a deeply emotional exile that I made my homecoming to a competition that has always been very dear to my heart.

Since making my debut in 1979, the Ryder Cup has acquired 'Major' status and has become one of the most eagerly awaited events on the sporting calendar. I had watched the intervening eight contests on television as avidly as any armchair sports fan but relished the prospect of pitting my wits against American captain Tom Lehman and his assistants, Corey Pavin and Loren

Roberts, three long-time rivals on the US Tour. This, then, is the diary of my return to Ryder Cup duty:

Sunday 17 September: Jolande and I flew from Glasgow to Dublin for dinner with Woosie and two other members of his advisory team, Peter Baker and Des Smyth, plus their wives.

On the plane, I glanced through the *Sunday Times* to discover an article in which Tony Jacklin named me in his Ryder Cup All-Time 'Dream Team', comprising Seve Ballesteros, Arnold Palmer, Sam Snead, Bernhard Langer, Ben Hogan, Nick Faldo, Lee Trevino, Jose-Maria Olazabal, Billy Casper, Raymond Floyd and Ian Woosnam.

According to Tony: 'Sandy Lyle is a forgotten hero. His achievements – and what an enormously talented golfer he was – tend to be overlooked. But when he had confidence in his putting, he was a great player. Everything looked so easy. As Peter Alliss said, his ball striking was "nonchalant power".'

Palmer, Hogan, Snead and Lyle, eh? 'Remind me to buy Tony a drink the next time we see him,' I said to Jolande.

On arrival in Ireland, the Arnold Palmer-designed course at the K Club appeared the perfect setting for a Ryder Cup contest while the five-star hotel attached to the club would have been the ideal place to spend a relaxing week, if only we had time to enjoy the facilities. Set in 550 acres of lush County Kildare countryside on the banks of the River Liffey, it offered fly-fishing and clay pigeon shooting in addition to horse-riding, a gym and spa.

But we weren't at the K Club on holiday.

Monday 18 September: From the plane you could almost hear the instantly recognisable strains of 'The Entrance of the

Gladiators', echoing around Dublin airport to welcome the players. The Americans' flight was delayed for four hours, incidentally, because their luggage was too heavy for the plane's maximum fuel load and another jet had to be wheeled out. Tom Lehman explained that he had crammed 200 packets of taco chips into a suitcase as a reminder of American 'cuisine' for his players, and perhaps that was responsible. My suspicions, however, were focused more on the wives' and girlfriends' luggage. Who knows, maybe tacos really do weigh that much.

Not being much of a fashion guru (remember the kilt incident?), I am reliably informed that Ralph Lauren was responsible for the Americans' natty tweed jerkins, blue shirts, red knitted ties, patterned woollen tank-tops and cavalry twills to recreate the 'Great Gatsby' 1920s look. The Europeans, by comparison, wore suede jackets on top of grey zip-up tops which, according to one observer, 'made Paul McGinley look even more like the elder brother of Oasis's Noel and Liam Gallagher'.

Always an emotional wee tyke, before our first team dinner with the players in the hotel wine cellar, Woosie screened the premiere of the inspirational video he had 'directed', containing clips of famous European victories, to the soundtrack of BBC radio commentator Tony Adamson reciting Kipling's 'If'.

While we were entertained by team psychologist, Jamil Qureshi, who used to work as a stage hypnotist and magician, elsewhere in the hotel, the Americans held a 'traditional Irish BBQ' (with taco chips and salsa?) at which many of their number were introduced to the delights of Guinness and during which – a highly embarrassed Tiger Woods included – everyone had to give a rendition of their college song. I was told that the star of the show, not surprisingly, was Mrs Chad Campbell (aka Amy

Lepard), a successful pop-soul recording star. Ah, but they've never heard Jolande's version of 'Tulips From Amsterdam'.

Tuesday 19 September: The first day of official practice and, although Woosie undoubtedly had an idea of his preferred pairings some weeks ago, an opportunity to see how the various permutations gelled on the course. Given that golf is such an individual sport, coming up with the correct combinations is probably the hardest task facing any Ryder Cup captain. An estimated crowd of 40,000 – an amazing number for a practice day – followed the players round; heaven knows how many will turn up when we get down to serious business.

As I said earlier, some successful partnerships are made in heaven: Arnold Palmer and Billy Casper in 1961, Jack Nicklaus and Tom Watson (1977), Seve Ballesteros and Jose-Maria Olazabal (1987). Yet others appear the work of divine madness. What persuaded Tony Jacklin, for instance, to send out Woosie and Nick Faldo – fire and ice – in tandem at Muirfield Village in 1987 when they contributed 3½ points out of four in Europe's historic 15–13 victory? Or for that matter, Bernhard Langer and A.W.B. Lyle, who emerged with a 100 per cent record from their three outings in the same contest? Hal Sutton probably thought he had come up with a cunning plan at Oakland Hills in 2004 when he persuaded the world's top ranked two players – Tiger Woods and Phil Mickelson – to join forces, only for them to lose both their opening day matches.

While we were hard at work, the European and American Wags, as the wives and girlfriends of all sports teams have since become known, following England's World Cup campaign in Germany over the summer, went off for a day at the races at the

Curragh (all their winnings going to charity!) before rejoining us for the welcome dinner in honour of our guests. In the past, some people have criticised the dizzying round of social occasions that accompanies the Ryder Cup but it is my belief the dinners, parties and get-togethers contribute greatly to the unique atmosphere of this biennial trans-Atlantic clash.

Wednesday 20 September: Jolande and I were awoken by the tail-end of Hurricane Gordon, which had been battering the Azores, passing over our corner of the Emerald Isle. There was no let-up in the rain the following morning when practice was delayed for the best part of four hours – and the course closed to spectators and all non-essential staff for their own safety – as the wind gusted at up to 40mph until Hurricane Gordon finally moved away to terrorise someone else.

The players were therefore restricted to just nine holes of practice but with even bigger crowds than Tuesday (like the Scots, they're a hardy lot these Irish), they cheerfully lined up under their umbrellas to sign a mountain of autographs. It was particularly pleasing to see how well our two Swedish rookies – Henrik Stenson and Robert Karlsson – adapted to what, for them, must have been highly unusual surroundings. Great players as they are – both won twice in Europe this year and Stenson was joint leader at the halfway stage in the US PGA Championship before finishing joint fourteenth – there is nothing quite like your first Ryder Cup to induce a feeling of sheer panic. Golf being an inherently selfish game, it requires a major readjustment to look upon eleven guys you regard as your fiercest rivals week in, week out as your 'family'.

As for the Lyle family, I have employed my two elder sons, Stuart and James, to act as my (unpaid!) chauffeurs at the wheel of my buggy, much to the outrage of Lonneke and Quintin who have been left behind in Balquhidder. I'm afraid schoolwork is more important than even the Ryder Cup at their age. Stuart and James have another role to play as my minders. When I went out in the buggy on my own to monitor the first day's practice session, I hopped out at one hole and returned to find that a souvenir-hunter had made off with the umbrellas! Perhaps I'll be able to buy them back on eBay.

Thursday 21 September: The morning after the night before. Despite the fact that we were dressed in our matching white tuxedos and red bow ties, the Gala Dinner in the Citywest Hotel descended into something of a bun-fight. Over 1400 people crammed into the ballroom – many having acquired their tickets via the various hospitality deals on offer – and at times both teams were buried under an avalanche of autograph seekers.

According to rumours, former US president Bill Clinton was to have been among the VIP guests but if he was I never saw him. I did, however, catch fleeting glimpses of Arnold Palmer who had flown in at the controls of his private jet. Although I would have enjoyed renewing acquaintance with the great man, who was one of my boyhood heroes, every time I spotted him he was surrounded by a forest of waving arms proffering commemorative menus to be signed. After being served Wexford rack of lamb, we were entertained by Irish singer Van Morrison – who was the surprise top-of-the-bill attraction.

But no time for a morning lie-in; the final practice session beckoned before a leisurely lunch then the chance to play darts or pool in the team room, or simply chat, although every conversation inevitably turned to the three days ahead. Padraig

Harrington has a nice way of describing 'the Ryder Cup Experience'. 'The Ryder Cup is like a rollercoaster. When you're on the damn thing you're looking round thinking "what am I doing putting myself through this? Let me off right now!" You scream your head off throughout the ride but, of course, the further away you get from it you start thinking "that was great – I can't wait to do it again".'

After last night's white tux, it was into our green jackets (well, we were in Ireland, after all) for the Opening Ceremony, which I thoroughly enjoyed. In days of yore, of course, only the national anthems of Britain, Ireland and the United States were played but such is the changing face of golf that in recent contests the flags of Sweden, Spain, Germany, France, Denmark, Italy and Finland have all fluttered alongside that of Europe. How long will it be, I wonder, before we have the first Russian in the Ryder Cup? That day will come, believe me.

Friday 22 September: Come Sunday, to someone – hopefully a European – will go the honour of being The Man Who Holed The Putt That Won The Ryder Cup. But seasoned campaigners that they are, when Padraig and Colin Montgomerie teed off against Jim Furyk and Tiger Woods at 8 a.m. in the opening fourballs, they knew that every half point would be precious. The first match – and every one in between for that matter – is equally as important as the last in any Ryder Cup contest.

Being our 'rock', there was never any question that Monty would be asked to strike the first blow. As Woosie put it over a beer (just the one, honest): 'Nothing in golf compares to standing on the first tee on the opening day. You feel like throwing up. I always had a swift look round to check the whereabouts of the nearest bush.

Well, you don't want to be sick all over your opponents' shoes, do you?' Playing in the Open or the Masters is relatively easy by comparison because the only person you can let down is yourself. But screw it up in the Ryder Cup and you let yourself down, your eleven team-mates, the country and the whole continent.

So when Tiger Woods sent his opening drive into the water, it told you everything you needed to know about the unique pressures of the Ryder Cup. Harrington and Monty beat the Tiger when he played with Mickelson at Oakland Hills two years ago, but this time, alas, the tables were turned on the final hole.

To the rookies, it almost goes without saying that the pressure is intensified tenfold, which is why my heart went out to Robert Karlsson – all six foot five of him – when he lined up with Paul Casey in the second fourballs against Stewart Cink and J.J. Henry. I know, I was that knee-knocking rookie at The Greenbrier in 1979. Karlsson emerged with what could be a priceless half point thanks to a red-hot putter. And I'll let you in on a little secret which may explain the Swede's superb touch on the greens – he recently spent an entire sleepless night, knocking in ten-foot putts on his carpet while a friend rebuked him for every miss (something Mrs Lyle and I might try when we get home to Balquhidder). He also underwent a two-week fast in preparation for the Ryder Cup during which he existed solely on milk – given my love of hearty stews and puddings, that is not something I'll be trying!

And what can I say about Monty? Out on the course at eight in the morning, he was still there ten and a half hours later, holing a treacherous eight-foot putt on the eighteenth green to earn him and Lee Westwood a half against Phil Mickelson and Chris DiMarco to send Europe into day two with a 5–3 advantage. Had he missed, our lead would have been one slender point.

Saturday 23 September: Monty's Ryder Cup record is truly remarkable: a member of four victorious European teams and fourth in our all-time list of points scorers with 22 (Nick Faldo has 25, Bernhard Langer 24 and Seve Ballesteros 22½), while remaining unbeaten in all seven singles appearances.

If anyone deserved a rest it was him and so we stood him down for the morning fourballs. He's forty-three now, after all, and one day soon he will find out – just as Woosie and I did – that the older you become, the more the muscles don't quite react how you'd like them to after a long day on the course. We have a very, very powerful twelve in depth, and we have to keep an eye on Monty with Sunday's singles in mind.

Enter Sergio Garcia as our substitute 'rock'. Having won both matches yesterday – including a two-hole defeat of Woods and Furyk in tandem with Luke Donald in the fourballs, the Spaniard made it four points out of four with two more heroic victories. Teamed with compatriot Jose-Maria Olazabal, Sergio whipped Mickelson and DiMarco 3 and 2 in the fourballs, then rejoined forces with Donald to defeat Mickelson and David Toms in the foursomes.

It was Martina Navratilova's belief that you are either committed to your sport, or merely involved. 'And therein lies a world of difference,' she explained. 'Think of ham and eggs. The chicken is involved, the pig is committed.' When it comes to the Ryder Cup, Sergio is certainly committed, personifying the 'spirit' of the European team as did his countryman Seve Ballesteros before him.

I was enjoying the Ryder Cup rollercoaster ride from the comfort of my buggy and dropped by the fourteenth tee where Paul Casey and David Howell were a handsome five up, with five to play, against Zach Johnson and Stewart Cink in their four-balls. If the Americans were harbouring any notions of a come-back they were sorely disabused when Paul holed out off the tee with a 4-iron and his celebrations were long and understandably lusty. The most important hole in one I enjoyed came on the twelfth hole of the 1993 US Open at Baltusrol. An hour later on the par-three sixteenth, my ball flew straight and true, hit the pin, thought about dropping but opted to stay above ground, denying me a second ace in the space of four holes.

Europe 10, United States 6. Aye, we sank a few pints of Guinness that night as we drew up our battle plans for 'Super Sunday'.

Sunday 24 September: After the United States had won the Ryder Cup for the fourth successive time, in 1977, it was Jack Nicklaus's idea that GB and Ireland might consider the possi-bility of embracing the notion of a European team. After Europe's third win a row – with a whopping 18½–9½ – then maybe the Americans should consider joining forces with Australia or South Africa if they are to make a match of it at the Valhalla Club, Louisville, two years hence. Only joking.

The US might have come to Ireland with the top three ranked players in the world in Tiger Woods, Phil Mickelson and Jim Furyk, but the Ryder Cup is a team competition and, as a *team*, we were in a different class throughout the week.

Each and every one of our twelve players was a hero; Sergio Garcia, Padraig Harrington and Robert Karlsson may have been our only losers on a wondrous final afternoon of golf, but Woosie and his advisors had been at pains to foster a 'family atmosphere' and they were greeted like the heroes they were when they returned to the bosom of their 'family'.

'Baby' of the team he may be, but Sergio, the young Spaniard – like Seve before him – has emerged as the 'spiritual leader' with his fist-pumping aggression. It was Henrik Stenson who holed the climactic putt on this occasion but no one did more to make our latest victory possible than Garcia. And here's a thought that will bring a warm glow to future captains: at the tender age of twenty-six, he could still be playing come 2020!

Field Marshal Montgomerie, now unbeaten in eight Ryder Cup singles and our third highest points scorer of all time, led from the front as has become his custom. Paul Casey was magnificent. David Howell pitched and putted like a demon. Lee Westwood issued his statement of intent by birdieing five of the first seven holes. And then there was Darren Clarke, still grieving over the recent death of his wife, Heather, reducing all of Europe to tears with his courage and skill. The team of 2006, I salute you, it was a pleasure and privilege being with you all.

And what of my own ambitions to be Ryder Cup captain one day? To Nick Faldo will go the honour in 2008 but if a Welshman can lead the team in Ireland, then why not a Scotsman in Wales come 2010, or even in Scotland at Gleneagles four years later? As one of the so-called 'Big Five of European Golf' – along with Seve, Faldo, Bernhard Langer and Woosie – I am the only one still awaiting the call and if I am to be brutally honest, the Ryder Cup captaincy is an honour I think I deserve in recognition of my past achievements. It would mean everything to me, even as much as my Open Championship and Masters victories.

The Ryder Cup has now attained Major status and, to me, serving as captain would represent my third Major. If Europe needs me, then I am ready.

CAREER RECORD

The Roll of Honour

Year   **Tournament**

Amateur

1975   English Amateur Open Stroke-Play Championship (Brabazon Trophy); English Boys' Amateur Stroke-Play Championship (Carris Trophy)

1977   British Youths Open Amateur Championship; English Amateur Open Stroke-Play Championship

Professional

1978   Nigerian Open

1979   Scottish Professional Championship; British Airways Jersey Open; Scandinavian Enterprise Open; European Open

1980   Coral Welsh Classic

1981   Paco Rabanne French Open; Lawrence Batley International

Year	Tournament
1982	Lawrence Batley International
1983	Madrid Open
1984	Kapalua International, Hawaii; Casio World Open, Japan; Italian Open; Lancome Trophy
1985	Benson & Hedges International Open
1986	Greater Greensboro Open, US
1987	The Tournament Players' Championship, US; German Masters
1988	Phoenix Open, US; Greater Greensboro Open, US; Dunhill British Masters; Suntory World Matchplay Championship
1991	BMW International
1992	Lancia Martini Italian Open; Volvo Masters

European Tour Order of Merit: Winner: 1979, 1980, 1985

The Open:

Year	Venue/Winner	Position	Score
1974	Royal Lytham (par-71)	=75	75, 77, 84 (missed 4th round cut as amateur)
	Gary Player (South Africa) 282		
1977	Turnberry (par-70)	=118	75, 80 (missed cut as amateur)
	Tom Watson (US) 268		
1978	St Andrews (par-72)	=86	72, 78 (missed cut)
	Jack Nicklaus (US) 281		
1979	Royal Lytham (par-71)	=18	74, 76, 75, 70 = 295
	Severiano Ballesteros (Spain) 283		
1980	Muirfield (par-71)	=12	70, 71, 70, 73 = 284
	Tom Watson (US) 271		

Year	Venue/Winner	Position	Score
1981	Royal St George's (par-70)	=14	73, 73, 71, 71 = 288
	Bill Rogers (US) 276		
1982	Royal Troon (par-72)	=8	74, 66, 73, 74 = 287
	Tom Watson (US) 284		
1983	Royal Birkdale (par-71)	=64	73, 71, 74 (missed 4th round cut)
	Tom Watson (US) 275		
1984	St Andrews (par-72)	=14	75, 71, 72, 67 = 285
	Severiano Ballesteros (Spain) 276		

1985 Royal St George's (par-70)
Leaderboard:

282 – Sandy Lyle		68, 71, 73, 70
283 – Payne Stewart (US)		70, 75, 70, 68
284 – Mark O'Meara (US)		70, 72, 70, 72
Bernhard Langer (Germany)		72, 69, 68, 75
David Graham (Australia)		68, 71, 70, 75
Jose Rivero (Spain)		74, 72, 70, 68
Christy O'Connor Jnr (Ireland)		64, 76, 72, 72
285 – Tom Kite (US)		73, 73, 67, 72
D A Weibring (US)		69, 71, 74, 71
Anders Forsbrand (Sweden)		70, 76, 69, 70
286 – Fuzzy Zoeller (US)		69, 76, 70, 71
Jose-Maria Canizares (Spain)		72, 75, 70, 69
Peter Jacobsen (US)		71, 74, 68, 73
Gary Koch (US)		75, 72, 70, 69
Eamonn Darcy (Ireland)		76, 68, 74, 68

Year	Venue/Winner	Position	Score
1986	Turnberry (par-70)	=30	78, 73, 70, 74 = 295
	Greg Norman (Australia) 280		
1987	Muirfield (par-71)	=17	76, 69, 71, 70 = 286
	Nick Faldo (UK) 279		
1988	Royal Lytham (par-71)	=7	73, 69, 67, 74 = 283
	Severiano Ballesteros (Spain) 273		
1989	Royal Troon (par-72)	=46	73, 73, 71, 72 = 289
	Mark Calcavecchia (US) 275		
1990	St Andrews (par-72)	=16	72, 70, 67, 72 = 281
	Nick Faldo (UK) 270		
1991	Royal Birkdale (par-70)		79, disqualified
	Ian Baker-Finch (Australia) 272		
1992	Muirfield (par-71)	=12	68, 70, 70, 72 = 280
	Nick Faldo (UK) 272		
1993	Royal St George's (par-72)	=109	70, 76 (missed cut)
	Greg Norman (Australia) 267		
1994	Turnberry (par-70)	73	71, 72, 72, 72 = 287
	Nick Price (Zimbabwe) 268		
1995	St Andrews (par-72)	=76	71, 71, 79, 75 = 296
	John Daly (US) 282		
1996	Royal Lytham (par-71)	=55	71, 69, 73, 73 = 286
	Tom Lehman (US) 271		
1997	Royal Troon (par-71)	=116	78, 75 (missed cut)
	Justin Leonard (US) 272		
1998	Royal Birkdale (par-70)	=18	71, 72, 75, 72 = 290
	Mark O'Meara (US) 280		
1999	Carnoustie (par-71)	=141	85, 81 (missed cut)
	Paul Lawrie (UK) 290		

Year	Venue/Winner	Position	Score
2000	St Andrews (par-72) Tiger Woods (US) 269	=127	71, 78 (missed cut)
2001	Royal Lytham (par-71) David Duval (US) 274	=69	72, 71, 77, 81 = 301
2002	Muirfield (par-71) Ernie Els (South Africa) 278	=75	68, 76, 73, 75 = 292
2003	Royal St George's (par-71) Ben Curtis (US) 283	=84	73, 79 (missed cut)
2004	Royal Troon (par-71) Todd Hamilton (US) 274	73	70, 73, 81, 79 = 303
2005	St Andrews (par-72) Tiger Woods (US) 274	=32	74, 67, 69, 75 = 285
2006	Hoylake (par-72) Tiger Woods (US) 270	=91	73, 73 (missed cut)

The 1988 Masters:

281 – Sandy Lyle		71, 67, 72, 71
282 – Mark Calcavecchia		71, 69, 72, 70
283 – Craig Stadler		76, 69, 70, 68
284 – Ben Crenshaw		72, 73, 67, 72
285 – Greg Norman		77, 73, 71, 64
Fred Couples		75, 68, 71, 71
Don Pooley		71, 72, 72, 70
286 – David Frost		73, 74, 71, 68
287 – Bernhard Langer		71, 72, 71, 73
288 – Raymond Floyd		80, 69, 68, 71
Severiano Ballesteros		73, 72, 70, 73

The Ryder Cup:
1979: Greenbrier, West Virginia

Europe	United States
Sandy Lyle	Lee Trevino
Tony Jacklin	Hale Irwin
Nick Faldo	Tom Kite
Peter Oosterhuis	Lanny Wadkins
Severiano Ballesteros	Hubert Green
Bernard Gallacher	Larry Nelson
Brian Barnes	Fuzzy Zoeller
Ken Brown	Andy Bean
Mark James	Gil Morgan
Des Smyth	John Mahaffey
Antonio Garrido	Lee Elder
Michael King	Mark Hayes
John Jacobs – captains –	Billy Casper

Day I: Afternoon Foursomes
Lyle & Jacklin   halved   Trevino & Morgan

Day II: Morning Foursomes
Lyle & Jacklin   beat   Elder & Mahaffey   5 & 4

Afternoon Fourballs
Lyle & Jacklin   lost   Irwin & Kite   1 hole

Day III: Singles
Lyle   lost   Trevino   2 & 1

Result: US 17, Europe 11

1981: Walton Heath, Surrey

Europe		United States
Sandy Lyle		Jack Nicklaus
Nick Faldo		Tom Watson
Bernhard Langer		Lee Trevino
Peter Oosterhuis		Johnny Miller
Mark James		Ray Floyd
Sam Torrance		Hale Irwin
Bernard Gallacher		Tom Kite
Manuel Pinero		Bill Rogers
Howard Clark		Jerry Pate
Eamonn Darcy		Ben Crenshaw
Des Smyth		Larry Nelson
Jose-Maria Canizares		Bruce Lietzke
John Jacobs	– captains –	Dave Marr

Day I: Morning Foursomes
Lyle & James   beat   Rogers & Lietzke   2 & 1

Afternoon Fourballs
Lyle & James   beat   Crenshaw & Pate   3 & 2

Day II: Morning Fourballs
Lyle & James   lost   Nelson & Kite   1 hole

Afternoon Foursomes
Lyle & James   lost   Rogers & Floyd   3 & 2

Day III: Singles

Lyle	lost	Kite	3 & 2

Result: Europe 9½, US 18½

1983: PGA National, Palm Beach Gardens, Florida

Europe		United States
Sandy Lyle		Tom Watson
Severiano Ballesteros		Ray Floyd
Nick Faldo		Ben Crenshaw
Ian Woosnam		Tom Kite
Bernhard Langer		Fuzzy Zoeller
Bernard Gallacher		Craig Stadler
Sam Torrance		Lanny Wadkins
Gordon J Brand		Jay Haas
Brian Waites		Gil Morgan
Jose-Maria Canizares		Bob Gilder
Paul Way		Calvin Peete
Ken Brown		Curtis Strange
Tony Jacklin	– captains –	Jack Nicklaus

Day I: Morning Foursomes

Lyle & Gallacher lost   Watson & Crenshaw 5 & 4

Day III: Singles

Lyle	lost	Crenshaw	3 & 1

Result: US 14½, Europe 13½

1985: The Belfry, Sutton Coldfield

Europe	United States
Sandy Lyle	Ray Floyd
Severiano Ballesteros	Lanny Wadkins
Nick Faldo	Craig Stadler
Manuel Pinero	Tom Kite
Ian Woosnam	Peter Jacobsen
Paul Way	Hal Sutton
Bernhard Langer	Andy North
Sam Torrance	Mark O'Meara
Howard Clark	Calvin Peete
Jose Rivero	Hubert Green
Jose-Maria Canizares	Fuzzy Zoeller
Ken Brown	Curtis Strange
Tony Jacklin – captains –	Lee Trevino

Day I: Morning Foursomes
Lyle & Brown   lost   Wadkins & Floyd   4 & 3

Day II: Morning Fourballs
Lyle & Langer   halved   Stadler & Strange

Day III: Singles
Lyle   beat   Jacobsen   3 & 2

Result: Europe 16½, US 11½

1987: Muirfield Village, Columbus, Ohio

Europe	US
Sandy Lyle	Tom Kite
Severiano Ballesteros	Curtis Strange
Nick Faldo	Dan Pohl
Jose-Maria Olazabal	Andy Bean
Ian Woosnam	Larry Mize
Sam Torrance	Mark Calcavecchia
Jose Rivero	Payne Stewart
Eamonn Darcy	Scott Simpson
Bernhard Langer	Larry Nelson
Ken Brown	Hal Sutton
Howard Clark	Lanny Wadkins
Gordon Brand Jnr	Ben Crenshaw
Tony Jacklin – captains –	Jack Nicklaus

Day I: Afternoon Fourballs
Lyle & Langer   beat   Bean & Calcavecchia   1 hole

Day II: Morning Foursomes
Lyle & Langer   beat   Wadkins & Nelson   2 & 1

Afternoon Fourballs
Lyle & Langer   beat   Wadkins & Nelson   1 hole

Day III: Singles
Lyle   lost   Kite   3 & 2

Result: US 13, Europe 15

Other Team Appearances:

Walker Cup – 1977

World Cup (Scotland) – 1979, 1980 (Individual Winner), 1987

Dunhill Cup (Scotland) – 1985, 1986, 1987, 1988, 1989, 1990, 1992

Awards:

MBE – 1987

Henry Cotton Trophy (Rookie of the Year) – 1978

INDEX